Women who obtain abortions
are married + wish to terminate
Pregnancy as a means of family
Planning.

?

ABORTION IN PSYCHOSOCIAL PERSPECTIVE

PREVIOUS TFRI MONOGRAPHS

David, H. P. Family planning and abortion in the socialist countries of Central and Eastern Europe. New York: The Population Council, 1970.

David, H. P. (Ed.). Abortion research: International experience. Lexington, Mass.: Heath, 1974.

David, H. P., & Cambiaso, S. (Org.), Epidemiology of abortion and practices of fertility regulation in Latin America: Selected reports. Washington: Pan American Health Organization, 1975.

van der Tak, J. Abortion, fertility, and changing legislation: An international review. Lexington, Mass.: Heath, 1974,

Transnational Family Research Institute

Henry P. David, Herbert L. Friedman,
Jean van der Tak, and Marylis J. Sevilla, Editors

ABORTION IN PSYCHOSOCIAL PERSPECTIVE
Trends in Transnational Research

Springer Publishing Company
New York

Springer Publishing Company, Inc.

200 Park Avenue South

New York, N.Y. 10003

78 79 80 81 82 / 10 9 8 7 6 5 4 3 2 1

Library of Congress Cataloging in Publication Data

Main entry under title:

Abortion in psychosocial perspective.

  Bibliography: p.
  Includes index.
  1. Abortion-Psychological aspects--Addresses. essays,
lectures. 2. Abortion--Social aspects--Addresses,
essays, lectures. I. David, Henry Philip, 1923-
HQ767.A185   301   78-7784
ISBN 0-8261-2470-4
ISBN 0-8261-2471-2 pbk.

Printed in the United States of America

CONTENTS

IV: ABORTION DENIED

V: SERVICE PROVIDERS

VI: COMMENTARIES

INDEXES

FOREWORD

Legal abortion, hailed by some as a blessing for desperate women carrying unwanted pregnancies and condemned by others as government-sanctioned mass murder, has become one of the most emotional, divisive, and polarizing public issues in a number of countries, including some in which restrictive laws are still enforced and other in which a few years ago the battle for reproductive freedom appeared to be won. Discussion has turned into debate, debate is turning into confrontation. Even in pluralistic societies such as ours, no compromise is in sight because victory for one side means unconditional surrender for the other.

In this context, it is doubly welcome to encounter a book that places research before rhetoric, empathy before emotion, and professionalism before propaganda. The editors and the distinguished group of scholars assembled have made a major contribution to the field. Abortion is more than a medical issue, or an ethical issue, or a legal issue. It is, above all, a human issue, involving women and men as individuals, as couples, and as members of societies. This fact, often overlooked or neglected, requires that abortion be studied from a psychosocial perspective; and, because abortion is a worldwide phenomenon, it must be approached on a transnational basis if it is to be understood rather than merely used as a political football.

My own views on the abortion issue are well known to friend and foe alike. I am a partisan, but I do not like to be a blind partisan. This book has extended my horizon, broadened my understanding, and deepened my commitment. I hope it will do the same for many other readers.

Christopher Tietze

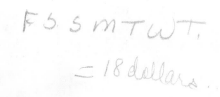

PREFACE

At this time more than two-thirds of the world's population lives in countries in which induced abortion is legally and safely available on social as well as medical grounds during the first trimester of pregnancy/ Only about eight percent of people live in countries where abortion is prohibited without exception. Sociocultural ambivalence and political sensitivities continue to inhibit abortion-related research in many lands, particularly psychosocial studies designed to assess determinants and consequences associated with the choice of abortion within the total context of human fertility-regulating behavior. It is the purpose of this monograph to consider, review, and share more widely psychosocial research experience gained in selected developed and developing countries of Africa, Asia, Europe, and North and South America.

The monograph evolved from the activities of the Cooperative Transnational Research Program in Fertility Behavior, initiated in 1970 and informally coordinated by the Transnational Family Research Institute (TFRI), a multidisciplinary, nongovernmental, and nonprofit research organization. One of the objectives is to separate fact from emotion through jointly conducted research designed to increase understanding of psychosocial, demographic, epidemiological, and public health aspects of abortion-seeking behavior, and of the abortion/contraception relationship in fertility regulation.

The studies reported from Czechoslovakia, Dominican Republic, Israel, Jamaica, Nigeria, and Yugoslavia were cooperative projects conducted in association with a research center from each country. Every project was designed and conducted jointly, directed by a local colleague, with TFRI consultation available throughout the data gathering, analysis, and reporting phases. Research priorities were determined by national needs and the potential utility of eventual findings. A frequent goal was to elicit current information, heighten awareness of sociocultural concerns, and contribute to the attainment of societally desired birth planning.

TFRI and its associates do not espouse specific solutions to population problems. Instead, when invited, an attempt is made to explore in depth areas of common interest and, when feasible, to provide consultation on prospects for effectively joining people, ideas, and funding. Emerging research concepts and methodologies have been refined at workshops convened in Africa, Asia, and Europe. Advances in abortion techniques and services, social research findings, as well as legislative trends and relevant new publications, are reported periodically in <u>Abortion Research Notes</u>, published by the International Reference Center for Abortion Research, a unit of the Transnational Family Research Institute.

Many colleagues contributed their knowledge and skills to this monograph, from the initial discussion of the idea through the final delivery of the edited manuscript. We are especially pleased to acknowledge the constructive suggestions of Raymond L. Johnson, J. Joseph Speidel, and Tema S. David, as well as the superb manuscript typing skills of Ann G. Rosendall. It is with sadness that we note the untimely death of "Tonita" Ramirez who took major responsibility for the initial TFRI cooperative research study in the Dominican Republic: hers was a bright star whose brilliance will be long remembered.

The cooperative studies reported in this monograph are expected to help clarify--for service providers, researchers, policy makers, and social change agents--the complexities of the decision-making process in fertility regulation, and the socioeconomic and cultural environmental influences impinging on couple communication and choice behavior. It is with the hope of further improving transnational communication of shared experience and encouraging future research that this monograph is presented. All royalties have been waived to reduce the sale price.

H.P.D.
H.L.F.
J.vd T.
M.J.S.

January 1978

LIST OF CONTRIBUTORS

Christopher G. M. Bakare, Ph.D.
  Department of Guidance and Counselling, University of Ibadan,
  Ibadan, Nigeria

Henry P. David, Ph.D.
  Transnational Family Research Institute, 8307 Whitman Drive,
  Bethesda, Maryland 20034, USA, and Department of Psychiatry,
  University of Maryland School of Medicine, Baltimore,
  Maryland, USA

Zdeněk Dytrych, M.D.
  Psychiatric Research Institute, Bohnice, Prague 8,
  Czechoslovakia

Anibal Faundes, M.D.
  Faculty of Medical Science, University of Campinas, Campinas
  SP., Brazil, and Population Council Representative in Brazil

Herbert L. Friedman, Ph.D.
  Psychology Department, Claybury Hospital, Woodford Bridge,
  Essex, 1G8 8BY United Kingdom; Scientific Director (1971-
  1975), Transnational Family Research Institute, Geneva,
  Switzerland

Ezequiel García, Ing.
  Universidad Nacional Pedro Henriquez Ureña, Santo Domingo,
  Dominican Republic

Marion Hall, M.D.
  Aberdeen Maternity Hospital, Aberdeen, Scotland, United
  Kingdom

Ellen Hardy, M.D.
  Faculty of Medical Science, University of Campinas, Campinas
  SP., Brazil

Raymond Illsley, Ph.D.
  MRC Medical Sociology Unit, Institute of Medical Sociology,
  Westburn Road, Aberdeen AB9 2ZE Scotland, United Kingdom

Raymond L. Johnson, M.S.
  Transnational Family Research Institute, 8307 Whitman Drive,
  Bethesda, Maryland 20034, USA

Nila Kapor-Stanulovic, Ph.D.
  University of Novi Sad, 21000 Novi Sad, Njegoseva 1,
  Yugoslavia

Jean M. Kellerhals, Ph.D.
Department of Sociology, University of Geneva, Geneva, Switzerland

András Klinger, Ph.D.
Hungarian Central Statistical Office, Keleti Karoly U. 5-7, 1525 Budapest, Hungary

Zdeněk Matějček, Ph.D.
Postgraduate Medical Institute, Department of Pediatrics, Thomayer Hospital, 146 29 Prague 4, KRC, Czechoslovakia

Minoru Muramatsu, M.D., Dr. P.H.
Department of Public Health Demography, Institute of Public Health, 4-6-1 Shirokanedai, Minato-Ku, Tokyo, Japan

Alberto E. Noboa Mejia, Dr.
Instituto Nacional de Educación Sexual, Danae No. 8, Santo Domingo, Dominican Republic

Willy Pasini, M.D.
Unit of Psychosomatic Gynecology and Sexology, University of Geneva Medical School, Geneva, Switzerland

Tsiyona Peled, Ph.D.
The Israel Institute of Applied Social Research, 19 George Washington Street, P.O. Box 7150, Jerusalem, Israel

Malcolm Potts, M.B., Ph.D.
International Projects Assistance Services, London, United Kingdom, and International Planned Parenthood Federation, 18-20 Lower Regent Street, SW1Y 4PW London, England, UK

*Antonía Ramírez M., Dra.
Universidad Nacional Pedro Henriquez Ureña, Santo Domingo, Dominican Republic

Cándida E. Ramírez E., Lic.
Universidad Nacional Pedro Henriquez Ureña, Santo Domingo, Dominican Republic

Antoinette Russin, M.S.W.
Kennedy-Russin Associates, 3601 Idaho Avenue, N.W., Washington, D.C. 20016, USA

---

*deceased

Vratislav Schüller, CSc
  Psychiatric Research Institute, Bohnice, Prague 8,
  Czechoslovakia

Marylis J. Sevilla, M.A.
  Transnational Family Research Institute, 8307 Whitman Drive,
  Bethesda, Maryland   20034, USA

Karl A. Smith, M.B., Ch.B., Dr. P.H.
  Department of Social and Preventive Medicine, University of
  the West Indies, Mona, Kingston 7, Jamaica

Egon Szabady, Ph.D.
  Central Statistical Office, Hungarian Academy of Sciences
  Demographic Committee, Buday L. U. 1-3. 1525 Budapest,
  Hungary

Jean van der Tak, M.A.
  Population Reference Bureau, 1337 Connecticut Avenue, N.W.,
  Washington, D.C.   20036, USA

Christopher Tietze, M.D.
  The Population Council, 1 Dag Hammarskjold Plaza, New York
  New York   10017, USA

Genevieve Wirth
  Faculty of Medicine, University of Geneva, Geneva,
  Switzerland

PART ONE

RESEARCH PERSPECTIVES

1

Transnational Trends:
An Overview

Henry P. David, Herbert L. Friedman,
Jean van der Tak, and Marylis J. Sevilla

The contributions to this monograph are drawn from a
broad spectrum of social, cultural, economic, and political
conditions. The people whose behavior, thoughts, and feelings
about abortion and fertility regulation are described come
from settings that are variously urban and rural, developed
and developing, highly traditional and very modern--represent-
ing a full range of abortion policies and family planning practices. In some of these societies abortion is considered a
morally unacceptable act; in others, it is seen as a common-
place aspect of reproductive control. In some, overpopulation
is feared; in others, a decline in the population growth rate
has created concern. Despite considerable diversity, however,
those immediately involved express a surprising degree of consensus about psychosocial factors associated with induced abortion and fertility regulation.

FINDINGS

All the studies cited in this monograph confirm that
abortion is a universal phenomenon. For many women, especially
in societies where modern contraceptive methods are only gradually attaining wide acceptance and dissemination, abortion is
often the primary mode of fertility regulation. There is some
evidence for this observation, now or in the recent past, in
parts of Hungary, Czechoslovakia, Yugoslavia, Jamaica, the
Dominican Republic, and Nigeria. Abortion is rarely a psychologically traumatic event, even when it is socially disapproved
and legislation is restrictive. If there are psychological sequelae, the most common one, by far, is that of relief. This
is not to say that abortion is regarded casually. Where legislation makes it difficult to obtain, the burdens are considerable, ranging from finding and paying an abortionist to
risking complications that may lead to sterility or death. In
all societies those most vulnerable to the hazards of clandestine abortion are poor, very young, and uneducated women. For
the young, unmarried, and economically disadvantaged, a lack
of knowledge about how to proceed, fear of social (or parental)

disapproval, and/or insufficient funds often lead to delayed
second trimester abortions, thereby unnecessarily increasing
the discomfort and health risks involved. The poor and uneducated of whatever age all too often must make do with whatever they can afford, and that may mean exposure to dangerous
self-induced abortion.

Despite the physical, legal, and social costs encountered, the motivation to control fertility is strong enough
that women who are otherwise law-abiding, have little or no
money to spare, and are concerned about their health (the most
common reason given for not using modern contraceptives) are
willing to break the law (if necessary), borrow the money, and
risk illness or death to avert unwanted births. The reports
from the Dominican Republic and Nigeria tell their own story.
The cost in health care services is high. As noted in Chile
and the Dominican Republic, expenses associated with caring
for women admitted to public hospitals for incomplete or septic abortion frequently exceed the costs of cleanly performed
induced abortion.

In societies where restrictive legislation is accompanied by a de facto acceptance of abortion, as in Israel prior
to 1977, some of the problems are alleviated but others remain.
There may be a limitation of services, which are provided only
by those willing to assume some risk, even if more social than
legal. This effectively reduces the availability and accessibility of qualified practitioners, increasing the price and
creating hardship for the poor. That a useful service can be
provided with sensitivity to patients' needs is apparent from
the Chilean experience.

Societies that permit legal access under conditions
that enable most women to have safe, simple, low-cost abortions
have avoided the problems associated with clandestine illegal
abortion. Other difficulties--perhaps less severe, but important in their own right--then arise. The research findings
presented in this monograph suggest that even among women with
comparatively easy access to abortion, few choose to rely on
it to regulate fertility. This is clearly so in Yugoslavia
and is apparent in Japan as well. There is some evidence from
Hungary and the United States that the repeated abortion seeker
experiences circumstances that she feels somewhat helpless to
avoid, dislikes, and would prefer to change.

Overall, the findings suggest that a liberal abortion
policy is likely to reduce many problems besetting the public,
and especially the young and the poor, when abortion legislation is highly restrictive. They also indicate the need for
efforts to help couples avoid having to resort to abortion, by

facilitating more successful contraceptive practice. Although the availability and accessibility of modern contraceptives are clearly important, changing behavior requires a better coordinated public health strategy, which might benefit from the results of some of the experience reported in this monograph.

RESEARCH PROBLEMS

Successful contraception requires the coordination of three distinct human forces: the drive to have sexual intercourse, the wish to have or not have a child, and the will to regulate the fertility consequences of sexual behavior. While these forces may be <u>logically</u> linked, they are not <u>psychologically</u> related; coordinating them requires a considerable and ever-vigilant effort. Abortion does not. Abortion obviates the need for advance planning, and for frequent action with no immediate reward, or long-term reward that appears only in the guise of the <u>absence</u> of an event. Availability of abortion also avoids interference with sexual activity, and reduces perceived health dangers posed by modern contraceptives and reinforced by media reports. Where guilt is associated with abortion, it is often also associated with modern contraception; the latter requires continual violation of the code whereas abortion does not. Although these advantages alone might suffice for many to choose abortion as a preferred method, it appears more likely that abortion remains somewhat distasteful (albeit not traumatic) to the majority of women who use it. It is chosen not in preference to contraception but because it is the only possible way to avoid giving birth <u>at that stage</u>. As noted earlier, making abortion illicit does not eliminate it, but simply drives it underground at considerable cost to society. Those currently and potentially providing abortion services, as sampled in these studies, generally do not believe in restricting abortion. Their concern is how to enable couples to supplant abortion with effective contraception.

One of the monograph's major findings is the importance of consensus within the couple, as evidenced by studies in Switzerland, Yugoslavia, Israel, and Czechoslovakia. If husband and wife share the same views, and if they accurately perceive their partner's views, a major impediment to family planning is removed. Unwanted pregnancies occur perhaps most often when the couple relationship is unstable, as frequently noted among adolescents, or where the psychological distance between the man and the woman is great, as may be the case in very traditional societies. In these situations it is the woman alone who must take action after a pregnancy is suspected. Abortion is deemed to be in her domain while contraception is still perceived as the man's responsibility. Modern contraceptives,

however, are designed for women. In societies where the woman
traditionally is subservient to the man, she may be unwilling
to raise the topic of contraception or take upon herself the
decision to contracept. Japan appears to be the exception to
the rule. Enhancing couple communication and awareness of what
is often a shared but unexpressed belief--that there is a need
to avoid or delay another baby--might be a powerful vehicle in
introducing and achieving acceptability of more efficient modern contraceptives or improving the practice of more traditional methods where there is equal access to safe and legal
abortion.

A second problem associated with the acceptability of
modern contraceptives is the widespread feeling, especially
prevalent among non-users, that the pill and the IUD are dangerous to the woman's health. This is apparent in the Dominican Republic and in Yugoslavia. Sickness is something the poor
cannot easily afford, especially in developing societies. Women
are often vital to caring for the family and for producing income. The tendency among many family planning workers to minimize side effects of modern contraceptives contributes to a
climate of suspicion, which acts as a subtle but powerful de-
terrent and can be a major contributor to the discontinuation
of contraception. Honesty and openness appear to be a much
surer way to achieve realistic method acceptance.

A third problem is created by the wide gap between
awareness of modern contraceptives, in a general way, and specific information tailored to meet the needs of the individual
who must risk the unknown--as seen, for example, in Israel.
The concerns may have little to do with physiological aspects
of a method but more with uncertainty about how it will affect
sexuality, appearance, or health in ways that are not necessarily method related (and thus seldom discussed by the professional informant) but are very relevant to the individual's
perceptions. How to get the right questions asked and answered
in a supportive atmosphere is an important and perhaps overlooked task.

A fourth research problem is that sources of information are often psychosocially inappropriate. General practitioners, midwives, and social workers are seldom qualified, by
their own admission, to discuss questions about sexual behavior.
They are not normally asked such questions; yet among these
practitioners may lie the key for successful adoption of contraceptive measures, especially for the young. It is to members of their peer group, or to those slightly older, that
young people are more likely to turn for help--which may not be
the most reliable kind. Awareness of the informal communication
network among the young, and strengthening the process of

disseminating correct information among trusted sources, might
help to prevent unwanted pregnancies and teenager resort to
abortion.

A fifth contributor to abortion, as demonstrated in the
Yugoslav report, is a personal sense of lack of control over
destiny and circumstances. The relatively passive act of requesting an abortion supersedes active prevention. This is
sometimes true of couples as well but, although more subtle,
may not be a hopeless problem. Couples can often exercise control over areas of their lives other than fertility regulation.
Demonstrable success of that kind needs to be emphasized in a
way that can be generalized to fertility control. Other personal characteristics likely to make abortion more common than
contraception include a lack of future orientation or of planning behavior, and a subsequent dulling of aspiration through
lack of success.

Planning and choice behavior can be taught. An important point at which to enter the lives of couples is at the beginning of their fertility careers, i.e., when they are first
married or joined in a permanent union and are--for the first
time in their lives--acting jointly rather than as individuals.
This population is relatively limited in numbers. Although
abortion is probably least common for the first pregnancy, the
pattern of planning or its absence is established early. By
the time the couple becomes interested in spacing the next
birth, a lack of planning behavior may have resulted in an unwanted pregnancy, which is either terminated by abortion or
carried to term as an unwanted child. Efforts designed to enhance planning behavior in major areas of the couples' lives
early in their fertility career may help to introduce planning
habits that encourage contraception and reduce resort to
abortion.

Although improvements have been and continue to be made
in contraceptive methods, techniques that would significantly
enhance acceptability are not yet widely available. A long-
lasting but fully reversible method, free of all side effects,
would be high on the list of those most likely to succeed: it
would require the least effort and place the burden on a deliberate choice to conceive rather than to contracept. A male
method with similar characteristics would be particularly acceptable in some populations subgroups. Further reduction of
the side effects and discomfort associated with currently
available major reversible methods will be another step forward. However, as long as human needs vary, it is unlikely
that any single method will provide the perfect solution.

These then are the problems which motivated the cooperative research program and this monograph: policy needs

versus the public health wisdom of abortion legislation, service provision as a facilitator or inhibitor of the use of contraception in place of abortion, and communication of information or its absence and how this may lead to unwanted pregnancy and termination. No single factor explains the choice of abortion when contraception is possible and no single solution is likely to be found, but neither is abortion a mysterious phenomenon, as the research reported in this volume amply demonstrates.

CHAPTER ORGANIZATION

The major purpose of this monograph is to present a broad background and spectrum of research into the psychosocial aspects of abortion, with attention both to findings and to innovations in research methodology. Part I offers a research perspective, including this overview and the discussion of additional selected issues in psychosocial research presented by Illsley and Hall. The focus of Part II is on psychosocial dynamics with reports from Switzerland, Israel, and the United States. These represent countries in which abortion is obtainable, although social and/or legal obstacles may vary and affect accessibility of abortion services. The United States chapter endeavors to summarize findings from major American studies, including determinants of fertility choice behavior, psychological sequelae of abortion, and the special concerns of adolescents.

Choice behavior is further considered in Part III with reports from Yugoslavia, Japan, and Hungary. These represent countries with a relatively long and liberal tradition of ready availability of legal abortion, and more recent introduction of modern contraceptives. The successful Japanese experience in reliance on widespread usage of the condom is especially instructive. Part IV features studies of effects associated with denying abortion requests. The report from Czechoslovakia is an unusual study of children born to women twice denied abortion for the same pregnancy, and matched controls. The chapter from the Dominican Republic documents the high socioeconomic and public health costs associated with the choice of illegal abortion in preference to carrying an unwanted pregnancy to term.

The three chapters of Part V on Service Providers reflect concerns from Jamaica, Nigeria, and Chile, where abortion is a common phenomenon but often obtainable only under difficult illegal circumstances. The attitudes, behaviors, and practices of those who may provide abortion services are reported. Part VI offers commentaries on methodological approaches used in several of the studies reported, followed by a discussion of issues faced when endeavoring to translate available knowledge into more effective service programs.

Although the studies reported are quite diverse, they reflect the continuing interaction of ideas that characterizes the Cooperative Transnational Research Program in Fertility Behavior, coordinated by the Transnational Family Research Institute. Most of these concepts have been discussed at technical seminars convened in Africa, Asia, and Europe, as cited in the suggested readings.

It is recognized that the contributors to this monograph do not provide definitive answers to the many problems posed. It is nevertheless hoped that policy makers, service providers, researchers, and social change agents will be stimulated to consider relevant psychosocial research findings within the context of their priority needs. In this crowded world we share, the common goal of assuring access to legal and safe abortions must be among the realistic alternatives provided to women and men everywhére.

SUGGESTED READINGS

David, H. P. (Ed.). Proceedings of the conference on psychology and family planning, Nairobi, Kenya, August 1971. Washington: Transnational Family Research Institute, 1972.

David, H. P., and Bakare, C. G. M. (Eds.). Summary report of the workshop on psychosocial research in abortion in Africa, Accra, Ghana, December 1973. Washington: Transnational Family Research Institute, 1974.

David, H. P., and Bernheim, J. (Eds.). Proceedings of the conference on psychosocial factors in transnational family planning research, Geneva, Switzerland, April 1970. Washington: American Institutes for Research, 1970.

David, H. P., and Lee, S. J. (Eds.). Proceedings of the technical seminar on social and psychological aspects of fertility, Choonchun, Korea, November 1973. Washington: Transnational Family Research Institute, 1974.

David, H. P., and Shashi, B. (Orgs.). Proceedings of the Asian regional research seminar on psychosocial aspects of abortion, Kathmandu, Nepal, November 1974. Washington: Transnational Family Research Institute, 1975.

David, H. P., and Szabady, E. (Eds.). Proceedings of the re-
    search planning conference for transnational studies in
    family planning, Budapest, Hungary, September 1969.
    Washington: American Institutes for Research, 1970.

Friedman, H. L., and David, H. P. (Eds.). Summary of the con-
    ference on cooperative transnational research in fertility
    behavior, Rostock, German Democratic Republic, October
    1971. Washington: Transnational Family Research Institute,
    1972.

Friedman, H. L., and David, H. P. Choice behavior in fertility
    research: Summary of the Warsaw technical seminar, Warsaw,
    Poland, October 1972. Washington: Transnational Family
    Research Institute, 1973.

2

Psychosocial Research in Abortion:
Selected Issues*

Raymond Illsley and Marion Hall

*Editors' Note: The authors consider the con-
fusing international abortion literature within
the context of cultural, religious, and legal
constraints prevailing in a particular society
at a given time. Where careful pre- and post-
abortion assessments are made, the evidence is
that psychological benefit commonly results;
serious adverse emotional sequelae appear to be
rare. Research on the administration of abortion services suggests that counseling is often
of value, and that distress is frequently
caused by delays in decision making and by un-
sympathetic attitudes of service providers.*

INTRODUCTION

In reviewing selected issues of psychosocial research
in abortion we propose to interpret the term "psychosocial"
widely. We are not just concerned with "psychiatric indications for, or psychiatric sequelae of, induced abortion." We
take the word "psychosocial" not to refer merely to pathology
but to comprehend states of feeling, motivation, and responses
(whether they be sick or healthy), and the social context from
which they arise and by which they are influenced. Moreover,
our concern is not with the value questions of whether abortion is or is not justifiable on psychiatric grounds (although
this inevitably arises), but with the events leading to unwanted pregnancies, the decision-making processes, the clinical procedures, and the supporting services in so far as they
relate to the psychological state of the woman and her family.

*Adapted with permission from the Bulletin of the
World Health Organization, 1976, 53, 83-106.

11

Several research implications flow from our view of
the sociocultural and legal context of abortion that have a
bearing on the interpretation of the literature.

1. Because of differing cultural, religious, and legal rules, and the strength of their enforcement, abortion has
a different meaning from country to country and from one period
to another. Research studies that are all formally concerned
with an event called abortion may, in fact, be measuring different phenomena. Scientifically, therefore, the literature
cannot be aggregated but must be treated as a historical
sequence.

2. Much past literature, even though relatively recent,
is not fully applicable to contemporary problems. The social
situation and psychological orientation of women, families, and
doctors have changed, and we are now concerned with legal, administrative, clinical, and welfare problems of a different
order. For many countries the problem is no longer strictly a
matter of legality or morality but of the most humane and effective method of organizing an abortion service within a
health system.

3. In epidemiological terms, findings about the few
patients who are referred for abortion in a restrictive system
cannot be equated with the results of large-scale studies of
patients in a society in which abortion is performed upon
request.

4. Guilt about abortion has been, and in most societies continues to be, deliberately induced as part of a traditional system of social control. In such circumstances it
is superfluous to ask whether patients experience guilt--it is
axiomatic that they will.

5. In restrictive systems, persons who penetrate the
control barriers to obtain an abortion must automatically be
regarded as "deviant," being a highly selected group with
strong motivation, exceptional social situations, or overt
severe pathology.

6. Only in recent times and in a limited number of
societies has it been possible to distinguish the intrinsic
effects of abortion or repeated abortion from other socially
induced consequences.

GENERAL PROBLEMS OF THE PSYCHOSOCIAL RESEARCH FIELD

The Flux of Psychiatry

Psychiatry, rather than psychology or sociology, has been the dominant discipline concerned in past research about the psychosocial aspects of abortion. Research on psychiatric factors has built up over several decades during which psychiatry as a discipline has itself changed considerably in its theoretical, conceptual, and methodological bases. Early literature was heavily influenced by the psychoanalytic approach, with its emphasis on unconscious or subconscious sexual drive, Oedipus complex, pregnancy as fulfillment, etc. The later development of behavioral and sociocultural approaches to psychiatry—based on quite different premises concerning etiology, diagnosis, and treatment—meant the coexistence of a spectrum of psychiatric perspectives. The request for abortion could be seen as intrinsically indicative of psychopathology, a rejection of the feminine role, overidentification with a father figure, a conscious or unconscious desire to take revenge on either self or another, response to situational factors, avoidance of stigma, or just the desire not to have a baby at that time.

The conflict of theoretical perspectives is compounded by terminological and methodological uncertainties. Practicing psychiatrists have usually become concerned with abortion research because they have had to decide on a course of action for a patient. National laws and professional ethics have usually forced clinicians (and most research reports are conducted by clinicians on their own patients or those of their clinics) to formulate the problem in terms of health or illness rather than of motivation or feeling. "Illness" hides a variety of symptoms, indications, types of behavior, and feelings. Even a cursory glance at the literature reveals that under the terms "psychiatric indications or sequelae" are included categories as diverse as schizophrenia, depression, generalized states of anxiety, disturbance or stress, aspects of personality (e.g., vulnerable personality, psychiatric insufficiency, sadomasochism), feelings of distress that are not necessarily indicative of personality problems or of mental illness (e.g, regret, guilt), and behavior variously capable of being treated as rational or as indicative of psychopathology (e.g., suicidal threat, marital conflict).

Problems of interpretation are complicated by the fact that the criteria for diagnostic judgments are not usually spelled out or validated by independent observers. Moreover, it is clear that psychiatric indications and sequelae have been influenced by legal criteria: "psychosis" was an acceptable term for both action and publication, but termination

for reasons of distress was a cause for prosecution rather
than publication.

Methodologically, the psychiatric research problem is
inherently acute quite apart from the softness of psychiatric
theories and terminology. At the point of pregnancy referral,
several possibilities as regards the patient's psychiatric
state may apply:

1. The patient may have been previously treated for
psychiatric disturbance. Such disturbance, however, may have
been temporary, non recurrent, or situational, and it may re-
cur with or without renewed stress. The clinician is dealing
with probabilities of recurrence.
2. The woman may have had a previous psychiatric disturbance, which, however, has never been identified and treated.
Here the clinician must attempt to reconstruct prior events at
a point when the patient is already under stress.
3. The woman may have had no history of psychiatric
abnormality but may be judged (variously by different observers)
to be especially vulnerable. Again, therefore, the clinician is
predicting.

Even post-hoc interpretation of the dynamics of the
case must also be in terms of probabilities. Women referred
for abortion are, by any definition, different from those not
so referred. One may also expect a higher incidence of psychiatric disturbances among women with a history of previous
psychiatric problems. The post-abortion or post-partum prevalence of mental illness in this group is thus likely to be
high. How can cause and effect be established? It seems in-
escapable that every judgment made by a psychiatrist involved
in a particular case must be a mixture of scientific knowledge,
clinical hunch, personal temperament, moral stance, and professional ideology. In effect, the psychiatrist has frequently
been placed in an impossible position. To avoid political or
moral debate, society has often recruited the psychiatrist,
with his indefinable but humane perspective, to soften the
harsh provisions of the law. While psychiatry has played a
by no means ignoble role, its medical-scientific component is
debatable; indeed it is the very "softness" of its data that
fits it for this role. It is, therefore, unreasonable to expect conclusive scientific findings.

The implications from this discussion are:

1. That future research should be formulated, designed,
and reported to give the maximum of descriptive, factual, and
observational materials, so that its reliability can be tested,
its assumptions validated, and its findings replicated.
2. That as long as decisions are made by persons other
than the woman herself, research should identify and allow for
the built-in assumptions of professional decision makers.

SEXUAL BEHAVIOR AND FAMILY PLANNING

Introduction

In its psychosocial context, abortion may be seen as one choice in a series of events, decisions, and pathways that begin with sexual relationships. At the point of expected or unexpected sexual intercourse at least four "choices" need to be made: whether intercourse should occur, who should be the partner, whether or not contraception should be employed and, if so, what kind of contraception. "Choice," however, is frequently a misleading term because choice was either not perceived as existing or had a priority so low that it was effectively nonexistent. The existence or perception of choice and the values attached to each option are determined culturally and psychologically.

If ultimately, through unprotected intercourse or contraceptive failure, pregnancy occurs, a further range of choices confronts the woman. If she is unmarried, should she, can she, marry and thus bear a child that, though unexpected, finally may not be unwanted? Should she bear an illegitimate child and accept the role of motherhood? Or should she bear the child and have it adopted? Alternatively, should she seek an abortion, legal or illegal? If she is already married to the father of the child, her choices are limited to continuation (with or without adoption) or termination. Involved in these decisions is a constant interaction between individual psychology, social pressures and constraints, and individual actions that precipitate societal responses which, in turn, have an impact on the social and psychological state of the woman and her partner.

Research on abortion should always be formulated in full cognizance of this context. It involves consideration of the possible relevance of the following factors.

Family Size. Where, as in most advanced industrialized countries, norms or aspirations for education and material rewards compete with children, the desired size of families becomes much smaller than it would be at natural levels of natality. Abortion is likely to raise serious policy issues when the desired family size is such as can be obtained only by mobilizing antinatal techniques.

The Status of Contraception. Here we refer to the technical properties, availability, and practical and moral acceptability of contraception. The historical sequence of family reduction, contraception, and abortion is clearly an important determinant of attitudes to abortion among women, the medical profession, and society generally. It thus influences the characteristics--both medical and social--of the population

groups that seek abortion, the frequency of abortion use, and
the structure of medical and supporting services.

The Status of Alternatives. If illegitimate pregnancy carries
a stigma, other alternatives automatically appear to be more
attractive, and the single girl may opt for a marriage that
would otherwise seem undesirable. Research on total populations
designed to demonstrate the relative frequency of each "pathway"
would provide good indications of the availability and perceived
acceptability of each alternative.

The Status of Women. Societies in which women are wage-earners
on an equal footing with men not only confer a degree of inde-
pendence in decision making upon the woman but are also likely
to make available the nursery and care arrangements that make
unmarried motherhood more supportable. We are aware of no studies that explicitly examine the influence of the status of women
or of supporting services on the abortion decision.

Freedom of Sexual Relationships Before and After Marriage. The
sharp rise in out-of-wedlock pregnancy in Western Europe and
North America is evidence of a changing attitude towards premarital chastity and extramarital sexual relationships (Illsley
& Gill, 1968a,b). It pre-dated the introduction and easy
availability of oral contraceptives and of relatively liberal
abortion laws, but may well have hastened liberalization. Kings-
ley Davis (1963), discussing Japanese and other experience, suggested that abortion represents one part of a massive demographic response to changed social and economic conditions in a
process of demographic change and response in which change in
one component is eventually altered by the change it has induced
in the other components. Each of the factors listed above represents one component in this complex process, and the tempta-
tion has been to treat abortion separately from these other
aspects of sexuality, reproduction, and population.

REFERRAL AND DECISION-MAKING PROCESSES

        Most empirical research inquiries concerning the possi-
ble effects of the decision to terminate or to continue a pregnancy are based on the patients referred to a particular gynecologist, psychiatrist, clinic, or hospital. The findings are
likely to reflect the rules and procedures of that specific
situation and to provide few results of general applicability.
In the extreme instances where abortion is possible only on
grounds of danger to life, the small number of identifiable
cases may not justify research, but the volume of illegal abortions may be large. Where only clear-cut medical grounds are
acceptable, the population of potential or actual abortees will
include a high proportion of women who accept abortion reluc-
tantly on medical advice and where therefore little enthusiasm
about the operation can be expected. Where wider grounds of

mental health are allowed, the composition of the group of aborted women will exhibit greater heterogeneity and one can expect the population to show, after abortion, a variety of psychopathological manifestations. At the other extreme of abortion on demand, the population of abortees is likely to reflect the culture of the society, its ideas about family size and spacing, and the availability and use of contraception. This section of the report is intended to identify the pitfalls and methodological problems deriving from differences in referral and decision making.

With the exception of spontaneous abortions and those performed on medical grounds, all aborted pregnancies fall within the category of unwanted pregnancies. They may, however, form only a small proportion of the total of "unwanted pregnancies." Depending on the time and place of the research, they are likely to exclude one or more of the following categories (some of which overlap).

1. Women whose motivation for termination was weak.
2. Women who were unaware that termination might be possible or who considered themselves as ineligible.
3. Women whose religious or other principles prohibited termination.
4. Women deterred by spouse or partner, relatives, friends, or advisers.
5. Women who made up their minds too late in pregnancy or were delayed too long by administrative procedures.
6. Women who raised the possibility of termination with their doctors too tentatively or indirectly to get a response.
7. Women who were refused termination.
8. Women who changed their minds after a positive decision.
9. Women who procured an illegal abortion.
10. Women who decided to marry rather than accept the stigma of other alternatives.
11. Women who decided to continue the pregnancy and have the baby adopted.
12. Women who aborted spontaneously.

Each of these groups may differ from the others in such a way that its inclusion in or exclusion from a study would seriously affect the social, psychological, and health composition of any population of aborted women or of women refused an abortion. For example, depending on the circumstances, the groups might be biased in terms of age, parity, education, social class, financial status, area of residence, mental and physical health, personality characteristics, marital status, or previous abortion experience. Moreover, where the decision is taken by medical advisers, selection would

occur on the basis of the legal, medical, and other criteria
acceptable as indications, the professional ideology and moral
stance of the doctor, and the availability of beds and
facilities.

In the literature reviewed in the next two sections,
authors most frequently describe their studies in such terms
as the following: "the author followed up 32 cases referred
for abortion on psychiatric grounds compared with 48 women who
were refused an abortion and a control group of 50 pregnant
women who did not apply for termination." Such a design or
description may at times be adequate for highly specific and
limited purposes. Clearly, in view of the selectivity indicated above, it would be of little value outside the clinic
concerned.

Ideal experimental conditions rarely exist in research
on human subjects. The next best alternative is to adopt comparative methods of empirical investigation that permit, by
their very design, definitive answers to specific questions.
Such studies only arise accidentally out of routine clinical
practice. The comparative method often requires collaboration
among centers that differ from each other in specified ways,
and methodological considerations demand the participation of
specialists with skills not usually present in a clinical team.

PSYCHIATRIC AND PSYCHOLOGICAL CORRELATES
AND CONSEQUENCES OF ABORTION

The status of the psychiatric literature has been discussed under "General problems of the psychosocial research
field." It is sufficient, at this point, to remind the reader
of the extreme divergence of views among psychiatrists on what
constitutes a psychiatric indication for abortion, as is also
described more fully by David in chapter 5. A review of the
international literature (Illsley & Hall, 1976) suggests the
following observations:

Suicide. Although suicide in pregnancy is rare, the rate of
suicide in unwanted pregnancy is unknown and would be extremely
difficult to determine. The risk of suicide in women seeking
abortions seems to be small but real. Psychiatric referral is
indicated where suicide is threatened because such women need
detailed pre-abortion assessment and careful follow-up whether
abortion is performed or not. Further research in this field
does not seem likely to be profitable.

Psychiatric Indications. Much research reported on abortion
for psychiatric indications is unreliable because it was done

in a situation in which a woman seeking abortion on mainly social grounds had to show psychiatric disturbance in order that
the abortion should be legally acceptable, and indeed was
likely to become genuinely disturbed by the possibility of not
obtaining it. In countries such as the USA, where there is now
no legal restriction upon the performance of abortion, it seems
that research on the purely psychiatric aspects of the problem
in women with psychiatric disease will become easier. Clear
definitions of criteria for diagnosing and labeling psychiatric diseases would be a prerequisite for useful research, but
may be difficult to achieve.

Even in conditions such as schizophrenia, where the
diagnosis is relatively clear-cut and the natural history of
the disease is well documented, there is a wide range of opinions among psychiatrists on the correct management of a schiz-
ophrenic woman who seeks termination of an unwanted pregnancy.
Evaluation of the literature is made difficult by the failure
of many authors to distinguish different forms of severe psychiatric disease when describing their abortion-seeking
patients.

Medical Indications. Patients who have an abortion on medical
grounds form less than five percent of most reported series,
and have been excluded from many studies of psychiatric sequelae of abortion. Research should be directed towards determining methods of minimizing the traumatic nature of the
termination procedure for these women.

Guilt and depression have been noted in women having
abortions because fetal malformation is suspected. Research
should be directed towards providing more adequate emotional
support.

WOMEN WITHOUT OVERT PSYCHIATRIC DISORDER

There is considerable doubt whether women who seek
abortion differ from other women in any respect other than
having an unwanted pregnancy with which they have decided not
to continue. Several difficulties arise in answering this
question. First, assessment of personality traits should
ideally be made prior to the crisis of the unwanted pregnancy,
since assessment at the time when abortion is sought may be
biased towards abnormal results that are due to the pregnancy
itself, to the fact that it was unplanned or unwanted, or (as
in the case of rubella infection) doomed to an unsuccessful
outcome. Disturbed personalities may be attributable to adverse social circumstances, such as unemployment or poor housing, that make the continuation of the pregnancy impossible,

to the break-up of the relationship with the putative father
that has led to the abortion request, or to pregnancy resulting from rape.

A further problem is that assessment by psychiatric
interview may be biased by the opinions and background of the
interviewer and produce results difficult to measure, whereas
"objective" psychological and personality tests, although
easier to score, are relatively crude. The selection of control groups for studies giving as assessment of pre-operative
personalities has never been ideal and has sometimes been
quite bizarre--for example, Kenyon (1969), in stating that
women seeking pregnancy termination tended to be promiscuous,
was comparing them with routine psychiatric referrals. Olley
(1970), in Aberdeen, compared 207 married women seeking termination with 80 normal pregnant women matched for age, social
class, and gestation. His control group for 163 single women
seeking termination is less satisfactory in that it consisted
of 700 nonpregnant student nurses. He found that the married
abortion seekers, tested before they knew whether their request would be granted, showed neurotic personality patterns
compared with the control group, whereas the single women
showed psychopathic features with "accident-prone" tendencies.

Reports of the psychiatric sequelae of abortion in
women who are not suffering from obvious psychiatric disease
at the time of seeking an abortion vary from the pessimism of
Bolter (1962), who has never seen a patient who did not have
guilt feelings about a previous abortion, to the optimism of
Osofsky et al. (1971), who describe relief as the usual sequel.
The wide range of opinions seems to be due to the failure of
some authors to take into account (a) previous psychiatric
illness of the patient; (b) the stigma attached to unwanted--
particularly illegitimate--pregnancy, irrespective of whether
it is aborted; (c) the marital discord or break-up of sexual
relationships that often precipitates the decision to seek
abortion but persists as a stress whether or not abortion is
performed; (d) the traumatic effect on the psyche of all surgery, particularly on the genital tract; (e) the possible adverse psychological effects of sterilization, which is often
combined with abortion; (f) the distressing effect of hostile
clinic and hospital staff and other ward patients; (g) the potential trauma of administrative problems, such as delays in
decision making and in admission for abortion after the decision has been made, and admission to maternity wards where the
patient may see and hear neonates; and (h) ignorance of patients regarding the likelihood of somatic sequelae.

There is now a substantial body of data reported from
many countries, suggesting, after careful and objective

follow-up, that there is a low incidence of adverse psychiatric
sequelae following abortion and a high incidence of beneficial
reactions.

Only a few examples will be given here. One of the
earliest thorough studies was that of Ekblad (1955), who personally interviewed 479 women having abortions on psychiatric
or social grounds in Stockholm in 1949 and 1950, both before
discharge from hospital and two-to-five years later. He found
relatively serious self-reproach in eleven percent of the women
but he considered their depression to be mild in psychiatric
terms. It occurred more often when sterilization had been
made a condition for the abortion to be performed, and was at
least partly due to the sterilization. Only four women (one
percent) were unable to work because of impaired mental health,
and Ekblad considered that the break with the male partner was
probably the cause of the depression. He also stated that it
was likely that they would have developed equally severe symptoms of insufficiency even if they had not been granted legal
abortions. In the United Kingdom, Pare and Raven (1970) followed up (mostly by interview one-to-three years later) 250 to
270 abortion seekers who had been referred for a pre-abortion
psychiatric opinion. Of 128 whose pregnancies were terminated,
all but two were glad to have had the operation, although mild
guilt lasted for more than three months in thirteen percent.
In Aberdeen, Aitken-Swan (1973) conducted a sociological interview prior to abortion and four-to-five months later. Of 50
single women, 21 felt sadness or guilt, but 46 were convinced
of the rightness of their decision. Of 52 married women, 48
were sure that abortion had been the right decision. Psychiatric interview and psychological testing in Aberdeen before and
13-43 months after abortion showed that fifteen percent of
single women and thirty percent of married women were depressed
and anxious. However, the post-abortion depression was frequently due to stresses other than those resulting from abortion.
The psychological tests showed a marked improvement at follow-
up on women who had had an abortion. In summary, it seems that
where careful pre- and post-abortion assessments are made, the
balance of the evidence is that psychological benefit is common; guilt does occur, but serious adverse sequelae are very
rare. It should be remembered that the woman with an unwanted
pregnancy finds herself in a situation in which all the available solutions have some possible disadvantages. There certainly does not seem any real basis for a fear that adverse
psychiatric sequelae will commonly result if she and the physician choose abortion as the solution.

OUTCOME OF REFUSED ABORTION

Outcome for the Mother

Reports of adverse emotional reactions following induced abortion have often ignored the possibility that adverse reactions can also result from refusal of abortion. Comparison of the incidence of adverse reactions in these groups is of limited value for the following reasons.

1. Patients whose requests for abortion on any medical, psychiatric, or social ground are refused are likely to be, in the opinion of the deciding doctors, healthier and more "stable," and to have better social and financial circumstances than those whose requests are granted (Olley, 1970).

2. There is a high incidence of illegal abortion, or legal abortion obtained elsewhere, in many studies of refused abortion. This means that the residual group of women who continued their pregnancies tends to include more of those who were less strongly motivated towards abortion in the first place, or who are less able to cope with the difficulties of seeking another opinion (Dytrych et al., 1975).

3. Follow-up of refused abortion is often incomplete, since the women concerned often do not want to cooperate with the staff of the hospital who refused them the help that they sought.

Thus it cannot be suggested that the outcome of refused abortion represents what would have happened to the women whose pregnancies were terminated, had they been refused. Study of the outcome of refused abortion is nevertheless of great interest, since the sequelae of refused abortion for the mother are likely to be of a different order altogether from those of termination. The latter is a surgical operation that lasts at most an hour and can often be concealed from friends and family, although it may have great emotional significance for the mother, whereas the former involves a much longer period of incapacity for work during the pregnancy, is usually obvious to all with whom the mother comes in contact--frequently with unpleasant connotations, if the pregnancy is out of wedlock--and, finally, there is usually a period of responsibility for the child, which will last 15-20 years.

A review of the available literature (Illsley & Hall, 1976) suggests that many women who are refused abortion adjust to the situation and grow to love the child, almost half would still have preferred abortion, a large minority suffer considerable distress, and a few develop severe disturbance.

Outcome for the Child and the Family

The potentially damaging effect of a continued pregnancy on the child, other children, and the family unit in general is now widely accepted as a factor to be considered in termination decisions. Many authors have commented, or produced some incomplete research material, on the outcome for the child. It is significant, however, that only two major controlled studies have been reported in the literature-- Forssman and Thuwe (1966), Dytrych et al. (1975).

In 1966, Forssman and Thuwe reported a twenty-year follow-up study of 120 children born to Swedish women whose requests for abortion on psychiatric grounds had been denied by the medical authorities. The control children were same-sex babies born in the same hospital immediately after the delivery of the unwanted child. An examination of available records twenty years later showed that many more of the unwanted children than control children "had not had the advantage of secure family life during childhood." They were registered more often with psychiatric services, had engaged in more antisocial and criminal behavior, and had received more public assistance. The results obtained pointed to the unwanted children "being born into a worse situation than the control children."

Matching of the unwanted children and their controls was limited primarily to sex, age, and place of birth. There were, however, some major differences between the groups. For example, 26.7 percent of the unwanted children were born out of wedlock compared to 7.5 percent of the control children. Of the 120 unwanted children, eight were adopted by others, compared to none of the controls. Similar differences existed on such variables as mother's age and parity, and the family's socioeconomic status. These methodological flaws make the reported findings more difficult to interpret. There is also a suggestion that the mothers of the unwanted children included more women who were "mentally vulnerable."

As reported in greater detail in chapter 9, unique circumstances in Prague, Czechoslovakia, combined to make available for detailed assessment 120 boys and 120 girls born in 1961-63 to women twice denied legal abortion for the same pregnancy, and a similar number of matched controls whose mothers had not applied for abortion. Unwantedness was operationally defined in terms of requesting or not requesting an abortion. The study children were born to women whose request for abortion had been denied on original application and on appeal-- usually for reasons of health, because the pregnancy was of more than twelve weeks duration, or because the applicant had had another abortion during the previous twelve months.

The research study was conducted when the children were about nine years old. They were matched insofar as possible with a control group of children of the same sex, age, birth order, number of siblings, and school class. The mothers were matched for age, marital status, and socioeconomic status (as determined by the husband's occupation and his presence in the family). The research staff was not involved in the matching process and did not know which child belonged to which subgroup. The findings suggest that "compulsory childbearing has varied and sometimes unfavorable consequences for the subsequent life of the child."

Clearly, there cannot be a single answer to the question whether "refused-abortion-children" differ developmentally from other children. The answers will vary across societies and from time to time within a society according to the applicability of the factors listed above. The research problem is further complicated by the fact that whether a child is overtly wanted or not wanted will itself be affected by the freedom with which abortion can be obtained and hence the perception by the mother of alternatives to continuation.

Research projects that attempt to determine the effect of a refused abortion on the state of the child 10-15 years later must encounter severe methodological problems because of the intricate developmental sequences occurring over a long period. It is essential to know the social and psychological circumstances in which children of unwanted pregnancies are reared (separate subgroups of unwanted pregnancies being treated separately). This knowledge, together with what is generally known from social pediatrics, developmental psychology, and the sociology of the family, will enable us to predict the cause-and-effect relationship.

ADMINISTRATIVE ASPECTS

Pre-abortion Counseling

Although in many countries abortion is legal only on ethical grounds, it is generally recognized that unwanted pregnancy is not a "disease" for which "treatment" can be prescribed, and that a careful evaluation of the woman's motivation and background is essential.

Unlike many decisions the woman will have to make in her life, the decision to terminate or to proceed with an unplanned pregnancy is irreversible. In addition, the possibility of discussing the advantages and disadvantages of abortion with friends and relatives may be very restricted. Lambert (1971), in a survey of 3,000 unwanted pregnancies seen in

London, reports that only 34 percent of single girls had informed their parents and in 33 percent of cases the putative
father either had not been told of the pregnancy or had taken
no interest in the decision. Osofsky and Osofsky (1972) reported that 47 percent of their patients considered the decision a difficult one to make. It seems therefore that pre-
abortion counseling may be not only a helpful but a necessary
service.

        It has not yet been established by whom such counsel-
ing might best be given. Pre-abortion counseling may be given
mainly by the woman's personal physician or general practitioner, who is likely to have some knowledge of her social
background and medical history and of the possible effect upon
her and the child of the available alternative. However,
Farmer (1973) notes that in Aberdeen most of the practitioners
tended to strongly dissuade their patients from seeking abortion and to refer them to a consultant gynecologist only re-
luctantly. Considerably doubt may be cast upon the suitability
of the general practitioner as a counselor in the United Kingdom by the fact that large numbers of women go directly to the
Pregnancy Advisory Services set up in Birmingham and London,
in order to seek advice about pregnancy termination.

        Gynecologists have often performed pre-abortion coun-
seling, partly because they are usually called upon to perform
the pregnancy termination and partly because they have a special knowledge of the somatic complications of abortion and of
the factors involved in selecting the best operation for the
woman whose pregnancy is to be terminated. It is often felt
that they also understand the emotional significance of pregnancy because they deal so much with pregnant women. However,
their capacity to weigh up the adverse emotional sequelae of
abortion against those of continuing an unwanted pregnancy is
more doubtful. Certainly there is little evidence of awareness of the possible problems associated with refused abortion
among leading British gynecologists. In restrictive systems,
the gynecologist until recently accepted the responsibility
for controlling abortion and has tended in consequence to adopt
a conservative approach.

        In many countries, prior to abortion law reform, rou-
tine referral to psychiatrists was common, mainly because psychiatric illness or disturbance had to be demonstrated by the
woman in order to qualify her for an abortion. Recent publications have tended to suggest that routine psychiatric consultation is unnecessary. The American Psychoanalytic Association stated in 1970 (Pasnau, 1970) that the legitimate
position of the psychiatrist and psychoanalyst is to serve as
a consultant where there is a question of a contraindication

to the proposed procedure. Pasnau (1970) himself suggests psychiatric evaluation only for women exhibiting psychosis, suicidal ideas, depression, or severe personality and behavior disorders. The consensus seems to be that psychiatric evaluation is necessary or helpful in only a small proportion of women seeking abortion.

Committees of doctors (sometimes with lay members) have often been used to provide pre-abortion evaluation (usually leading to the decision whether or not to abort the pregnancy). However, some committees were set up not to provide pre-abortion counseling but to "reduce the number of undeserving requests for abortion and provide impersonal judgement on the applications" (Hammond, 1964). Committees are useful devices for reaching impersonal and anonymous decisions, but are of doubtful value for purposes of counseling.

There is considerable doubt whether pre-abortion counseling is best done by doctors at all. Barnes et al. (1971) noted that many patients resented being judged by doctors. It may well be that, where the doctor judges, he is not well placed to give counsel. Asher (1972) considers that, in the USA, the need for counseling can be, and is being, met by a wide range of individuals possessing a variety of skills and experience. He suggests that certain personality traits are important in a counselor: "empathy, nonpossessive warmth and genuineness. . .maturity, flexibility, and willingness. . .to let the woman make her own decision."

Counseling by medical personnel arose largely because they controlled decisions, not because they had been shown to give good counsel. Counseling by nonmedical personnel has now arisen in many countries on an ad hoc basis, not primarily because lay people had been shown to perform the task better but because doctors were unwilling or unable to cope with the increased load resulting from legislative changes. Experience seems to show that counseling can be done adequately by both nonmedical and medical personnel who are interested in the problem. However, further research seems to be required into the qualifications, background, qualities, and training necessary for a pre-abortion counselor. In systems where medical personnel make the termination decision, their suitability as counselors needs special examination.

Decision Making

In many countries, the decision whether abortion is granted to a woman who seeks it is now left entirely to the woman herself, provided that the pregnancy is not too advanced. Comparison of the relative efficacy or success of different

methods of decision making is difficult, since the characteristics required of the decision maker will depend on the legal
framework within which he or she is required to operate. For
example, if abortion is legal only on psychiatric grounds,
then clearly a psychiatrist must make the decision; if abortion is always legal, except when gestation is to far advanced,
then a gynecologist should make the decision. However, within
the legal framework of any particular country, research with
long-term follow-up might be fruitful to determine the somatic,
emotional, and social sequelae of decisions made by any particular group of doctors or counselors, since there are often
great variations in the implementation of any particular law.

Timing of Abortion Procedure

Once a decision to perform abortion has been taken,
there seems little doubt that, from a strictly gynecological
point of view, the more quickly the operation is performed the
better, since the morbidity and mortality from the operation
rises with gestation. Furthermore, many women find the delay
in admission that often occurs very distressing. It has not
been established whether women who change their minds have
made a realistic or sensible decision. Aren and Amark (1961)
reported on 162 women in Sweden who were granted an abortion
but decided not to have it. Although six regretted this later,
and the outcome for the children in many cases was unsatisfac-
tory, the authors felt that the decision to abstain was usually right. Research into methods of identifying those with
sufficient ambivalence to merit some delay and further consideration would be helpful.

Type of Procedure

The decision as to which method of termination should
be adopted is primarily a gynecological one, based on the relative safety of different procedures at different stages of
gestation. There have been very few reports published on the
adverse emotional effects of different procedures. Several
authors have commented on the unpleasant experience undergone
by patients subjected to amniotic infusion, especially if they
are left unattended when abortion occurs. However, it should
be remembered that operations of this sort are usually performed on patients who attend late for pre-abortion consultation and who seem to be more ambivalent about abortion than
the group who attend early and therefore obtain vaginal termination. Their distress may be due at least partly to their
ambivalence. However, ignorance of what the procedure involves is also a factor, and the importance of educating the
patient in what to expect of the procedure is emphasized by
Asher (1972).

Place of Abortion

        Where abortion law reform has resulted in a large in-
crease in the number of abortions being done, there are often
major problems in providing hospital beds, operating room
time, and staff to perform the operation; unless special facilities are expanded, abortion patients inevitably use facilities
that would otherwise be available for other gynecological admissions. Since most abortion patients are clearly not ill,
nurses may have difficulty in considering them as patients and
may not perceive the operation as therapeutic. Furthermore,
since a pregnancy termination can be performed only within a
very limited time, abortion patients have to take priority over
ordinary waiting-list admissions, and this may further increase
nurses' resentment of them. An additional problem for nurses
(particularly operating room staff) is that they often do not
know the details of the case and therefore find it difficult to
sympathize with the problems of what seem to them to be healthy
women. There have been no systematic studies of the effect of
these factors on the treatment of abortion patients, but there
have been many reports of hostility or of problems experienced
by abortion patients (e.g., Tanner et al., 1971).

        Pion et al. (1970) suggested that women who had the
most difficulty in coming to terms with their abortions were
most likely to be dissatisfied with the services. However, it
could also be postulated that their difficulty in adjusting to
the abortion was exacerbated by the guilt-promoting effect of
the hostility experienced. Particularly unpleasant experiences
seem to be undergone by abortion patients who are admitted to
maternity wards.

CONCLUSIONS AND RECOMMENDATIONS

        Our review of issues, research studies, and findings
fully corroborates the already widespread opinion that past
research in this field has been inadequate in scope, faulty in
methodology, unsystematically organized, and in general motivated and directed towards problems posed by ideological rather
than scientific considerations. Consequently research into
such problems has been either impossible or limited in its application. Many of the theories, concepts, and categories used
to clarify issues about abortion have been so problematic that
they themselves need prior clarification. And the range of
disciplines used in research has been restricted because the
problems were too narrowly conceived in terms of illness rather
than of sociological processes and psychological states.

        We do not consider it part of our task to suggest de-
tailed research design because, at the cross-cultural level,

so much depends upon local knowledge, personnel, and opportunities. Instead we offer some general remarks on conceptual and methodological issues.

1. Future scientific understanding will not be furthered by ad hoc epidemiological studies of incomplete clinic or hospital populations in which the basic data for rigorous epidemiological analysis are not available or not reported.

2. Future research must be based on: (a) the occurrence of naturally arising innovations or experimental situations; (b) the application of experimental techniques designed to create situations in which specific questions can be answered; (c) surveys specially designed and conducted to provide answers to limited and defined questions; and (d) methodological studies designed to clarify concepts and system differences.

3. The preoccupation with mental health or illness and psychiatric pathology must give way to broader studies that are either descriptive or rigorously analytical, in which the focus will be on psychological states and their description and measurement in a variety of social, marital, administrative, and clinical situations. Abortion should be seen not as a separate phenomenon but as one possible course of action, the necessity for which arises out of prior and possibly preventable events and behavior.

4. Much research in the past has been centered on whether abortion should or should not be legalized. Many of these questions were not scientifically researchable. Research needs to be broadened to concentrate on abortion services, service providers, and patients' responses.

5. Since there is some tendency towards uniformity within national boundaries, international comparisons are well suited to pick up the variety of procedures and processes potentially available and to assess their implications. Cross-national research, if carefully designed, might therefore, at this stage, be worthwhile.

6. The nature of the problem must naturally dictate the choice of research method. Much past research has been epidemiological in nature but has totally lacked the known scientific rules for valid epidemiological enquiry. This must be rectified. Furthermore, we need far more descriptive and observational studies of the processes involved at each stage-- e.g., what referral pathways women follow under different systems and how they perceive them and feel about them, and what counseling services are available.

Studies of this kind would contribute in various ways, but particularly in identifying issues of concern to patients, the study of decision making as opposed to decisions, the reformulation of old problems in researchable terms, and the introduction of nonmedical disciplines.

In this review we have not attempted to cover all possibilities, preferring to confine outselves to major areas. Additional relevant references can be found in our original publication (Illsley & Hall, 1976) and in other chapters in this volume. Our general recommendations, arising from our immersion in a confusing research literature, are for simple, observational, descriptive research directed towards laying an information basis on which more ambitious theoretical work can be built later, and for the use of experiemtnal research wherever it is practically or ethically appropriate. Methodology is all-important. Research on a cross-cultural basis would clearly be profitable because it most easily permits the comparative study of management systems and the identification of experimental situations.

REFERENCES

Aitken-Swan, J. In G. W. Horobin (Ed.), Experience with abortion: A case study in north-east Scotland. London: Cambridge University Press, 1973.

Aren, P., & Amark, C. The prognosis in cases in which legal abortion has been granted but not carried out. Acta Psychiatrica et Neurologica Scandinavica, 1961, 36, 203-278.

Asher, J. D. Abortion counselling. American Journal of Public Health, 1972, 62, 686-688.

Barnes, A. B. et al. Therapeutic abortion: Medical and social sequels. Annals of Internal Medicine, 1971, 75, 881-886.

Bolter, S. The psychiatrist's role in therapeutic abortion: The unwitting accomplice. American Journal of Psychiatry, 1962, 119, 312-316.

Davis, K. The theory of change and response in modern demographic history. Population Index, 1963, 29, 345-366.

Dytrych, Z., Matejcek, Z., Schüller, V., David, H. P., & Friedman, H. L. Children born to women denied abortion. Family Planning Perspectives, 1975, 7, 165-171.

Ekblad, M. Induced abortion on psychiatric grounds. Acta Psychiatrica et Neurologica Scandinavica, 1955, 99, Supplement.

Farmer, C. In G. W. Horobin (Ed.), Experience with abortion: A case study in north-east Scotland. London: Cambridge University Press, 1973. Pp. 333-357.

Forssman, H., & Thuwe, I. One hundred and twenty children born after therapeutic abortion refused. Acta Psychiatrica Scandinavica, 1966, 42, 71-78.

Hammond, H. Therapeutic abortion: Ten years' experience with hospital committee control. American Journal of Obstetrics and Gynecology, 1964, 89, 349-355.

Illsley, R., & Gill, D. G. New fashions in illegitimacy. New Society, 1968, 12, 709-711. (a)

Illsley, R., & Gill, D. G. Changing trends in illegitimacy. Social Science and Medicine, 1968, 2, 415-433. (b)

Illsley, R., & Hall, M. H. Psychosocial aspects of abortion: A review of issues and needed research. Bulletin of the World Health Organization, 1976, 53, 83-106.

Kenyon, F. E. Termination of pregnancy on psychiatric grounds: A comparative study of 61 cases. British Journal of Medical Psychology, 1969, 42, 243-263.

Lambert, J. A survey of 3,000 unwanted pregnancies. British Medical Journal, 1971, 2, 156-160.

Olley, P. C. Age, marriage, personality and distress: A study of personality factors in women referred for therapeutic abortion. Seminars in Psychiatry, 1970, 2, 341-351.

Osofsky, J. D. et al. Psychological effects of legal abortion. Clinical Obstetrics and Gynecology, 1971, 14, 215-234.

Osofsky, J. D., & Osofsky, H. J. The psychological reactions of patients to legalized abortions. American Journal of Orthopsychiatry, 1972, 42, 48-59.

Pare, C. M. B., & Raven, H. Follow-up of patients referred for termination. Lancet, 1970, 1, 653-658.

Pasnau, R. O. Psychiatric complications of therapeutic abortion. Obstetrics and Gynaecology, 1972, 40, 252-256.

Pion, R. J. et al. Abortion request and post-operative re-
    sponses. Northwest Medicine, 1970, 69, 693-698.

Tanner, L. M. et al. Attitudes of personnel: Determinants
    of or deterrents to good patient care? Clinical Obstet-
    rics and Gynecology, 1971, 14, 1282.

PART TWO

PSYCHOSOCIAL DYNAMICS

3

Abortion Seeking in Switzerland*

Jean Kellerhals and Willy Pasini
with Genevieve Wirth

*Editors' Note: Availability of abortion has
long differed among Swiss cantons. In Geneva,
for example, there is usually one request for
pregnancy termination for every two births;
about half are approved. The study here reported was conducted during 1970-1971 with a
representative sample of 906 women requesting
legal abortions. The perceptive analysis
considers evolving meanings of a child for
the family, psychosocial determinants of contraceptive practice, psychodynamics of abortion seeking, and the legal decision-making
process in Geneva. Six years after the conclusion of this study, the Swiss Parliament
liberalized abortion legislation by empower-
ing cantonal abortion commissions to consider
the "social situation" associated with the
pregnant woman's request to terminate an
unwanted pregnancy.*

INTRODUCTION

At the time the study was conducted, the legal procedure for requesting authorization to interrupt a pregnancy in
Geneva was as follows: the medical practitioner certified
the woman's pregnant condition and, in consultation with the
woman, determined whether there were grounds for requesting
an induced abortion. Should this be so, the pregnant woman

---

*This study was conducted through the facilities of
the Faculty of Medicine, University of Geneva, under the spon-
sorship of Professors J. Bernheim and W. Geisendorf with
agreement of the College of Advisors and in consultation with
the Transnational Family Research Institute.

35

had to apply to a second physician or "advisor" for authorization to obtain an abortion. This medical advisor was especially commissioned by the cantonal government and had to be either a psychiatrist or a specialist in the particular medical area the woman cited as grounds for pregnancy interruption. Under this prevailing legislation (Switzerland, 1973), authorization to terminate was granted if the woman's "health" would be seriously impaired and permanently injured by pregnancy continuation. Different cantons applied different interpretations to the definition of "health." Whereas some considered only serious illnesses as grounds for legal abortion, the Canton of Geneva included consideration of socioeconomic problems associated with pregnancy. The Geneva procedure was thus deemed rather liberal in Switzerland.

Following Parliament action of June 1977 and a subsequent referendum, abortion decisions will be made by a specific commission established in the canton of the pregnant woman's residence and required to act within the prescribed 12 week limit. The commissions are empowered to consider the "social situation" associated with the pregnant woman's request for termination of an unwanted pregnancy, thus placing Swiss legislation among the more liberal in Europe while retaining cantonal interpretation.

The aim of our research was to determine (1) the social features of the women requesting an abortion, (2) the motives for the interruption, and (3) the chronological and emotional stages of the decision. The study was conducted on the basis of 906 interviews during the period 1970-1971. One woman out of two requesting an interruption of pregnancy was asked to participate. The interview took place before the appointment with the advisor, as illustrated in the diagram following. Every precaution was taken so that the patient would know that: (1) she was absolutely free to refuse the interview; (2) the interview had nothing whatsoever to do with the decision made by the advisor; and (3) none of the information given during the interview would be communicated to the advisor.

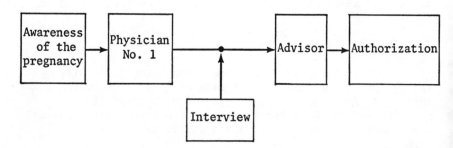

The rate of interview refusal was low, about three percent. We can therefore state that our sample is representative of the population applying for a legal interruption of pregnancy in Geneva. (This includes Swiss or foreign women, married or single, who have been residents of the canton of Geneva for at least three months.) A questionnaire containing open as well as closed questions served as a guide for the interviews which were conducted by a small team of women having a background in psychology or social research.

UNDERSTANDING ABORTION

Since abortion is used so frequently as a method of birth control, we must try to understand it. Two elements seem to be important: (1) the social meaning of the child in contemporary Swiss society, which provides a strong motivation for fertility limitation, and (2) the high rate of "contraceptive failures" resulting in unwanted pregnancies.

Let us first examine what the child means sociologically for contemporary Swiss families. This will help us understand the general motivation for resorting to interruption of pregnancy.

Motivation for Childbearing: The Meaning of the Child

The social identity of the child proceeds mainly from his "social visibility" and from the social functions he fulfills. Both elements have varied considerably in Switzerland during the change from preindustrial to advanced industrial society.

Social Visibility. Social visibility refers to the number and size of the groups that control the fertility of a given couple and whose structure can be affected by the birth of another child. One can easily see how this visibility has shrunk because of three structural aspects of the contemporary family: (1) its nuclear and neolocal nature entails that the new child does not disturb the pattern of tasks and leadership division in the family of origin; (2) the bilateral nature of the filiation entails that no steady and definite group can be formed as a cooperative unit beside the nuclear family; (3) marriage by affinity implies that, as a rule, the families of origin, as they loosen their control over the new spouses, loosen it as well over the new family's offspring.

To sum up, the contemporary child tends to have meaning for the parents only and no longer affects the equilibrium and dynamics of much more extended groups, as was the case in previous situations. Of course, there remain ties between the extended family and one or another child, but these ties cannot be compared in their nature to those existing in a large number of preindustrial societies (Michel, 1972). We shall later expound on the consequences of this.

Social Functions. First, let us define the social functions fulfilled by the child for the family, as differentiated from a societal role. In preindustrial Switzerland, the child had an economic function for the family. In many cases, e.g., agriculture, shops, cottage industries, a child represented usable manpower from early age. Secondly, there was an insurance value: in the absence of social insurance parents expected children to look after them when they got older. Thirdly, the child functioned as a provider of status. In many contexts, the prestige of the family depended partly on the number of children born to the couple. More frequently, the mother found her social identity in procreation. She existed, socially speaking, only if she had children.

In addition, there was a religious function attached to the child, who was frequently perceived as a link between the "lower" world and the "higher" one. The child was thought to be a positive reward, a benediction from God. Finally, of course, the child provided powerful emotional gratification to the parents.

On observing contemporary society, one notices that these various functions have been toned down considerably, or have disappeared completely. Most people have become wage earners, social security systems have been developed, and religion is often less influential than in the past. Urbanization and geographical mobility have combined to bring a major change in the social personality of the child, whose status has changed from being a form of capital to one which has an essentially affective function.

The identity of the child is greatly affected by this "socially restricted visibility" and the loss of some social functions. Procreation has become entirely the decision of the couple or the woman. It is no longer dictated by external factors. This makes the birth of a child rather less inevitable. This arbitrariness is reinforced by the fact that most of the costs involved in procreation are borne by the couple alone. The assistance given by other members of the family or by social security is of minor importance compared to the material (and psychological) responsibilities of the couple or the unmarried mother.

Childbirth has two aspects, a concrete one and a symbolic one. In traditional Switzerland, as well as in other societies, the concrete aspect proceeds from the "material" functions of the child, while the symbolic one lies in the expression of the couple's relationship with God or the extended group. In our present society, the concrete aspect lies in the emotional gratifications expected by the couple from their child, while the symbolic aspect lies in the expression of the emotional relationship between husband and wife, of which the child is the token.

As a consequence, the child has meaning only if the couple agrees that the quality of their relationship is such that it justifies being symbolized in procreation and that the investment involved in raising a child is more rewarding than other activities with which it is in competition, e.g., travel, professional involvement of the woman, improvement of the couple's standard of living, etc. If these two conditions are not present, having a child may appear to be an unbearable burden.

In one sense the child has become more valued as an individual. In this light, the whole status of childhood changes. The child is no longer seen as someone who must submit, as a "lesser" human being or as an individual-to-be who will only take on meaning once grown up. Childhood becomes a privileged age endowed with its own wealth, its own value, and its own mode of balance qualitatively different from that of the adult. But, in another sense, this privileged child is also vulnerable. Existence depends entirely on the extent to which the parents believe the child will gratify them. Moreover, this "leisure child" can fulfill anticipated concrete and symbolic roles only if endowed with all the attributes of normality and modernity expected by the parents.

All these considerations are important because they reflect an area of potential conflict between the point of view of society as a whole, as reflected in the penal code, and the point of view of couples or unmarried women with respect to abortion. There were times when the interests of society and those of couples regarding fertility coincided quite clearly. Such is no longer the case (Kellerhals, 1975). It happens often that society deems it necessary to protect values which appear meaningless to individuals, and neither point of view can be ruled out. Furthermore, if these assumptions are correct, it becomes evident that material help to couples, such as birth allowances, financial assistance to mothers, and better social security coverage, may not help radically to reduce the number of abortion requests. The problem lies more in the cultural status of the child than in

the narrow material costs of the baby. Similarly, various
forms of psychological counseling can help clarify the causes
of ambivalence towards procreation, but not eliminate them.
Moreover, clarifying the ambivalence might lead to an increase
in conflict rather than to a solution.

Chance: The Accidents of Birth Control

The contemporary social status of the child allows us
to understand why, in Switzerland as well as in other industrialized countries, the desire for "large families" has been
replaced by the wish for families with no more than two or
three children. It seems, however, that the techniques used
to achieve the desired family size have not always been
adequate.

Within the population resorting to abortion, the practice of birth control is relatively inadequate. This is shown
clearly in Table 3-1.

Table 3-1

Birth Control Methods Used by the Applicants	(N=906)
No method	31.2%
Rhythm methods	27.6%
Coitus interruptus	16.0%
Pill, IUD, diaphragm, condom	16.5%
Other methods	8.7%
	100.0%

It is important to note that the rather low level of
birth control use is not unique to our sample. Other studies
conducted in Geneva on the same subject show similar findings
(Bassand, Kellerhals, & Wirth, 1974). Our study on abortion,
as well as the ones on fertility, show that effective contraception relates to several concepts.

The Degree and Quality of Communication between Partners. The
importance of communication between partners is clear from
the following observation: the less stable the couple's relationship, the worse their contraceptive behavior. In our

study, 80 percent of the "occasional or accidental" couples
practiced no birth control, against 15 percent of the married
ones. Since "occasional or accidental" relationships are
quite frequent in urban contemporary society, the "risk" involved in this kind of relationship is considerable.

The Absence of Norm Conflicts with Respect to Birth Control.
Norm conflicts regarding methods of birth control can take two
rather different aspects. First, there can be a role conflict.
Most of the modern birth control methods involve the woman
primarily. This is the case for the pill and the IUD. Now it
could be observed that the autonomy these methods give the
woman regarding her fertility does not always correspond to
the role norms which in many of the cultures present in Geneva
give the man dominance in the control of fertility. For example, the principle of birth control is accepted by the Italians and Spaniards living in Geneva, but they choose coitus
interruptus as their contraceptive method in 80 percent of the
cases. Among Swiss couples, only 20 percent prefer this
method.

Ideological conflict is the other type of norm conflict. It is clear that the attitude of the Catholic Church
with respect to fertility control has continued to have certain impact. This explains why one notices an overrepresenta-
tion of the Ogino-Knauss and temperature rhythm methods in the
Catholic subsample. Again, this ideological conflict is better
illustrated among the migrants. It is added to the effect of
the role conflict mentioned earlier. It may take a few more
years before more modern methods of contraception become acceptable to this group (Bassand, Kellerhals, & Wirth, 1974).

Sufficient Knowledge of Birth Control Methods. Formal education plays a role in effective contraception. Although the
pill is used by almost 40 percent of those belonging to the
managerial classes, it is used by no more than 10 percent of
blue collar workers. It is also quite possible that the correct use of the rhythm techniques depends largely on the degree of education of the couple. Social status may also be
significant because informal (social) communication may be important in obtaining correct information about contraceptive
use. Thus, those of lower social status may not have adequate access to needed information unless their circle includes
some well-informed people.

*Lack of Psychological Ambivalence with Respect to Preventing
the Next Birth.* The fact that only 3 percent of the 906 women
in our survey had planned to use legal interruption of pregnancy as a primary method of birth control leads us to ask why
the other 97 percent ended up with a situation which was both

physically and psychologically uncomfortable for them. It
quickly became evident that induced abortions are often the result of previous difficulties associated with poorly integrated
sexuality and of psychological conflicts concerning contraception. We did not study the first of these two points, but
other clinical research has shown that the emotional reaction
to sexuality--the denial of the simple nature of pleasure--can
build up a state of ambivalence, of emotional tension, or of
temporary confusion that may influence the control of fertility (Pasini, 1974).

     There is a cluster of psychological factors that give
rise to conflicts about birth control. Abortion, although a
more active intervention medically, is psychologically more
passive than contraception. Contraception requires planning
and action by the individual or couple; abortion is performed
by outsiders. Anticipating the consequences of one's own actions is sometimes difficult and, as mentioned earlier, may be
associated with educational deficiencies. More often, however,
it is due to difficulty in assuming an active and responsible
control of one's own fertility, which is defined as an adult
behavior but which may also arouse more guilt feelings when
norm conflicts exist. In our study, for instance, many people
were able to justify, a posteriori, their request for an interruption of pregnancy--on the grounds of economic difficulties,
the well-being of existing children, etc.--but could not overcome the psychocultural taboos that went with the decision to
practice contraception.

     A second kind of psychological factor determining the
acceptability of contraception is the presence of a deep desire
for pregnancy, sometimes so visceral and emotional that it can
thwart any endeavor towards family planning. Particularly
among women from cultures where maternity represents the essential realization of femininity, a conscious or unconscious ob-
stacle to the control of fertility will proceed from the idea
that birth prevention will interfere with womanly development.
The social function of the child has already been described;
from a psychological point of view, one could add that pregnancy and a child fulfill many symbolic functions, representing
normality, fulfillment, power, expiation, and the like. Sometimes the desire for pregnancy exists, but not the desire for
a child, as we have found in our sample--especially among
adolescents and women over forty.

The Acceptability of Specific Contraceptive Methods. It is
evident that the acceptability of different contraceptive methods is subject to many physical factors, such as effectiveness
and the presence or absence of side effects. But the way contraceptive information is transmitted is also important. After

the first simple euphoria, family planning centers have had to organize genuine contraceptive education classes in order to overcome the inhibitions and the distortions stemming from traditional information.

From this point of view, the most striking result shown in Table 3-1 remains the fact that about one-third of the 906 women (31.2 percent) were practicing no form of contraception at all. Table 3-2 shows how they justified their behavior.

Table 3-2

Reasons for Not Practicing Contraception

Reason	Number	Percentage
Unforeseen or imposed act	84	29.68
Thought conception impossible	81	28.62
Poorly informed about contraception	33	11.66
Moral aversion to contraception	26	9.19
Physical contraindication to all forms of contraception	18	6.36
Voluntary conception	11	3.89
Other reason	30	10.60
Total	283	100.00

These answers are interesting because they show us the rationalization of unconscious motivations for abortion. In the first place, the desire for a passive solution is expressed in terms of magical surprise. More than 28 percent of the women said, "I thought it was impossible for me to get pregnant." This surprise differs greatly from that of the woman who describes the failure of the method she was using and believed effective. Physical contraindication to all forms of contraception is an even more unlikely justification put forward by 6.36 percent of the women. Insufficient information and an aversion to contraception resulted in passivity in the use of contraception but did not restrict sexuality. Finally, the number of voluntary conceptions which end in pregnancy termination (3.89 percent) allows us to cite desire for pregnancy as another motivation which causes women to "prefer" abortion to contraception.

The unconscious choice of abortion over contraception may sometimes satisfy pathological needs, especially those of a sadomasochistic variety. This is the case of women whose chief pleasure comes not from being pregnant, but from aborting. They thus satisfy their hostility toward the embryo, the symbolic resuscitation of little brothers who were early childhood rivals. Sometimes, the termination of an otherwise desired pregnancy represents the epiphenomenon of a failure-oriented behavior pattern, or the implicit punishment of guilt-ridden sexual relations. These sadomasochistic tendencies are much more frequent among repeat abortors (Pasini, 1974), who comprise about 15 percent of the sample and who are clearly different from the women requesting a first legal termination of pregnancy. However, it must be reiterated that these cases involving sadomasochism are not representative of the group. The study, as a whole, points out that abortion is not preferred to contraception. Resort to the procedure is often only a consequence of resistance to effective contraception, which arises from conflicts involved in behaving in an active and voluntary manner to control fertility.

Who Are the Applicants for Abortion?

Abortion requests are the result of two main forces: (1) the need for fertility limitation and (2) contraceptive failure. The requests are by no means confined to special subgroups in the population, such as the poor or adolescents. Nevertheless, certain types of social situations, such as low socioeconomic status (Table 3-3) or being unmarried (Table 3-4) do increase either the immediate need for fertility limitation or the likelihood of contraceptive failure.

Despite these correlations, it is quite easy to see, from a descriptive point of view, that no part of the population can avoid having to resort to abortion from time to time. Among the married population, it is important to note that 40 percent of the abortions appear to serve a spacing function: more children are wanted, but at some other time. The result of this situation is that, in any given period, a large majority of the requests are made by people whose social situation, age, fertility, etc., are median rather than extreme (see Tables 3-5 through 3-7). This is in clear contradiction to the whole social image of abortion in Switzerland, where many political and social leaders think that abortions are mainly requested by women 18 years old or younger, or those who already have four or five children and whose family incomes are less than 1000 SFRS a month. The fact that the women requesting abortion in Geneva can be considered near average, therefore, has deep implications for social policy.

Table 3-3

Percentages of Pregnancies Terminating in Live Births
(in the Population as a Whole) According to
Order of Pregnancy and Social Status

Monthly Family Income (SFRS)	1st Conception	N	4th Conception and Over	N	Difference between the Percentages of Live Births
Less than 1000	89.5%	153	50.0%	18	-39.5%
1000-1250	88.1%	594	57.4%	54	-30.7%
1251-1500	88.0%	408	60.0%	44	-28.0%
1501-2000	86.8%	608	63.0%	54	-23.8%
more than 2000	78.4%	324	84.2%	19	+ 5.8%

Note. From M. Bassand, J. Kellerhals, & G. Wirth. <u>Familles urbaines et fécondité</u>. Geneva: Georg, 1974.

Table 3-4

Comparison between the Civil Status of Applicants for
Abortion and of the Whole Population of Women
Residing in Geneva, Aged 15-45

	Applicants	All Resident Women
Single	54.9%	36.7%
Married	37.5%	63.3%
Widowed, divorced, separated	7.6%	

Note. From Bureau Cantonal de Statistiques, Geneva, 1971.

Table 3-5

Comparison between the Nationalities of the Applicants
for Abortion and those of the Whole Population
of Women Residing in Geneva, Aged 15-45

	Applicants	All Resident Women
Swiss women	50.4%	62.7%
Foreign women	49.6%	37.3%

Note. From Bureau Cantonal de Statistiques, Geneva, 1971.

Table 3-6

Number of Children Born to Married Applicants for
Abortion at the Time of the Request

No child	10%
1 child	31%
2 children	44%
3 or more children	15%

Table 3-7

Monthly Family Income of Married Women Requesting
Interruption of Pregnancy

Less than 1000 SFRS	2.6%
1000-1500	22.0%
1500-2000	33.0%
2000-2500	16.0%
2500-3000	8.0%
More than 3000	10.0%
Unknown	8.4%

Motivation for Abortion

The social composition of the population requesting abortion helps us to understand why the motives put forward by the applicants to "justify" their requests are not primarily economic, or based on illness, overfertility, fear of taboos, etc. Most motives refer to the cultural and psychological implications of motherhood. Following is the distribution of the main motives for the request:

Somatic Motive (11.6 percent). The health of the applicant is or would be severely impaired by the pregnancy, or she believes that it would. The request proceeds from the illness itself.

Psychological Motive (3.5 percent). The applicant was already psychologically ill and under treatment before the pregnancy. In these cases, the illness and its correlates entail the request. This does not include psychological difficulties caused by the awareness of the pregnancy and the social and psychological difficulties to which the pregnancy will give rise.

Economic Motive (18.5 percent). Here, the financial situation of the household or of the single woman is the problem. The applicant believes that she does not have the financial assets to accept the child. We divided the economic arguments into the following categories:

1.	Housing too small; impossibility of finding another	1.3%
2.	Family income inadequate	3.5%
3.	Single woman's income inadequate	4.4%
4.	Outside activity of the wife absolutely necessary to the family income	3.0%
5.	Economic design for the future (will be impaired by a birth at this time)	0.4%
6.	Uncertainty of future economic situation	1.8%
7.	The woman is the sole earner of the family income	2.1%
8.	Other reasons	2.0%
	Total	18.5%

Family Motive (35.1 percent). This motive was put forward by married women or unmarried mothers refusing a pregnancy in order to avoid aggravating family trouble or endangering a fragile equilibrium with their already-existing children. The different items are:

48 ABORTION IN PSYCHOSOCIAL PERSPECTIVE

1. Continuing education or professional training of the mother — 2.9%
2. Continuing education or professional training of the father/partner — 1.2%
3. Fear of gossip and taboos — 6.0%
4. Loneliness, immaturity of mother — 8.9%
5. The unmarried couple wants to gain stability before having children — 2.8%
6. Temporary or definitive refusal of maternity for other aspirations or ambitions — 3.1%
7. The child-to-be has no meaning because the couple's relationship is also meaningless — 9.5%
8. Other social motives — 0.7%

Total — 35.1%

Coercion Motive (1.0 percent). Another person (husband, father, etc.) compelled the applicant to request an abortion; otherwise, the woman would probably have kept the baby.

Eugenic Motive (8.8 percent). The idea that the child-to-be will be deficient physically, mentally, or affectively, is entailed in the decision. Here, as a rule, the interests of the mother or the couple play no part. The main items are:

1. Fear of physical deficiencies — 2.3%
2. Fear that the child shall be unhappy because he has no father — 6.5%

Total — 8.8%

Constellation of Motivations (8.1 percent). In some cases, there is a constellation of motivations in which not one is clearly dominant. Following are sample cases:

1. The young unmarried girl, whose age, lack of money, and lack of professional education make up a constellation that cannot be disentangled — 2.6%
2. The old mother whose failing health, grown children, fears for the new baby, and reluctance to take anew the social role of the mother create a tangle of motivations — 2.4%
3. Other cases — 3.1%

Total — 8.1%

The generally normal situation of the applicants suggests that if one used the outward signs of social emergency
as criteria, the majority of the requests would be refused.
But, in spite of the relative "social ease" of the applicants,
it is evident that most of them believe they have serious
grounds for resorting to abortion. This presents a considerable problem for the advisor who must make a wise decision
about whether or not the referral is acceptable.

What criterion will he use? His duty is all the more
complicated by the fact that very few abortion referrals are
based on situations that the legislators have foreseen as acceptable. Severe threats to health that are clearly identifiable by medical science comprise less than 15 percent of the
motivations for referral. All the others belong in the social
and psychological domain.

The contradiction between the social image of abortion
and the motives put forward by the applicants, moreover, give
rise to certain guilt feelings associated with the abortion
request.

The Decision and Its Conflicts

In this section we will examine three aspects of the
process of the abortion decision: (1) the mother's perception
of the fetus; (2) the guilt feelings associated with the decision; and (3) the ease of the decision.

The Mother's Perception of the Fetus

A large part of the discussion about abortion proceeds
from the fact that it is very difficult to define the identity
of the fetus. Is it perceived as a human being or not? The
mother's perception of it partly determines the way she will
experience abortion and, particularly, the level of the conflict she will feel between the subjective necessity of an
abortion and the identity she gives to the child-to-be.

The law--as well as the Catholic Church--starts from
the idea that the fetus is, from conception on, a "person-to-
be" whose life must be protected. Now it is evident that
among the population we interviewed this fundamentalist outlook is not shared by the majority. Two other kinds of outlook are observed. There is the relational view. To the question, "When does the fetus become a human being?" the relational viewpoint answers that the threshold is defined as the
moment when the parents recognize the fetus as a human being.
There is no other threshold than the definition that each

person gives·the identity of the fetus. For some parents, it
may be when the fetus stirs and the mother senses the fetus as
a partially autonomous entity. For others, the moment may be
at birth, when society recognizes the presence of a new member.
The third outlook can be called positivist because in its es-
sence it proceeds from the idea that one can define thresholds
in embryogenesis, stages when the fetus changes in its nature.
One will then say that the fetus becomes a human being "when
it is complete," or "at three months," or "when it is given a
brain." No matter the ingenuousness of these images, the basic
idea is that a definite stage in the development of the fetus
marks the passage from the simple object or tissue to existence as a person. The fundamentalist outlook includes about
20 percent of the answers; the relational one, 43 percent; the
positivist, 25 percent. Twelve percent are unclassifiable.

        Two elements are of interest in this distribution:
first is the existence of a rather wide gulf between the legal
position and that of the interviewees. Of course, it is not
certain that if the question were put to the whole population
the same proportions would be found. But neither can we say
that the fundamentalist outlook would prevail. Second is the
relative importance of a relational perception of the child,
i.e., of an identity dependent on the mother-child relationship rather than on the child alone. It is evident that this
relational image of the fetus proceeds directly from the social significance of the child as discussed earlier. The
child's lower social visibility and mainly emotional function
contribute to this outlook.

        In a given subgroup, the predominance of a particular
image does not seem to be explained by the main sociological
factors generally in use. There is no variation in terms of
civil status, socioprofessional position, national of origin,
etc. Religious observance alone is related to a more marked
frequency of the fundamentalist outlook.

The Sense of Guilt
        There is a clear relation between the type of percep-
tion and the sense of guilt associated with the decision of
interrupting the pregnancy. Thus, 93 percent of those having
a fundamentalist outlook say that abortion is morally reprehensible or, in any case, is a moral offense. The proportion
falls to about 60 percent for the women who have a relational
or positivist outlook.

        The existence of a fundamentalist outlook, however,
is not the only factor leading to a sense of guilt. Wider cultural features have an influence here, even when the fetus is

not seen as a human being. Thus, 85 percent of the Italians and Spaniards sampled voice a negative moral judgment of abortion, while only 64 percent of the Swiss and 53 percent of respondents from other European countries and the United States do so.

This relationship between nationality and negative moral judgment is not due to religion, nor to a fundamental outlook. It is linked, rather, with the cultural image of the voluntary control of fertility. We can then say that the moral judgment about abortion has at least two sources: (1) the direct one, springing from the perception of the fetus, and (2) the indirect one, dependent on the current public opinion about fertility and its control. This is important because it shows that the sense of guilt does not always depend on the subjective meaning of the behavior itself, but more often on the context--social, legal, etc.--in which the behavior takes place.

For the married women, the sense of guilt is stronger if she already has children. Among those who do not have children, 57 percent express a negative judgment of abortion. In contrast, 70 percent of women with two children and 86 percent of those with three think negatively of abortion. In one sense, this result is unexpected; one could have foreseen the opposite. But it looks as if the presence of children, which does not influence the perception of the fetus, makes the women more sensitive towards the possible moral aspects of abortion.

Among the single women, we observe that the nature of the relationship with the partner correlates with the sense of guilt towards abortion. This is in accordance with our point of view about the symbolic meaning of the child. Negative moral judgment of abortion occurs among 81 percent of the women with steady relationships with their respective partners. When the relationship is only occasional, this proportion decreases to 61 percent.

Among the Swiss women--the only population for which comparison is possible--religion itself does not seem to play a role in the moral judgment of abortion. Among the married women, 70 percent of the Catholics and 62 percent of the Protestants say that abortion is morally reprehensible or is a moral offense. For single women, these proportions are 71 and 72 percent, respectively. Religious practice, for the same subsamples, show only a minor effect.

The Homogeneity of the Decision to Abort

We have already mentioned the ambivalence about sexuality, and especially about contraception, that can result in the

use of abortion. But, with respect to abortion itself, the decision is sometimes the problem. The personal self-acceptance
of the woman is an essential element conditioning her decision
to terminate a pregnancy and the contingent aftereffects of
abortion. A state of conflict (most of the time intrapsychic
and sometimes intracouple) existed in 36 percent of the cases
observed in the Geneva study, as shown in Table 3-8.

Table 3-8

Ease of the Decision

Was The Decision An Easy One To Come To?	N	%
Yes	564	62.3
No (intrapersonal or intracouple conflict)	317	35.0
No (fear of physical consequences)	12	1.3
No answer	13	1.4
Total	906	100.0

        Sometimes termination of pregnancy is decided ration-
ally, but this solution may nevertheless be in conflict with a
deep-seated desire for pregnancy. For 15 percent of the married and 24 percent of the single women, the first reaction to
the knowledge of pregnancy was very positive: they were happy
and/or proud. For single women--but not for married ones--
this positive reaction is rather strongly related to nationality: 20 percent of the single Swiss women, compared to 40
percent of their Italian and Spanish counterparts, expressed
positive reactions. Among the single women, the quality of the
relationship with the partner again plays a major role. When
a stable and strong relationship exists, 45 percent of them express happiness at the pregnancy; only 5 percent do so when the
union is only occasional. Among the married women, reaction
to the pregnancy was affected by the number of children already
existing. Although 26 percent of those without children expressed positive feelings, only 13 percent of the women with
two children and 8 percent of those who had three showed positive reactions.

What Are the Factors Affecting the
Ease of the Decision?

For single women, we again find the influence of nationality and the quality of the relationship. The decision was easy for 65 percent of the Swiss women and only 50 percent of the Italian and Spanish women. A stronger correlation exists with the quality of the couple's relationship. For those women with strong and stable relationships, the decision was easy in only 45 percent of the cases. Of those with unstable relationships, 79 percent found the decision easy. Among married women, nationality does not play a role, nor does the fact of having or not having children have a visible importance. For both married and single women, the decision is slightly easier for Protestants than for Catholics. Religious practice plays a role only among the single women; for those regularly practicing their religion, the decision was easy in 54 percent of the cases, as compared to 71 percent among those who do not observe religious practices. For both married and single women, the perception of the fetus is strongly associated with the ease of the decision. Seventy percent of those with a relational outlook and 61 percent of the positivists found the decision easy; only 47 percent of the fundamentalists made the decision with ease.

IMPLICATIONS

What are the main conclusions that can be drawn from the Genevan study?

1. With regard to abortion, there exists a considerable gap between the law's rationale and that of the applicants. The motives acceptable to the law and those acceptable to individuals differ widely and are clearly based on varying implicit or explicit perceptions of the fetus.

2. The consequence of this gap is the relative inefficacy of the legal procedure. Indeed, it is evident at once in Table 3-9 that the woman's own physician hardly plays a part in the decision to abort.

It is the woman herself who reaches the decision and the doctor only plays a technician's part. It is also clear that other types of potential counselors, such as religious authorities, social workers, and the like, are hardly ever sought out for advice.

Table 3-9

Role of the Applicant's Physician in the
Decision To Abort

Persuaded the woman to interrupt the pregnancy	3.2%
Tried to dissuade the woman	3.8%
Confirmed the woman's decision	20.4%
Played no part in the decision	71.0%
No answer	1.6%

The role played by the second physician, the "advisor" commissioned by the government, is not at all clear. We must assume that the advisor has been chosen for this role because of his medical education. However, only in a minority of cases (less than 15 percent) is the motive related to the professional competence of the physician. In the majority of the cases, the advisor has to decide on cases based on (a) socioeconomic and (b) "subjective" criteria. Socioeconomic considerations include age, number of living children, income, and other factors that may be of great importance to the woman or the couple involved but do not call for the advisor's scientific competence. Moreover, some of these socioeconomic reasons may be considered unacceptable by the public at large. Subjective criteria refer to those personal factors that the advisor believes to be outside the bounds of his professional competence, and which he thinks only the woman herself can accurately evaluate. He thereby negates his role, or at least the one given him by society, by simply going along with the woman's decision. The situation could give rise to some identity problems among the advisors.

3. The role of the advisor is complicated still more by the fact that even if the applicant herself decides to interrupt the pregnancy, she is not always prepared to bear by herself the responsibility for the interruption. In many cases, she needs a kind of moral support from the advisor. Very often, the "therapy" proposed by the patient comes into conflict with her own opinions and those of her social community. Resort to abortion is still often disapproved of by common opinion. Sometimes the applicant herself possesses personal norms which are opposed to pregnancy interruption.

Thus, besides the technical help which the patient expects from the doctor, another role expectation stands out.

It consists of the doctor bearing the responsibility for the therapeutic act, not only in its technical aspect but also in the orientation towards the social values it stands for. The advisor must relieve the patient of the psychological weight of the decision she has taken. He is the authority justifying the behavior. He becomes a peculiar kind of judge, one who pronounces only acquittals.

It is essential to note that a large majority (60 percent) of the women, though they made their decisions without consulting a physician, believe that abortion should not be left entirely to the patient's will.

Sixty percent of the respondents ask for the intervention of a physician or of another specialist as a justification for abortion. The contradiction existing between the fact that the woman makes the decision alone and her own attitudes toward the liberalization of abortion can probably be explained by its social image and its institutional status in Switzerland. From many points of view, such a contradiction is unhealthy.

In Switzerland, the restrictive character of the legislation (not taking into account the more liberal cantons) has resulted in a large number of illegal abortions. These are much less safe and increase the effects of the social disparities. The current institutional status of abortion is mainly conducive to an increase in the sense of guilt and irresponsibility regarding fertility regulation, but is unable to prevent abortions (Graven, 1975).

4. The advantages of a counseling procedure against a referral procedure are obvious when one considers the following facts. We have seen that a certain number of cases were marked by ambivalence towards procreation. To the data given above, we can add that 30 percent of the married women and 39 percent of the single ones considered for a moment the possibility of having the baby. Among the single women, this idea occurred more frequently among the Italians and the Spanish (50 percent) than among the Swiss (37 percent). This correlation does not exist among the married women. However, in the latter subsample, it is mostly the women who have not yet had any children who, of course, consider more often the possibility of having the child (40 percent v. 29 percent). Among the single women, the wish to have the child depends also on the quality of the relationship with the partner. Fifty-six percent of those with steady relationships considered having the child; this idea was expressed by only 14 percent of those who had unstable relationships.

Resort to abortion is not, as a rule, considered as a behavior of slight consequence. Eighteen percent of the married and 27 percent of the single women consider going through the procedure as an essential event in their life; 62 percent and 60 percent of the married and single women, respectively, consider abortion an important occurrence. Only 15 percent of the total sample think that it is an unimportant act.

Considering the data, one may think that a procedure of counseling, given the present state of attitudes and behavior, could help the woman or the couple reach a decision. But it is evident that this procedure will not remove ambivalences or norm conflicts.

5. An investigation of the motives put forward makes it clear that the various welfare plans the state may set up to help married or single expectant mothers will hardly reduce the number of abortion referrals. The assistance is, of course, necessary, but can play only an incomplete role. The economic motive is often secondary, the principal one being psychocultural or familial.

6. Broadly speaking, we may consider that Swiss society has not yet completely assimilated the new historic fact represented by the currently available techniques allowing voluntary pregnancy intervention, which are changing the whole social status of human reproduction. In addition to helping the women who resort to abortion, any action aiming at increasing the responsibility of people facing procreation and its control shall, in the long run, reduce the contraceptive failures as well as the ambivalences towards maternity.

REFERENCES

Bassand, M., Kellerhals, J., & Wirth, G. Familles urbaines et fécondité. Geneva: Georg, 1974.

Graven, Ph. La législation suisse en matière d'interruption légale de la grossesse. Revue Internationale de Criminologie, 1975.

Kellerhals, J. L'avortement dans la société d'abondance. Revue Internationale de Criminologie, 1975.

Michel, A. Sociologie du mariage et de la famille. Paris: Presses Universitaires de France, 1972.

Pasini, W. Sexualité et gynécologie psychosomatique. Paris: Masson, 1974.

Switzerland, Government of. Penal Code of 21 December 1937, Sec. 2, Art. 120 and following, as revised by Parliament in June 1977.

4

Psychosocial Aspects
of Abortion in Israel*

Tsiyona Peled

*Editors' Note: Findings from two cooperative
studies are reported in this chapter. The
first study explored couple consensus in
abortion-seeking behavior in a society where
both modern contraception and safe (though
at that time nominally illegal) abortion
were available. The second study examined
Israeli population policy (which is implicit
rather than explicit) as perceived by three
population segments most directly involved:
service providers, users, and policy makers.
Conservative views on elective abortion, expressed in these sample surveys, were eventually reflected in the legislative changes
adopted by the Knesset in January 1977.*

INTRODUCTION

All approaches to population policy and fertility regulation in Israel are colored by the extreme diversity of the
population. Of some 3.3 million persons estimated in 1973,
85 percent were Jews (about a quarter of European or American
origin, another quarter Afro-Asian, and half native born) and
the rest were mostly Arab Moslems. (Approximately another
million non-Jews currently live under Israeli control in

*The studies reported were joint projects of the
Israel Institute of Applied Social Research and the Trans-
national Family Research Institute. They were supported, in
part, by the Demographic Center, Office of the Prime Minister
of Israel; Pathfinder Fund; the U.S. National Institute of
Child Health and Human Development; and the Rockefeller/Ford
Foundation Program in Social Sciences, Law, and Population
Policy. I am pleased to acknowledge the counsel of Elihu Katz
(Hebrew University) and TFRI colleagues.

occupied territories.) Immigration has been the main source
of Jewish population growth since the state's founding in 1948.
During the early years this immigration was massive and predominantly from modern Western industrialized countries, but
the waves slowed after 1951 and shifted to Jews from traditional Eastern societies. This shift exacerbated the socioeconomic and fertility differentials still evident in the
various population subgroups, with the highest fertility rates
being observed among the more traditionally oriented groups,
particularly Arabs, who are also poorer and less well-educated
generally. In 1972, total family size still averaged 7.3
among non-Jews (8.5 among the predominating Arab Moslems), actually up from 6.9 in 1955; in contrast to 3.2 among all Jews
(down from 4.0 in 1951), with Jews of Euro-American origin
averaging 2.7 children, the Israeli-born 3.0, and Afro-Asians
3.8. The 1972 non-Jewish rate of natural increase (annual
births minus deaths per 1,000 population) was 2.3 times that
of the Jewish population (39.0 and 16.7, respectively) (Israel
Central Bureau of Statistics, 1973).

Concern with the shifting volume and nature of Jewish
immigration and the growing gap between Jewish and non-Jewish
population growth provoked appointment of a government population committee in 1962. Their 1966 report recommended promotion of a generally pro-natalist atmosphere in the country and
more financial assistance to large families through increased
social welfare benefits, and led to the establishment of a
government demographic center in 1968, charged with implemen-
ting these policies.

Political and religious pressures prevented the committee's recommending the regular provision of public family
planning services. As of 1975, such services were still not
officially available within the country's otherwise extensive
public health system, and it appeared unlikely that the government would be prepared to endorse a national family planning program in the near future. In its report, the 1966
population committee did, however, recommend that the practice
of terminating unwanted pregnancies by induced abortion be reduced and publicly supervised, but was divided on how this
might be accomplished.

ABORTION LEGISLATION

Adapted from the prohibitive legislation in force during the British Mandate of Palestine, the Israeli abortion law
(until January 1977) permitted legal abortion only for strictly
medical reasons. Performers of illegal abortions were threatened with a penalty of five years' imprisonment. However,

following a 1952 court order, the law was rarely enforced; only one abortion prosecution was registered after 1960. For those able to pay, elective abortions were easily and safely available from private physicians. The relatively few legal abortions performed in hospitals required references from a general physician and approval by a hospital abortion committee, whose decisions were often deemed arbitrary. In response to public demand and the June 1974 report of a special committee appointed by the Ministry of Health to study the abortion problem, the Knesset actively considered revision of the restrictive law.

A Law Concerning Termination of Pregnancy was adopted by the Knesset on January 31, 1977 (Israel, 1977). Abortion must be performed in a "recognized medical institution" by a specialist in obstetrics/gynecology, acting upon the pregnant woman's written request, approved by a special committee consisting of a registered social worker and two qualified medical practitioners, one of whom must hold the title of specialist in obstetrics/gynecology. Termination may be approved if the woman is under the legal marriage age (17 years), unmarried, or over age 40; if the pregnancy results from extramarital relations; or on grounds of physical/mental health risks, socioeconomic difficulties, or juridical or eugenic circumstances.

FERTILITY REGULATION

Government policy to the contrary, it is evident from the fertility data that family limitation has been widely practiced, at least by the Jewish population. Data from the 1972-1973 population policy survey indicated that some 64 percent of Jewish married couples then of reproductive age were using contraception. Traditional methods, mainly coitus interruptus, were most common. Only 23 percent of a general sample of married women aged 20-45 were using pills or IUDs, although these are widely available through private channels. (Legally, pills can be bought only on physician's prescription, but in practice they are widely sold in pharmacies at a woman's request. The IUD is also available but requires fitting, usually by private physician.) Many respondents in this survey, among both the women and the service providers, expressed fear of potential dangers to a woman's health and fecundity from pills and IUDs; sterilization (especially vasectomy) was almost unanimously rejected. This and earlier surveys revealed that the use of contraception in general, and modern methods in particular, is more prevalent among the young, the economically advantaged, and better educated; the less religious; the couples of Euro-American origin; and the native-born. It is

less prevalent among Jews of Afro-Asian origin, although their
contraceptive practices improve with educational level and duration of residence in the country.

Because of the lack of effective contraception, coupled
with relatively low family size desires, abortion levels are
high in the Jewish population; use patterns by age, ethnicity,
and socioeconomic class parallel those of contraception. Surveys of the early 1960s indicated that the proportion of women
aged 40 or more who had had at least one abortion was 52 percent among Jewish women born in Europe or America, 30 percent
among the native-born, and 25 percent among the Afro-Asians,
with negligible percentages among non-Jewish women (Bachi,
1970). Comparable current percentages (reported in the two
recent studies to be described) were 27 percent among the
wives aged under 35 surveyed in 1970, and 31 percent among the
random sample of married women aged 20-45 queried in 1973, with
20 percent admitting to repeat abortions.

ABORTION-SEEKING BEHAVIOR: THE CASE
OF YOUNG, WELL-TO-DO ISRAELI COUPLES

The extensive use of abortion in Israel despite the
availability of modern contraception, and the highest rate of
use among women in higher socioeconomic classes, deserves further elaboration. During 1970, we studied a sample of 806
young, well-do-do, urban Israeli couples (Peled, 1970), representative of the segment of Israeli society previously identified as most sophisticated in its use of contraception. Although not the original aim of the project, the findings of a
secondary analysis presented here help identify some indicators
of abortion-seeking behavior. The study is also noteworthy as
one of the first to investigate repeated abortion-seeking, and
to focus on the couple rather than the woman alone as the para-
mount decision-making unit in family planning behavior.

Husbands and wives completed self-administered questionnaires simultaneously but independently of each other at
their homes; an interviewer was present to prevent any couple
communication. (Seventeen percent [181] of the original 806
couples who failed to answer the question on induced abortion
were excluded from the secondary analysis.) In the analysis
phase, the data gathered independently from each spouse was
combined in one couple file. This yielded objective measures
of couple agreement with respect to the various questionnaire
topics. The agreement scores were computed in terms of percentages of identical answers given by husbands and wives out
of all possible combinations of their individual answers. A
comparison of couples' consensus vis-à-vis various aspects of

family planning was made between two subgroups differentiated according to abortion experience: couples who had experienced at least one induced abortion (AG), and those who had not (NAG).

The 38 questions dealing with family planning practices and attitudes shared a common concept: they all measured directly a respondent's inclination to limit family size. Within this conceptual framework, a person was defined as higher in his inclination to limit family size the more he (1) preferred a relatively older age as ideal for marriage, (2) preferred a smaller number of children, (3) preferred longer spacing between children, and (4) expressed a preference for regulating fertility that was extremely committed to prior planning.

Our initial hypothesis was that the "closer" a topic gets to a couple's frame of reference the more agreement will be evident between spouses. "Closeness" of a topic was determined in terms of actuality (whether a particular question, even if general in nature, refers to a stage in the marriage cycle that the couple has either gone through or is confronting), and involvement (whether a particular question is general or relates to the respondent's own situation). For example, in terms of actuality, questions on ideal spacing between the first and second child, or between the second and third, were "closer" for the (relatively young) couples in our sample than those on spacing between third and fourth children.

This hypothesis was empirically confirmed for both the abortion group (AG) and the no-abortion group (NAG). Agreement between husbands and wives (AHW) was greater when they were responding to a question about desired family size of their own family under real circumstances than under ideal circumstances (see Table 4-1, left-hand panel). Regarding the ideal parental age for beginning or terminating family building or ideal child spacing, the findings showed that the earlier the stage of marriage referred to, the higher the AHW (see Table 4-1, right-hand panel). The hypothesis was also confirmed in responses to hypothetical questions on what decisions couples would make when having an additional child at a certain time might conflict with other family objectives, such as standard of living, academic careers, leisure time activities, etc. Regardless of the situation hypothesized, AHW was without exception higher where a second or third child was concerned, compared to a fourth.

More interesting than this total AHW for analyzing differences between AG and NAG couples is the subject matter provoking couple agreement or disagreement. Because it was found that most reported abortions were induced as a result of a mutual decision between spouses, it was hypothesized (but not

Table 4-1

Agreement between Husband and Wife Regarding Family Size and Spacing among Young, Well-To-Do Israeli Couples Who Have and Have Not Had Abortion Experience, 1970

	No. of Children Wanted		Ideal Spacing at Various Stages of Family Life			
	Under ideal circumstances	Under present circumstances	Between marriage and 1st child	Between 1st and 2nd child	Between 2nd and 3rd child	Between 3rd and 4th child
No Abortion Couples (n=487)						
Both want same number / Both agreed on same spacing	38%	53%	55%	42%	34%	30%
Husband wants fewer / shorter spacing	26%	23%	25%	34%	46%	46%
Wife wants fewer / shorter spacing	36%	24%	20%	24%	20%	24%
Couples with at Least One Abortion (n=181)						
Both want same number / Both agreed on same spacing	44%	63%	46%	41%	39%	20%
Husband wants fewer / shorter spacing	28%	17%	28%	42%	39%	48%
Wife wants fewer / shorter spacing	28%	20%	26%	17%	22%	32%

Note. T. Peled & H. Schimmerling. Consensus between husbands and wives in the area of family planning: A comparative analysis of couples who have and couples who have not performed an induced abortion. Paper presented at the Fourth International Congress for Social Psychiatry, Symposium on Family Planning, Jerusalem, 1972, Tables 1 and 2.

empirically proven) that as a result of the decision-making process itself AG couples will agree more than NAG couples on such topics as family size, spacing, time to end childbearing, etc. (It is true that not having an abortion does not exclude the possibility that NAG couples still went through a decision-making process with regard to fertility regulation or even abortion. But it was assumed that most of them did not experience such a process.) Though the differences found in total AHW between the two groups were small and inconsistent, a slight but consistent difference was revealed in regard to the subject matter agreed upon. A higher percentage of NAG than AG couples agreed that "when previous planning fails the woman should carry her pregnancy to term," preferred shorter child spacing, and considered a young age as ideal for marriage; agreement was higher among AG couples that two children at most was the desired size for a family.

Analysis of distributions of disagreement between husbands and wives (DAHW) was essential in revealing the source of pressure toward family size limitation within the decision-making unit. With both AG and NAG there was only slight evidence to suggest that, ideally, women prefer fewer children than men. The evidence that women prefer longer child spacing than do their spouses was more consistent (see Table 4-1). It is noteworthy that among AG couples the discrepancy between husbands and wives with regard to child spacing is greatest between the first and second child, the family life stage when abortions were most frequent. Data from the questions on hypothetical conflict situations revealed that DAHW here also stemmed from the greater inclination of wives to postpone or prevent a birth when this would interfere with other family objectives at that time--particularly among AG wives.

Also explored were differences between NAG and two subgroups of AG: a single abortion group (SAG) and a repeated abortion group (RAG). This analysis was carried out separately for men and women. Though the empirical differences found were not dramatic, the data showed quite consistently that the more experience a couple had had with abortions, the more the couple-- both husband and wife--preferred a relatively late age for marriage, preferred a small family, and expressed the intention to abide by their original plan even when undesired pregnancy occurred. Likewise, the husbands and wives of both the SAG and RAG groups preferred longer child spacing than their NAG counterparts.

Differences among these three groups were most interesting with respect to contraceptive practices. An identical pattern of contraceptive behavior was reported for two stages in the marriage cycle: prior to the first child and between the first and second chilren (Peled, 1975). This pattern

indicated that RAG couples were least regular in use of contraceptives, and most often used coitus interruptus (see Table
4-2). Within both the SAG and RAG groups, there was a higher
percentage of women who admitted that their first and second
children resulted from either contraceptive failure or negli-
gence (this in addition to their aborted pregnancies).

In sum, the evidence from this study--though taken
from a project that investigated the psychosocial correlates
of abortion in retrospect only--shows quite consistently that
the following psychosocial characteristics can be taken as indicators of abortion-seeking behavior: couples who, on the
aspirational-attitudinal level, have a high consensus on family planning issues (indicating an inclination to limit family
size) but who fail to achieve their aspirations (mainly because
they use primitive and unreliable methods of contraception) are
the most likely to seek either single or repeated abortions.

More extensive findings on the psychosocial aspects of
abortion seeking under changing conditions and among couples
in all levels of Israeli society were sought in a major study
launched in 1975 with funding from the (US) National Institute
of Child Health and Human Development, obtained in cooperation
with the Transnational Family Research Institute, entitled
"Contraception, Abortion, and Couple Decision Making." Data
were gathered from interviews with some 1,600 couples sampled
from various population subgroups (including urban Jewish cou-
les of varying ethnic origins and Arabs from both urban and
rural areas in Israel), ordered from low to high on multi-
variable modernity scales. Focus was on couples' subjective
assessment of fertility-regulating means, the interaction and
exchange of information between marital partners, and decision-
making processes leading to the choice of particular fertility-
regulating methods. Results (now being analyzed) are expected
to be of significance not only to Israel but also to other
countries where both modern contraception and safe abortion
are increasingly available and where the prevailing degree of
modernity resembles that of one or more of the Israeli
subgroups.

ABORTION POLICY AND PRACTICE IN ISRAEL: PERCEPTIONS AND
PREFERENCES AMONG POLICY MAKERS, SERVICE PROVIDERS,
AND WOMEN OF REPRODUCTIVE AGE

Of particular significance to the Israeli debate on
abortion law reform and publicly provided family planning services were the findings of a major study of population policy
conducted during 1972-1973 by the Israel Institute of Applied
Social Research, in association with the Transnational Family

Table 4-2

Contraceptive Practices before First and Second Child among Young, Well-To-Do Israeli Couples Who Have Experienced No Abortions (NAG), One Abortion (SAG), or Repeat Abortions (RAG)

Regularity of contraceptive use	Before First Child			Before Second Child		
	Regular	Irregular	Nonuse	Regular	Irregular	Nonuse
NAG (n=487)	32%	19%	49%	40%	19%	41%
SAG (n=106)	32%	24%	44%	38%	27%	34%
RAG (n= 75)	26%	28%	46%	22%	42%	37%

Reason for pregnancy	Before First Child			Before Second Child		
	Wanted child	Contraceptive failed	Negligent	Wanted child	Contraceptive failed	Negligent
NAG (n=487)	60%	6%	33%	71%	5%	23%
SAG (n=106)	51%	9%	41%	54%	13%	33%
RAG (n= 75)	50%	15%	35%	52%	14%	34%

Type of contraceptive being used[a]	Before First Child							Before Second Child						
	1	2	3	4	5	6	7	1	2	3	4	5	6	7
NAG (n=487)	27%	27%	22%	6%	3%	6%	9%	24%	24%	19%	9%	4%	10%	9%
SAG (n=106)	26%	20%	24%	7%	4%	5%	14%	20%	23%	20%	7%	3%	10%	18%
RAG (n= 75)	17%	36%	24%	8%	2%	2%	12%	16%	38%	8%	10%	8%	10%	10%

Note. From T. Peled & H. Schimmerling. Consensus between husbands and wives in the area of family planning: A comparative analysis of couples who have and couples who have not performed an induced abortion. Paper presented at the Fourth International Congress for Social Psychiatry, Symposium on Family Planning, Jerusalem, 1972, Table 10.

[a] 1 = rhythm; 2 = coitus interruptus; 3 = condom; 4 = diaphragm and/or jelly; 5 = intrauterine ring, coil or loop; 6 = pill; 7 = other, or several methods.

Research Institute.   Like others in the TFRI-coordinated Cooperative Transnational Research Program in Fertility Behavior,
the project was designed to draw upon multiple sources of data
about the same phenomena with a view to obtaining better vali-
dation of phenomena, particularly those of a subjective nature
(Peled, 1975).

     The original project employed the User-System Inter-
action Design (Friedman, 1973) to investigate the family planning situation within the same setting simultaneously but
independently from two sources of information: the providers
and the users, or potential users, of health and welfare services.   The basic assumption was that, regardless of the existing family planning policy of the various government and
public agencies (if indeed they had a definite and clear policy), the professionals employed by these institutions are the
actual gatekeepers of services and information.   In their interaction with the public they may give or withhold services
and information according to their own values, judgments, and
preferences.   It was also assumed that the provision of information and services is an essential aspect of the objective
environment in which such "goods" are consumed; unless the
clients are assured that family planning advice and means are
to be supplied in their encounters with various professionals
in public institutions, clients might not ask for these aids.

     Interviews were conducted with approximately 1,000
professionals employed by health agencies (hospitals, general
clinics of health insurance schemes, and mother and child
clinics) and municipal welfare agencies, drawn from the four
main urban centers and some additional towns whose maternity
centers also serve surrounding rural populations.   This sample
included about 200 gynecologists (some 65 working in health
insurance clinics, and the rest in hospitals), some 200 general practitioners, 250 nurses at mother-and-child clinics,
100 pediatricians, and 250 social workers at municiple bureaus.
(The sample included about a quarter of the general practitioners, two-thirds of the gynecologists, one-fourth of the
pediatricians, two-thirds of MCH nurses, and about half the
social workers employed by public and government agencies in
the sample areas.)   From these same communities approximately
800 women were drawn: half a random sample from the general
public of women of fertile age (20-45), who were interviewed
in their homes; half from hospital maternity wards where they
were interviewed shortly after giving birth.   (Fifty-four unmarried women in the general sample were excluded from the
data analysis.)   A third group of "elite" were added when it
became possible to add some specific population policy questions to another ongoing study.   This group comprised approximately 400 respondents of the political, administrative, and

cultural elite of Israel, representative of the policy makers and opinion leaders of the country.

The project probed a wide spectrum of perceptions and behavior with respect to population policy and all aspects of family planning. However, only findings most relavent to the abortion situation will be presented here. Details of the project have been reported by Peled (1975) and Peled and Friedman (1975).

Abortion Policy: Views of the Elite, Service Providers, and Women of Fertile Age

As shown in Table 4-3, the majority of each study group felt that the restrictive abortion law prevailing at the time of the study was not necessary. However, a considerable percentage among this majority would hesitate to demand its annulment. The elite sample was most strongly in favor of annulment (59 percent), with women--those most affected by the law--least liberal, especially the postpartum women (who were much younger and less advanced in their fertility careers than women of the general sample). Among the professionals, the social workers (who see the poor most often) and the gynecologists (who most commonly perform abortions), are more strongly in favor of annulment than are the general practitioners, the pediatricians, and the nurses. Differences of the same sort are reflected in respondent views toward evasion of the current law; gynecologists, social workers, public nurses, the elite, and the general sample of women are more tolerant of physicians who currently perform medically unjustified abortions than are general practitioners, pediatricians, and women who have just given birth. This pattern replicates findings on the necessity of providing free contraceptives to the public at large, with 72 percent of the elite group feeling this "necessary" or "very necessary," compared to 42 percent of postpartum women and other groups falling between these extremes.

Table 4-3 also shows that elite respondents affiliated with religious parties are least favorable towards annulment of the abortion law, are least tolerant of its evasion, and are considerably more dogmatic in this respect than women who describe themselves as religious--again replicating a gap found in attitudes towards the free supply of contraceptives.

Among those favoring annulment of the law, a main argument of both professionals and the female respondents was that a decision to have a child should be left to the woman. The women also argued that there are many reasons for justifying

Table 4-3

Views Regarding the Israeli Abortion Law among Women,
Professional Service Providers, and Members
of the Elite, 1972-1973

	Total (N)	Should the law be annulled?[a]			Should those who currently perform abortions be punished?[a]	
		(1)	(2)	(3)	(4)	(5)
Women						
Postpartum						
Total	(313)	45%	23%	32%	46%	55%
Religious	(110)	61%	23%	16%	62%	38%
Asian/African born	(107)	60%	21%	20%	53%	48%
In Fertile Age						
Total	(304)	33%	24%	43%	37%	63%
Religious	(78)	57%	25%	18%	52%	48%
Asian/African born	(108)	47%	27%	26%	51%	48%
Professionals						
General practitioners	(200)	34%	23%	42%	47%	53%
Gynecologists in health insurance clinics	(65)	23%	26%	51%	19%	81%
Gynecologists in hospitals	(105)	22%	22%	56%	28%	72%
Pediatricians	(94)	27%	33%	40%	43%	57%
Nurses	(267)	24%	30%	45%	34%	66%
Social workers	(215)	22%	25%	53%	33%	67%
Elite						
Total	(383)	18%	23%	59%	33%	68%
Religious party	(28)	79%	14%	7%	85%	14%
Asian/North African born	(31)	23%	32%	45%	24%	76%

Note. From T. Peled & H. L. Friedman. Population policy in
Israel: Perceptions and preferences among policy makers,
service providers, and the public. Jerusalem and Washington:
Israel Institute of Applied Social Research and the Transnational Family Research Institute, 1975, Table 15-12, p. 187.

[a](1) = law is necessary and should not be annulled
   (2) = law is unnecessary but should not be annulled
   (3) = law is unnecessary and should be annulled
   (4) = definitely, or perhaps should be punished
   (5) = perhaps not, or definitely should not be punished

abortion, while the professional dissenters stressed that legalization would permit proper control of abortion and would
be a legitimization of reality. Supporters of the law among
both professionals and women viewed it as a necessary hindrance
to the use of abortion as a means of birth control.

Interview data from all the service provider and
women's groups revealed a consensus regarding the extent to
which various reasons justify induced abortions. The majority
regarded abortion as absolutely justified for objective reasons such as rape, incest, possibility of genetic defects, unstable marriage, and out-of-wedlock pregnancy. It was deemed
absolutely unjustified when the reasons are purely subjective,
such as a couple's claim that they have no desire to raise
children or want longer spacing between children. There was
also a lesser tendency to approve abortion for such reasons as
a difficult economic situation, mature age of the woman, and
a couple's satisfaction with the number of children they already have. Thus, it would appear that the segments of the
population most concerned with abortion--service providers and
women of reproductive age--were not yet ready to insist upon
totally unrestricted legal abortion, a view eventually reflected
in the January 1977 Knesset legislation.

Professionals' Attitudes and Behavior Regarding
Provision of Induced Abortion

The various professionals (all employed by health and
welfare agencies) were asked how frequently they are consulted
on unwanted pregnancies and for help in obtaining abortions,
how they would tend to handle requests for abortion, and how
competent they believe themselves to be in dealing with such
requests.

As seen in Table 4-4, all professional groups (with
the exception of gynecologists) reported that in the year before the survey they had discussed unwanted pregnancies with
their clients more frequently than contraceptive methods, specifically the pill and IUD. Among general practitioners and
social workers, such discussions were even more common than
those on family size and spacing. This indicates that professional advice on family planning is sought more readily for
help in dealing with the undesired consequences of lack of
planning than for guidance in averting such situations. Indeed, the data from both the professional and women's samples
revealed that consultation on contraception within the existing health and welfare system is rare, especially among social
groups most in need of such guidance, such as poorly educated
women of Afro-Asian origin. When such advice is sought--most

Table 4-4

Frequency of Client-Service Provider Discussion on Various Topics Related to Family Planning During Year Preceding Survey, by Type of Professional, Israel, 1972-1973

	Total (N)	Never talked about it	Talked from time to time or only a few times	Talked many times or very many times
General Practitioners				
Frequency of discussion on family size and spacing	(204)	41%	47%	12%
Frequency of discussion on pill	(201)	36%	33%	31%
Frequency of discussion on IUD	(200)	51%	33%	15%
Frequency of discussion on unwanted pregnancy	(203)	25%	61%	15%
Gynecologists at Health Insurance Clinics				
Frequency of discussion on family size and spacing	(64)	15%	36%	49%
Frequency of discussion on pill	(64)	-	9%	91%
Frequency of discussion on IUD	(64)	2%	20%	78%
Frequency of discussion on unwanted pregnancy	(64)	3%	58%	40%
Gynecologists at Hospitals				
Frequency of discussion on family size and spacing	(101)	11%	46%	44%
Frequency of discussion on pill	(101)	1%	4%	95%
Frequency of discussion on IUD	(101)	2%	3%	95%
Frequency of discussion on unwanted pregnancy	(101)	4%	62%	35%
Pediatricians				
Frequency of discussion on family size and spacing	(97)	38%	39%	22%
Frequency of discussion on pill	(96)	68%	14%	17%

Frequency of discussion on IUD	(96)	70%	16%	13%
Frequency of discussion on unwanted pregnancy	(97)	52%	44%	5%
Nurses				
Frequency of discussion on family size and spacing	(273)	25%	47%	28%
Frequency of discussion on pill	(274)	36%	29%	35%
Frequency of discussion on IUD	(274)	35%	30%	35%
Frequency of discussion on unwanted pregnancy	(274)	30%	54%	16%
Social Workers				
Frequency of discussion on family size and spacing	(220)	45%	47%	9%
Frequency of discussion on pill	(222)	58%	25%	16%
Frequency of discussion on IUD	(222)	59%	29%	12%
Frequency of discussion on unwanted pregnancy	(222)	36%	52%	12%

Note. From T. Peled & H. L. Friedman. Population policy in Israel: Perceptions and preferences among policy makers, service providers, and the public. Jerusalem and Washington: Israel Institute of Applied Research and the Transnational Family Research Institute, 1975, Table 4-1, p. 32.

commonly from gynecologists--it is mostly at the initiative of
the clients. Among contracepting women, the primary source of
information for the method being used, even if an IUD or the
pill, was personal (husband, friends, parents, etc.) rather
than professional.

The majority of professionals (again excepting gynecologists, and with general practitioners divided half-and-
half) felt they lacked the relevant training and knowledge to
equip them for helping clients to decide whether or not to interrupt an undesired pregnancy.

All professional groups reported that their discussions
of abortion with clients concerned mainly the possible effects
of the abortion on a woman's health, and on her feelings and
those of her husband. Only gynecologists employed in health
insurance clinics had discussed to any extent questions of
legality and appropriate methods and timing. The possible consequences to parents and the child if the unwanted pregnancy
was carried to term was an aspect seldom discussed, even by
gynecologists.

The professionals' attitudes toward induced abortion
apparently reflect their views on dilatation and curettage
(D&C), since the majority (including gynecologists) mentioned
only this method; nearly all judged that this is the only
method practiced in the country. The majority felt that curettage involves a hazard to the woman's fecundity. The few
gynecologists who mentioned vacuum aspiration considered it
less harmful.

When asked how they would react to a couple's request
for a nonmedically justified elective abortion, gynecologists,
followed by general practitioners, more frequently replied
that they would try to dissuade the woman in every case (56
and 37 percent, respectively), compared to just 11 percent of
social workers. However, if pressed, gynecologists would more
often than the other professionals queried provide the address
of a private physician who would perform an elective abortion
(probably reflecting their greater acquaintance with such physicians). This seeming paradox may indicate that gynecologists
basically object to abortion as a family planning method but,
if clients persist, they are concerned to see abortions performed in the best possible clinical circumstances. However,
the majority of these public health professionals, including
gynecologists, responded that they would not in any case refer
women for elective abortions. It should be noted that positive responses could have implicated the respondents as law
breakers. It may be that despite the anonymity of the interview, and the fact that the question was posed hypothetically,
the responses should be taken with reservation.

Those professionals who had been explicitly requested to provide abortion advice in the preceding year (almost all gynecologists and the majority of the other groups, except pediatricians) reported that clients complained more of the difficulty of obtaining abortions within the law, that is, through regular health services, and of their high cost on the "free market," than of the difficulty of finding a compliant physician. Nevertheless, the great majority of these professionals (65 to 78 percent in the various groups) judged the public to be satisfied with the help they receive in seeking abortion.

Women's Experience with Abortion Seeking

Data from the two women's samples complete the picture of client-professional interaction in abortion seeking in Israel. Only 33 of the postpartum women (9 percent) reported having had an abortion, compared to 82 (31 percent) of the general sample of women of reproductive age. (As noted, the postpartum women were, on average, much younger than the general sample and could be expected to have more abortions later in their childbearing years.) Repeat terminations amounted to 47 percent among postpartum abortors, and 63 percent among abortors in the general sample. As expected, abortion experience was relatively more common among the less religious and secular and among Israeli-born women of European origin, while rare among the Asian-North African born. First abortions had occurred most frequently between a first and second child, and second abortions between the second and third. Unsuitable economic conditions and a desire for longer child spacing were the most frequent reasons mentioned for having abortions, followed by concerns for the health of the woman or child. In retrospect, only half the abortors recalled having had some fears prior to their abortions, mostly with regard to potential health hazards. The great majority (85 percent) reported no feelings of regret after abortions.

In addition to the acknowledged abortors, 55 of the postpartum women admitted to having first considered aborting the pregnancy just carried to term. Not surprisingly, their experience differed from that of the abortors in the two samples. The minority who had sought any professional advice had turned mainly to a general practitioner or a gynecologist within a health agency; they reported that in most cases the physician tried to influence them against an abortion. Among the abortors, a higher proportion sought early pregnancy confirmation and tended to consult with a gynecologist rather than another professional who could be expected to provide less specific help in obtaining an abortion. Also, nearly three-quarters of the women who subsequently terminated unwanted pregnancies applied directly to a private physician, doubtless aware that they did not have sufficient grounds for abortion within the legal scheme, preferring to preserve anonymity, or desiring to avoid formal procedures. In contrast to the 55 women who considered but did not implement an abortion, the great majority of abortors reported that their professional advisors made no effort to dissuade them from abortion. In fact, half reported that it was during the actual discussion that they definitely decided upon abortion. Among the women who had specifically consulted gynecologists about unwanted pregnancies, the majority claimed that the physician did not advise them to seek abortion through their health insurance scheme and gave them no address of another physician who would perform an abortion; these responses were proportionately higher among the 55 nonabortors.

It may be that in reconstructing the procedure both the abortors and the nonabortors were rationalizing their subsequent behavior. However, it may also be expected that if the abortors perceive the circumstances to have been favorable-- and 85 percent harbor no regrets--it is more likely for them to abort again, relative to the other group.

CONCLUSIONS

It is evident from the findings of these two surveys that abortion is regarded as a necessary evil in Israel, sought and easily obtained despite legal restrictions, by at least the more modernized segments of the Jewish population, who desire relatively small, planned families but are skeptical of the more effective contraceptive methods (IUDs and pills) and, like almost all Israelis, reject sterilization. Data from the three sources tapped in the recent population policy survey-- publicly employed health and welfare professionals, women of fertile age, and members of the elite--indicate that this situation is attributable to lack of publicly supported family planning services and information, which, in turn, probably stems from official uncertainty as to what would be the desirable birth policy for this heterogeneous, embattled country.

At the time of the survey, 1972-1973, the majority of those respondents who believed that the government had a birth policy (almost all the women, two-thirds of the professionals, but less than half of those closest to policy, the elite) perceived this policy as across-the-board pro-natalism. The elite and professionals based their perception on existing tax and welfare benefits tending to favor large families, while the women felt such a view was reflected in leaders' statements. The women in particular believe that such undifferentiated pro-natalism has little influence on fertility behavior (except among lower classes)--a perception borne out by low Jewish birthrates. However, the majority preference in all three groups is for a discriminating policy, aimed at bringing lower rates of growth to high fertility groups and higher rates to the low fertility groups. This was particularly true of the better educated and the professionals who work closely with families--social workers, pediatricians, and nurses.

Seventy-three percent of the women and 76 percent of the professionals agreed that "it is desirable that each child should come by previous planning by the couple," based on personal, rather than national, needs. The vast majority of the professionals and women respondents feel that the professional community is not now adequately serving the family planning needs of the public and that this discriminates against the poor, most needful segments of the population in particular. Most professional groups and women surveyed (82-95 percent), whatever their origin or religion, felt it "necessary" or "very necessary" that the general public be supplied with regular, undiscriminating family planning advice and services through the current framework, including schools, clinics, and the mass media. Only half the elite agreed to this although, as noted, they were much more favorable to the provision of free contraceptives than the professional and women's groups. Also, over 80 percent of the women and up to 97 percent of the professionals agreed that the initiative in family planning advice should come from the service provider, thus obviating the reluctance of socially and personally more inhibited women to discuss issues involving sex, and to ask for such advice (when they do not perceive that it should be supplied within the regular institutional framework). Well-documented in data from both professionals and women, fertility-regulating behavior not advised by qualified professional persons results in the use of primitive and inefficient contraceptive methods, or no contraception at all. (Over half the postpartum women, and a third of the others, indicated that they used no contraceptive method even when they did not want to become pregnant.) Subsequently, women find themselves with undesired pregnancies,

That broadening contraceptive education and services would reduce the number of induced abortions currently performed in Israel was explicitly stated by the great majority of professional respondents and could be implied from data obtained from the women. There was less certainty about the need to revise or annul the restrictive abortion law, although the majority of all respondent groups viewed the law as unnecessary. (The abortion law was, in fact, liberalized in January 1977 and abortion services are more widely accessible, as are facilities for contraceptive counseling.) In response

to a United Nations request for country statements on population growth and development in connection with the 1974 Population Year, the Government of Israel issued a formal document
stating that population policy for the coming decade, as implemented by the government Demographic Center, would include
among its aims the achievement of a better balance in family
size among the different sectors of the population (in contrast to former apparently undifferentiated pro-natalism),
mainly by putting more emphasis on "family counseling and advisory services."

REFERENCES

Bachi, R. Abortion in Israel. In R. E. Hall (Ed,), Abortion
    in a changing world (Vol. 1). New York: Columbia Uni-
    versity Press, 1970.

Friedman, H. L. Acceptability of fertility-regulating meth-
    ods: The user/system interaction. Paper presented at
    the First Cross-Cultural Conference on Psychology convened
    at the University of Ibadan, Ibadan, Nigeria, April 1973.

Israel, Government of, Central Bureau of Statistics. Abstracts.
    Jerusalem: Author, various years.

Israel, Government of. Law Concerning Termination of Pregnancy,
    Sefer Ha-Chukkim No. 842 of 9 February 1977.

Peled, T. Family planning behavior and preferences: Patterns
    of the young well-to-do social strata in Israel (in
    Hebrew). Jerusalem: Israel Institute of Applied Social
    Research, 1970.

Peled, T. Israel. In H. P. David & B, Sashi (Orgs.). Psycho-
    social aspects of abortion in Asia. Washington: Trans-
    national Family Research Institute, 1975.

Peled, T., & Friedman, H. L. Population policy in Israel:
    Perceptions and preferences among policy makers, service
    providers, and the public. Jerusalem and Washington:
    The Israel Institute of Applied Social Research and the
    Transnational Family Research Institute, 1975.

5

Psychosocial Studies of Abortion in the United States*

Henry P. David

Editors' Note: In tune with the broad definition of "psychosocial" advocated by Illsley and Hall in chapter 2, this chapter reviews American studies in terms of determinants and consequences, as well as sociodemographic and sociocultural characteristics associated with patterns of fertility regulation and pregnancy resolution. Special consideration is given to adolescent fertility and sociopolitical issues. The review of US statistical data and trends is followed by a discussion of fertility choice behavior with emphasis on couple communication and decision-making processes in first and second trimester abortions. Consideration of the abortion/contraception relationship precedes a review of repeated abortion seeking and potential prevention strategies. The risk of psychological sequelae after pregnancy termination is noted within the perspective of methodological assessment difficulties, clinical biases, and comparison to postpartum psychological problems. The last section of the chapter comments on current concerns, including personal and ethical dilemmas of service providers, implications of newer techniques of menstrual regulation, and abortion as a human right. A bibliography of over 170 references concludes the review.*

*Prepared, in part, with grant support from the Ford Foundation, the Rockefeller Foundation, and the Sunnen Foundation.

INTRODUCTION

Sociocultural Political Context

In an instructive historical review, Mohr (1978) documents that there was no abortion legislation in the America
of 1800. Abortion services were widely available. In the
1840s, advertisements appeared in the urban newspapers, rural
weeklies, popular magazines, and even religious journals. By
1900, however, "virtually every jurisdiction in the United
States had laws upon its books that proscribed the practice
sharply and declared most abortions to be criminal offenses."

Elective abortion did not again become an available
choice for American women until a decade ago. In 1967, Colo-
rado became the first state to reform its legislation by
broadening the conditions for permissible abortion, followed
by California, North Carolina, Maryland, Georgia, Arkansas,
Delaware, New Mexico, Oregon, Kansas, South Carolina, Virginia,
Hawaii, New York, Alaska, Washington, and the District of
Columbia (David, 1973a). Accessibility to legal and safe abortion across the country was greatly enhanced by the landmark
US Supreme Court Decision of January 1973, which ruled that
during the first three months of gestation the question of
terminating an unwanted pregnancy is to be resolved solely by
the pregnant woman and her physician (Institute of Medicine,
1975). State actions prohibiting abortion during the first
trimester were deemed unconstitutional by the Court. As abortion became legal in each of the 50 states, federal, state,
and local agencies gradually provided financial support through
public funds (Medicaid) for indigent women unable to pay medical costs, much as they already did for women carrying a pregnancy to term. It is estimated that by 1976 about one-third
of all reported legal abortions were funded by Medicaid (AGI,
1977a).

Several states refused to subsidize elective abortions
and were challenged in the courts. On June 20, 1977 the Supreme Court ruled that neither the Constitution nor the federal Social Security Act required the states to use public
funds to subsidize elective abortions for indigent women. The
Court also stated that public hospitals were not obligated to
provide abortion services (AGI, 1977a). At his July 12 press
conference, President Carter expressed the opinion that state
or federal financing was "an encouragement to abortion and its
acceptance as a routine contraceptive means," that any exception should be strictly defined, and that it was not the government's responsibility to equalize opportunities for poor
and wealthy women "particularly when there is a moral factor
involved" (Carter, 1977). After many months of heated debate

the United States Congress on December 7, 1977, voted to restrict federal funding of elective abortions for economically
disadvantaged women "except where the life of the mother would
be endangered if the fetus were carried to term" or for victims
of rapé or incest reporting "promptly" to a law enforcement
agency or public health service facility, or "where severe and
long-lasting physical health damage to the mother would result
if the pregnancy were carried to term when so determined by
two physicians." On January 26, 1978, the government announced
that federal health care funds may be used to pay for abortions
performed on victims of rape or incest if the incidents are reported within 60 days. Reports need not be made by the victim
but may be made by mail by any third party, apparently including private health facilities to which a victim may have gone
for medical treatment (AGI, 1978). Meanwhile, the struggle to
preserve access to safe and legal abortion for all women continues unabated. It is within this changing and often turbu-
lent context that psychosocial abortion research must be
considered.

The January 1973 Supreme Court Decision radically
changed the abortion climate in the United States, the sociocultural and medical atmosphere within which abortion services
were provided in major metropolitan centers, and societal acceptance of abortion as a human right. The June 1977 Supreme
Court decisions place the responsibility for assuring equal
access for impoverished women to legal abortion, as well as
childbearing, on the Congress, the state legislatures, and
the body politic. Translating a constitutional right into
free choice and equal accessibility to services, regardless of
economic circumstances, has become part of the continuing abortion controversy in the United States. It is a particularly
troubling issue for a country with strong traditions of individual initiative and enterprise plus conservative views of
sexual behavior and societal service responsibilities.

Research Constraints in the United States

While more statistics are available on abortion than
on any other surgical procedure (Cates, 1977), difficulties
of interpretation persist. One major difficulty in obtaining
generalizable data on psychosocial aspects of legal abortion
in the United States is the problem of eliciting a representative sample with follow-up access to the woman and her partner
(Adler, 1976). There is, at present, no uniform national reporting system for recording sociodemographic information
other than age. Available reports by five-year age groups are
generally believed to be underestimates (Weinstock, Tietze,
Jaffe, & Dryfoos, 1976). The performance of pregnancy

terminations, as well as the provision of contraceptive services, in a range of public and private facilities (from clinics
and hospitals to physicians' offices) makes representative
sampling, monitoring of repeat abortions, and follow-up ex-
ceedingly complex and costly (Jaffe & Dryfoos, 1976).

These problems are compounded for teenagers because
statistics are not compiled by single age year cohorts. Differences believed to exist between younger and older adolescents are not too well reflected in the present system of
abortion surveillance. Additional sociodemographic data are
usually limited to marital status and parity. These and other
constraints constitute a caveat to undue generalizing from
many of the studies reported.

ABORTION-SEEKING BEHAVIOR

Sociodemographic Aspects

The number of legal abortions in the United States
passed the million mark in 1975, according to a survey conducted by the Alan Guttmacher Institute (AGI) and the reports
received by the Center for Disease Control (CDC) from the
states and the District of Columbia. However, the annual rate
of increase has declined from 21 percent in 1974 to 15 percent
in 1975 and a projected 8 percent in 1976 (Sullivan, Tietze,
& Dryfoos, 1976; Tietze, 1977c). Although some legal abortions were reported in every state, the availability of abortion services remains highly concentrated on the East and West
coasts and in a relatively few other metropolitan areas. In
several states legal abortion remains almost as unavailable as
it was during the era of illegality (AGI, 1977a).

More than 2 percent of all US women of reproductive
age (15-44 years) obtained abortions in 1975; about 25 percent
of all pregnancies were terminated by abortion (after excluding those ending in miscarriages). The US rate of 22 abortions per 1,000 women of reproductive age is slightly above
that reported for Finland (21) and Norway and Sweden (20), and
slightly below the rate for Czechoslovakia (26), Denmark (27),
and the German Democratic Republic (29). The US rate is considerably below Cuba (71), Bulgaria (65), and Hungary (42),
but substantially above England (11) and Scotland (8); all
figures are based on the AGI study reported by Sullivan,
Tietze, and Dryfoos (1976).

Of the one million 1975 abortions reported by AGI,
about 60 percent were performed in free-standing clinics, 29
percent in private hospitals, 8 percent in public hospitals,

and 3 percent in physicians' offices. __Of the nation's non-__
Catholic private hospitals, only one in three reported performing even one abortion in 1975; 18 percent of public hospitals
reported performing abortions. About 8 percent of procedures
were performed outside the woman's state of residence. Sullivan, Tietze, and Dryfoos (1976) suggest that poor, rural, and
very young women are most likely to fail in obtaining wanted
abortions; they usually lack the needed funds, time, or familiarity with the medical system to cope with the search for
accessible services.

     The 1975 Abortion Surveillance Report, prepared by the
Family Planning Evaluation Division of the Center for Disease
Control (CDC, 1977), shows that of the 854,853 women whose legal abortions were reported to CDC, 33 percent were under age
20, 47 percent had no living children, and 88 percent had the
procedure within the first trimester of pregnancy. Of the
teenage women, 5 percent (or about 14,000) were under age 15,
45 percent between 15 and 17, and 50 percent over age 18.
About 26 percent of the aborting women were married at the
time of the procedure, continuing the decline in married women
noted in previous years. The abortion ratio was about 17 times
higher for unmarried women than for married women (CDC, 1977).
Among the women obtaining abortions, 47 percent had no living
children at the time of procedure.

     During the period 1972-1974, the legal abortion rate
was 2.2 times higher, and the abortion ratio was 1.5 times
higher, among nonwhite women than among white women. The ratios suggest that abortion was less acceptable, available, or
accessible to black teenagers and to older black women than it
was to blacks in the prime reproductive years (Tietze, 1977a).
Other findings confirm that in areas where abortion services
are readily available, the legal abortion ratio among low income and minority group women is considerably higher than
among upper income women. In other geographical areas, low
income and minority women who want abortions are often unable
to obtain them.

     There is growing evidence that the frequency of sexual
intercourse is increasing and beginning earlier among young
people (Baldwin, 1976, 1977; Juhasz, 1976; Zelnik & Kantner,
1977). Premarital pregnancy and its resolution among early
adolescents (young women under age 16) remains one of the most
difficult public health concerns for US society, which has
otherwise demonstrated a trend toward increasingly effective
fertility regulation (AGI, 1976). Teenagers are underserved
in family planning clinics (Jaffe & Dryfoos, 1976); 27 percent
have had a pregnancy prior to receiving services (Day et al.,
1976). Approximately one-third of all abortion patients in

the United States are teenagers (CDC, 1977); those under 15 have the highest proportion of second trimester abortions compared to first trimester terminations (Tietze & Murstein, 1975). Although access to legal abortion temporarily reversed the rate of out-of-wedlock births, the rate for termination continued to increase, especially among the very young (Baldwin, 1976, 1977; Shelton, 1977; National Center for Health Statistics, 1976).

It is impossible to ascertain how current abortion figures compare with figures from the years when abortion was illegal except to save the woman's life. Because illegal abortions have seldom been recorded, except when the woman died or the practitioner was in legal difficulties, it is not possible to determine with certainty to what extent legal abortions are replacing illegal procedures. However, the number of women whose deaths were associated with illegal abortion has dropped considerably during the past decade--from about 200 in 1965 to 5 in 1975, the latest year for which figures are available (CDC, 1977; Tietze & Lewit, 1977a).

Fertility Choice Behavior

It is increasingly recognized that for most couples fertility regulation is risk-taking behavior or "taking chances" (Luker, 1975, 1977). As Miller (1972, 1973) and others have noted, there are recurrent hazard points in the sexual and procreational concerns of women, at which times the risk of unwanted pregnancy may be particularly high. Balancing of risks and probabilities is involved (Miller, 1976). Women with a history of successful contraception are candidates for abortion for an unwanted pregnancy. Risk-taking is not a thoughtless act but the product of conscious renegotiation of the costs and benefits of contraception compared to the costs and benefits of pregnancy, often accompanied by a misconception of the degree of objective risk involved (Luker, 1975, 1977).

Expectation and values, including estimated effectiveness, prospects for pregnancy, possibilities of medical and social side effects, and psychological costs and benefits, are considered in terms of level of sexual activity and prevailing life situation (i.e., frequency, predictability, and location of sexual intercourse). The pathway of decisions and the decision-making process from planned/protected or unplanned/unprotected coitus through pregnancy and pregnancy resolution has been well described by Diamond et al. (1973) on the basis of the experience of the Hawaii Pregnancy, Birth Control, and Abortion Study, and in more psychodynamic terms by Miller and Godwin (1977).

No woman becomes pregnant entirely by herself. The
decision to use or not to use a fertility-regulating method is
heavily influenced by the partner relationship. The partner's
attitudes and degree of control in the couple relationship are
likely to affect the type of method used and the information-
seeking process, especially among younger adolescents (Cahn,
1976a). As noted by Stycos, Back, and Hill (1956) over two
decades ago, and by Misra (1966) more than a decade ago, the
quality of couple communication has "a clear and consistent
relationship" with effectiveness of fertility regulation and
decisions about eventual pregnancy resolution.

Among adolescents, communication about pregnancy prevention occurs more frequently after intercourse than before
(Kirkendall & McDermott, 1970; Arnold, 1972; Goldsmith et al.,
1972). The lack of communication among unmarried partners is
even more apparent when compared with data on marital success
in contraceptive practice (Ryder, 1973). Yet most research
approaches to fertility-regulating behavior, pregnancy resolution, and adolescent decision making have concentrated on
women, largely because it is the woman who becomes pregnant
and is more readily available for study (e.g., Reiss, Banwart,
& Foreman, 1975; Shah, Zelnik, & Kantner, 1975; David, 1976).
Despite the evidence that the role of the male is of special
importance in sporadic adolescent sexual relationships (Kantner & Zelnik, 1972, 1973, 1975), and that condoms and withdrawal continue to be the method of choice among the youngest
teenagers (Zelnik & Kantner, 1977), many family planning agencies devalue the male role and tend to exclude male participation from service programs (Scales, Etelis, & Levitz, 1977).
There are few studies of decision making involving the male
partner; those males that are studied tend to be purposive
groups rather than representative or random samples (Scales,
1977). Cvetkovich, Grote, Bjorseth, and Sarkissian (1975)
were unable to find "a single in-depth analysis of male adolescents regarding contraception." The greater the restrictions on access to the most competent sources of information,
the less likely it is that adolescents will use one of the
more efficient methods, thus increasing the risk of unwanted
pregnancy (Cahn, 1976a). Compounded by a lack of goals and by
perception of limited life opportunities, there may be even
less reason to guard against pregnancy (Ross, 1977).

There have been numerous attempts during the past
three decades to explore the motivational bases of fertility
(Pohlman, 1969). The psychoanalytic approach was an earlier
favorite but proved resistant to systematic empirical investigation or policy utilization (Wyatt, 1967). A second approach
endeavored to assess motivation on the basis of attitudinal
questions. The general conclusion of research viewers is that
most of these studies relied on superficial conceptualization

of attitudes and used weak psychological assessment instruments
(e.g., Smith, 1973). When attitudes are measured in a simple
way, without benefit of the motivational framework in which to
interpret meanings, they are rarely predictive of actual behavior, and hence of little utility in identifying policy options
(Simmons, 1977).

The research orientation of the Transnational Family
Research Institute is that individuals are faced with many
choice points and alternative courses of action that will
largely determine the success of their efforts to control their
own fertility. The awareness of these choice points, the extent to which alternative courses of action are recognized,
and the degree to which choices are based on realistic ap-
praisals of benefits, costs, and consequences are held to be
the keystones of healthy fertility and fertility-regulating
behavior (Friedman, Johnson, & David, 1976).

The psychosocial model of fertility behavior, originally developed for TFRI by Friedman in association with
Kellerhals (University of Geneva), emphasizes the subjective
assessment of the environment by the individual and the importance of the two partners in a couple determining each other's
choice behavior. Subsequent extensions of this model and its
implications for research methodology have been delineated
elsewhere (David & Friedman, 1973; Friedman, 1974; Friedman,
Johnson, & David, 1976) and are briefly noted by Friedman and
Johnson in chapter 14. In adolescent women especially, the
social, interpersonal, and/or material support needed to cope
with an unwanted pregnancy is likely to be lacking (Zelnik &
Kantner, 1974, 1975; McCormick, Johnson, Friedman, & David,
1977).

Pregnancy Resolution

It may well be a truism that there is no psychologically painless way to cope with an unwanted pregnancy. Although an abortion may elicit feelings of guilt, regret, or
loss, alternative solutions such as forced marriage, bearing
an out-of-wedlock child, giving a child up for adoption, or
adding an unwanted child to an already strained marital situation are also likely to be accompanied by psychological problems for the woman, the child, the family, and society (David,
1972, 1973a).

Discussions with colleagues suggest two divergent psychological models of abortion. One assumes that abortion represents personal failure, holding that aborting women are more
"field-dependent" (Seeley, 1976), or less adequate in diverse

social contexts and sexual attitudes and behaviors (Arnold & Slagle, 1976), or are the product of poor family relationships (Abernathy, 1973). If the assumption of relatively immutable personal characteristics is verified, it may be concluded that such women are more prone to negative psychological consequences, social deviance, and pathology (Graves, 1975).

Another psychological model, shared by Steinhoff (1977), Miller (1977), and TFRI views abortion-seeking behavior as an effective means of coping with a personal crisis, a normal ego-enhancing development, more likely to have positive than negative psychological consequences. For example, in comparing aborting women with those who carried an unplanned pregnancy to term, whether in or out of wedlock, Steinhoff et al. (1972) found that abortion patients were more future and planning oriented, had higher personal aspirations, and were more idealistic about marriage and eventual motherhood. Successful crisis resolution becomes a learning experience. In sum, the only difference between an aborting woman and another woman may be an unintended pregnancy which she has decided not to continue.

Delayed Abortion-Seeking Behavior

One of the most important factors in the evaluation of psychosocial factors associated with induced abortion is the period of gestation at which the pregnancy is terminated. The major dichotomy is between first and second trimester abortions; that is, between those performed at or before the twelfth week of gestation and those at thirteen weeks or later. In the United States, late abortions occur most frequently among economically, educationally, and socially disadvantaged women and especially among very young teenagers. In the view of Tietze and Murstein (1975), "the strong inverse association of period of gestation and woman's age probably reflects the inexperience of the very young in recognizing the symptoms of pregnancy, their unwillingness to accept the reality of their situation, their ignorance about where to seek advice and help, and their hesitation to confide in adults."

Sociodemographic and psychosocial correlates of delayed decisions to abort have been extensively reviewed and studied by Bracken and his associates (Bracken & Kasl, 1975a, 1975b, 1975c, 1976; Bracken & Swigar, 1972). Women who delay seeking an abortion generally have been found to be young, single, primigravidas, experiencing their first abortion. Black women appear to present later for abortion, as do women from lower socioeconomic groups, those with lower levels of completed education, and the unemployed. Other studies, including interviews with 400 delaying patients by Kerenyi et al. (1973), suggest additional reasons that may be divided into external and internal conflicts. External conflicts. would include: lack of information on availability or location of services, financial difficulties, bureaucratic delays, and inaccurate physician or clinic diagnoses. Internal conflicts would include: ambivalence, fear of telling parents or partner, and late recognition and/or denial of pregnancy until signs and symptoms become obvious.

Nearly all available studies of second trimester abortions, including those by Bracken et al., Kerenyi et al., and the psychoanalytic observations by Denes (1976), were conducted in the period before the January 1973 Supreme Court decision, when first and second trimester abortions were legally available in only a few metropolitan areas and when there was considerable uncertainty about abortion procedures and their legal status among the health professions and the public. As noted by Bracken and Kasl (1976), their studies and those of other colleagues did not include women whose abortion decision was too long delayed and who were subsequently obliged to carry their pregnancies to term. The personal problems and conflicts perceived by women "caught" in such situations in the Metropolitan Washington area were noted by Hiatt (1976).

Although there is substantial agreement in the literature on the demographic characteristics of women demonstrating delayed abortion-seeking behavior, there is much less consensus on the interplay of lack of information, psychosocial factors in the decision-making process, the actual role of administrative and institutional barriers, and the woman's (or couple's) ability to cope with conflict, feelings of powerlessness, and an environment perceived to be hostile. There is a need for more data on social-environmental milieu influences, as well as on motivation and decision-making processes, if public health strategies are to become more effective in reducing the incidence of second trimester abortions.

Abortion Refused

There are two kinds of abortion refusals. An abortion request may be denied, or a woman may change her mind and decide to carry to term after an abortion request has been approved. It has never been possible in the United States systematically to follow women denied an abortion or the children they were compelled to bear (if there was no resort to illegal termination). Only two control studies, from Sweden and Czechoslovakia, appear in the research literature; they are summarized by Illsley and Hall in chapter 2. Results of the Czech study are fully delineated in chapter 9.

Insofar as can be ascertained, there has been only one US follow-up study of abortion applicant dropouts (Swigar et al., 1976, 1977). A checklist of reasons for remaining pregnant was developed. There were no statistically significant demographic or gynecological differences between women who changed their minds after requesting abortion and decided to carry to term and a control group of women who implemented their plans for abortion during the same time period. Public controversies about the morality of obtaining abortion influenced several couples' decisions; the second most important deciding factor was the partner's desire for a baby; fear of the procedure and possible complications ranked third. Implications for abortion counseling are cited.

Abortion/Contraception

Studies of abortion-seeking behavior are incomplete without considering the interrelationship between abortion and contraception as methods of fertility regulation. The notion of conception prevention is historically far more recent, requiring adherence to a new level of shared responsibility in sexual behavior, exposure to and acceptance of contraceptive information and education, and conscious precoital planning. Abortion requires little prior educational effort; a missed period and anxiety about an unwanted pregnancy usually provide sufficient motivation. Unlike most contraceptives, abortion is a 100 percent effective, one-time, coitus-independent operation, based on certainty rather than probability (Moore, 1971).

The research literature (Moore, 1974) suggests that women who have had an abortion are more likely to become contraceptors, and that women who use contraceptives are more likely to resort to abortion in contraceptive or other failures. Choice behavior under conditions where both safe abortion and modern contraceptives are equally readily available and psychologically accessible remains to be studied in depth. Available information from New York City women over age 20, most of whom were married, "lend no support whatsoever to the concern that relatively easy access to legal and safe abortion has led to neglect of contraception. Rather, the data suggest more general and/or more effective practice of fertility regulation" (Tietze, 1975).

The New York City data are confirmed by findings from the 1975 National Fertility Study. Westoff and Jones (1977) report "a substantial increase in the proportion of women currently using contraception" since 1973, the year in which the US Supreme Court ruled induced abortion legal for the entire country. Among the most recent cohort in the NFS, women

married in 1971-1975, only 5.2 percent never used contraception over an average marriage duration of 2.5 years. Noting
the 1965-1975 data on the proportion using contraception among
married white women 15-44 years of age, Tietze (1977b) confirmed his earlier observation of an acceleration rather than
decline in contraceptive practice following the Supreme Court
ruling. Similarly, in a nationwide sample, the percentage of
sexually experienced and active teenage women using contraceptives at last intercourse increased from 45.4 percent to 63.5
percent between 1971 and 1976 (Zelnik & Kantner, 1977, 1978).

        In reflecting on contraception, Moore (1977) observes
that it has been "both boon and bane to modern women." The
possibility of fertility regulation represents an important
advance, relieving women of unintended and unwelcome childbearing. But making available the means to lower fertility
does not necessarily provide the reasons or the incentive for
so doing. In the private area of fertility regulation, improvements in technology will be utilized only to the extent
to which they enhance genuine couple communication and shared
decision making toward common socioeconomic goals (David,
1974).

                    Repeated Abortion Seeking

        One of the few American studies including information
on repeated abortion seeking during the preliberalization era
is Lee's (1969) report of 69 "well educated, intelligent, and
sophisticated" women who had obtained medical advice on contraception after their first abortion, which had been performed
by a physician under illegal circumstances more than a year
before data collection. Of these 69 women, 28 (43 percent)
had had a second abortion; of the 28 repeaters, 9 (32 percent)
had a third abortion. Lee suggests that the repeated abortions
observed may have been an artifact of the study design and indicative of the difficulties unmarried women had in obtaining
and using effective contraceptives in the United States during
the late 1950s and early 1960s.

        On the basis of data received from 20 states and the
District of Columbia, the Center for Disease Control (1977) reports that in 1975 almost one in five women obtaining a legal
abortion had had at least one prior induced abortion. The proportion of women reporting one or more prior induced abortions
ranged from seven percent in Nebraska to 30 percent in the
District of Columbia. Hard data on the incidence of repeat
abortions for the entire country are unlikely to be forthcoming in the absence of a uniform national reporting system.
Moreover, interview questioning about prior abortions has

usually demonstrated selective "forgetting" rather than reliable recall (Hogue, 1975).

With increasing acceptance and utilization of legal abortion to terminate unwanted pregnancies, attention among public health specialists and politicians has gradually shifted to "problems" perceived to be associated with repeat abortions. For example, at his Yazoo City, Mississippi, Town Meeting on July 21, 1977, President Carter (1977) reiterated his opposition to public funding of abortions, stating "it is very disturbing how many of the recipients of federal payments for abortion in the past have been repeaters. They come back time after time for additional abortions, which shows it is not entirely ignorance" (AGI, 1977c). In actual fact, systematic research funded by the federal government has demonstrated that the proportion of married couples practicing contraception has significantly increased since the 1973 legalization of abortion; so has the proportion of sexually active unmarried teenagers using contraception at last intercourse (Westoff & Jones, 1977; Zelnik & Kantner, 1977). No studies have yet been reported on repeat abortions among recipients of federal reimbursement (Medicaid).

It is necessary to recall that current US abortion statistics reflect only legal and reported terminations. Women who have had one abortion and are fecund and sexually active become candidates for a repeat abortion if they do not use contraception, or practice it inconsistently or incorrectly and do not want to carry an unwanted pregnancy to term. Thus, the rate of repeat abortions among women with abortion experience tends to be higher than the first abortion rate (Tietze, 1977d). The proportion of repeat abortions is bound to increase until a stable plateau is reached. It has been estimated that repeat abortions may be expected to occur within one year among two-to-five percent of women using oral contraceptives with a reasonable degree of motivation. Women relying on less effective methods or practicing less efficient contraceptive vigilance would be expected to have a higher incidence, which would increase further over time (Tietze, 1974a).

What does it mean when a significant number of teenage women have a repeat abortion? The Margaret Sanger Center of Planned Parenthood in New York City did not observe any significant distinguishable demographic characteristics (Cahn, 1976b). Although abortion was not found to be the preferred form of fertility regulation, multiple abortors more frequently stopped using one method of contraception without adopting another. Demographic characteristics such as age, education, and parity were associated with the choice of specific methods. This may mean that contraceptive motivations are method specific, in part because clinics emphasize asking women to choose a particular method rather than a system of fertility regulation (including temporary back-up alternatives). In an earlier study, Cahn (1975) noted that many teenagers decided on method preferences before coming to the clinic; he raised the question of whether service providers know what information inquiring adolescents really want and need for effective contraception in diverse circumstances of sexual activity and life situation.

The research literature suggests that most repeaters are more likely to have used contraception at the time of conception than first time abortors (Bracken et al., 1972; Rovinsky, 1972). Schneider and Thompson (1976) compared repeat abortors with first time abortors, pregnant women carrying to term, and nonpregnant women presumably at risk of conception. Every repeat abortor was matched with a woman in each of the other three populations for parity (excluding previously induced abortions), marital status, and age. This and other studies confirm that women who have had one abortion tend to increase subsequent use of contraception and are more likely to continue contracepting than women about to have their first abortion; however, they are less effective or less vigilant in their contraceptive practice than a group of sexually active nonpregnant women.

Although contraceptive failure and "risk taking" are probably the major reasons for repeat abortions, it is likely that there is a small proportion of women who prefer abortion as their primary means of fertility regulation. For them abortion is a safe, one-time event with none of the "hassles" perceived to be associated with modern contraceptive methods. There is much to be said for "the 100 percent effectiveness that can be obtained by use of the condom and diaphragm when these methods are backed up by early induced abortion of all pregnancies that result from contraceptive failure" (Tietze & Lewit, 1977b).

The social science and medical research literature yields few systematic studies of the psychological dynamics of repeated contraceptive failures. The "chance taking" aspects of fertility regulating have already been noted (Luker, 1975, 1977; Miller, 1976). Cobliner et al. (1975) documented that a certain irreducible proportion of unintended pregnancies "inevitably arise from the interplay between contraceptive technology and human behavior." Sociodemographic and other background characteristics were similar among their subjects with planned or unplanned pregnancies and did not account for different outcomes in contraceptive practice. Their subsequent studies suggest a relatively lower frustration tolerance among some women, causing them to reduce contraceptive vigilance while believing in an illusion of continued safety; this psychological process, in turn, precludes the resurgence of the felt need for resuming more efficient contraceptive action (Cobliner et al., 1976). In a related study, Byrne (1977) showed that ideas of contraception or unwanted pregnancy are almost never present in students' erotic fantasies. And they are rarely considered in soft or hardcore pornography.

Preventive Strategies

In the late 1960s comprehensive service programs of prenatal, maternity, and newborn care for school-age mothers were developed in many US communities. Serving high school students 17 years of age or under, the Yale New Haven Hospital included a heavy complement of counseling and education, encouraging contraceptive practices. In a follow-up of a group of 180 adolescents served by this program six to eight years after their babies were born, Jekel, Tyler, and Klerman (1977) found, somewhat to their surprise, that over one-third of these women had used legal abortion to terminate some 80 subsequent pregnancies; an additional 16 young women had sought and received surgical sterilization. A high proportion (48 percent) of the young mothers obtained abortions during the second trimester, even for repeat abortions (37 percent). The abortion experience after the first pregnancy of 180 teenage mothers served by this special program was not significantly different from comparable groups of teenage mothers who had not participated in the program.

None of the variables tested in the Yale study was a good predictor of whether or not the young woman would subsequently seek a surgical termination. The only statistically significant patterns that emerged were that those young women who had stayed in school through graduation and/or remained single tended to use abortions, and those who dropped out of school and married were more likely to use sterilization. Acceptance of contraceptives postpartum and their reported use 26 months later were not associated with use of either abortion or sterilization. No answer could be given to the question of why existing methods of reversible contraception were inadequate to meet the fertility control needs of almost half of the population served (Jekel et al., 1977).

If the assumptions of Cobliner et al. (1976) are valid, mere knowledge of contraceptives or better sex education are unlikely per se to promote contraceptive vigilance and thus foster alternatives to unwanted pregnancy and abortion. A

clear and direct relationship between extent of sex education
and use of contraceptives among adolescents has not been established. Zelnik and Kantner (1977) likened this transfer of
knowledge to "carrying water in a basket." Scales (1977) suggests that one reason for the apparent failure of sex education among adolescents is that it does not help them talk
about the subject. Risk-taking may be preferable to interrupting lovemaking with such mechanical methods as the condom
or withdrawal. Might a "disruptive" element be perceived as
pleasurable, and related to sharing of the decision-making
process, if women were taught to place the condom on the male
partner, as is already practiced in Sweden and Japan?

If on the pill, motivation for continuation is likely
to require something more for some women than the reward of a
nonoccurring event--the absence of unwanted pregnancy. Frustration tolerance and self-reliance may be enhanced by more
frequent and systematic exposure to the dangers of reduced
vigilance and self-delusion. This will require a greater
willingness of the media, especially TV, to advertise and discuss contraception. Research suggests that attempts at health
education and persuasion appear to be more successful when the
behavior to be changed is frequent and occurs during the
course of the information campaign (e.g., Maccoby & Farquhar,
1975).

Luker (1977) contends that programs designed primarily to extend and/or improve contraceptive delivery systems
"are inadequate to significantly decrease risk-taking behavior
and the need for abortion." Efforts must be made to influence
attitudes toward sexual behavior and improve economic opportunities for women. A growing body of data suggests that with
increasing economic options women marry later, have smaller
families, and are more likely to define the children they have
as more planned and wanted (Blumberg, 1976; Hass, 1972; Hoffman, 1974; Kasarda, 1971; Salaff, 1976; Weller, 1968). Unless
women can anticipate real and gratifying alternatives to childbearing, the utilities of pregnancy will continue to be mixed
(Luker, 1977).

Effective Coping

Much attention has been devoted in the literature to
the relationship between sociodemographic variables and indicators of "dysfunction" (however defined), but relatively
little consideration has been given to mutable psychosocial
and socioeconomic variables impinging, for example, on healthy
family functioning, effective fertility regulation, and successful coping (David & Johnson, 1977; David, 1977b, 1978b).

Available knowledge tends to be used primarily by a minority of couples and adolescents who appear to engage in more efficient planning behavior encompassing diverse life aspects, from education and saving money to fertility regulation.

The basic unit of successful coping and effective fertility regulation is likely to be the young couple. There are major methodological advantages to studying recently formed family units. This population is relatively small in any given society and is usually definable and (with proper precautions) approachable. Samples can be readily obtained in most metropolitan areas, representing a cross section of the population (albeit at one particular point in their life cycles); information is likely to cut across all socioeconomic classes. The only longitudinal study of young couples married for the first time currently known to be in progress is now in its third year in the Canton of Geneva, Switzerland (Kellerhals, 1977). Initiated in 1974 with support from the Swiss National Fund, two rounds of interviews have been completed with a third scheduled for 1978. Related studies comparing newly married couples with couples living in stable, marriage-like unions of unmarried cohabitation are underway in Sweden (Trost, 1977). There is much to be learned from these efforts for consideration in the United States.

PSYCHOLOGICAL SEQUELAE

Prelegalization Studies

Of all the complications of abortion, psychological sequelae are the most difficult to assess (Potts, Diggory, & Peel, 1977). Early research on abortion of necessity focused on small groups of women who had been granted therapeutic abortions under restrictive conditions or who had procured illegal abortions in the United States or abroad (Osofsky et al., 1975). In reviewing the interpretative findings and conclusions of studies conducted prior to legalization of abortion, the Osofskys (1975) noted findings ranging from frequent and severe sequelae (Bolter, 1962; Galdston, 1958; Whittington, 1970), to occasional direct or indirect problems (Rosen, 1954, 1967), to no noticeable difficulty (Kummer, 1963; Hardin, 1968; Guttmacher, 1967). The limited objective data in these studies showed low incidences of psychological complications and, in several instances, suggested the therapeutic effect of abortion.

Psychological and psychiatric studies on alleged sequelae of abortion conducted in the era before liberalization demonstrated a lack of consensus on definitions of mental

health consequences, a plethora of impressionistic case reports, and, quite often, an absence of rudimentary methodological concerns (Simon & Senturia, 1966; Sloane, 1969; Callahan,
1970; Walter, 1970; David, 1973a; Moore, 1974; Illsley & Hall,
1976). Among the more frequent methodological problems noted
were: (a) failure to examine the psychological status of the
woman before the abortion; (b) poor sampling techniques;
(c) lack of attention to possible interviewer bias; (d) lack
of control groups to compare with aborting women, or even
agreement on what control groups would be appropriate.

Limited data only are available concerning the psychological sequelae of illegal abortion. None of the women interviewed by Whittemore (1970) regretted her decision, but two
patients expressed regret over having previously given birth
to an out-of-wedlock child apiece. In a better controlled
study, Gebhard et al. (1958) and his Kinsey Institute associates interviewed 442 women who admitted having had abortions,
mostly illegal terminations of unwanted pregnancies; "less than
ten percent reported psychological upset." In most cases this
"upset" was described in general terms: "only a few said they
were nervous for some time after abortion" (p. 209). Gebhard
et al. comment that their findings concur with those of Mandy
(1954), who reported little evidence in his obstetrical experience to justify the exaggerated warnings of psychiatrists
regarding the frequency of serious depressions following illegal induced abortions. "We have seen in our clinic a number
of patients who admitted as many as 15 or 20 self-induced
abortions without any evidence of guilt or serious depression
consequent to these acts" (Mandy, 1954). There seems little
doubt that women who sought and were able to obtain illegal
abortions were "determined, healthy, and socially mobile individuals" (Osofsky, Osofsky, & Rajan, 1973).

It would be logical to expect a higher incidence of
psychological problems in women receiving a therapeutic abortion for psychiatric reasons (whether genuine or not). In reviewing the literature, the Osofskys (1971, 1972, 1973, 1975)
noted that the stringency of prevailing laws and indicators
for therapeutic procedures usually resulted in only the most
psychiatrically disturbed women qualifying for abortions.
Some of the findings demonstrated a small incidence of post-
operative psychiatric disturbance in women with prior severe
psychopathology, "usually related to the already existing psychiatric disturbance rather than to the abortion procedure."
In most cases, psychiatric and psychological evaluations demonstrated considerable improvement in both attitudes and behaviors. Women denied an abortion because of insufficient
evidence of disabling psychiatric problems often fared considerably worse after carrying their pregnancies to term than did

the apparently more emotionally disturbed women following their pregnancy terminations.

Particularly noted by the Osofskys and by Illsley and Hall (1976) are the contributions of Peck and Marcus (1966); Kretzschmar and Norris (1967); Simon, Senturia, and Rothman (1967); Niswander and Patterson (1967); Niswander, Singer, and Singer (1972); Patt, Rappaport, and Barglow (1969); and Meyerowitz, Satloff, and Romano (1971). Additional references may be found in the Guide to the 1968-1972 International Abortion Research Literature (IRCAR, 1973). One of the best-designed studies, measuring multiple variables over four time intervals, was reported by Payne, Kravitz, Notman, and Anderson (1976); women most vulnerable to post-abortion conflict were those who were single and nulliparous, had a previous history of serious emotional problems, experienced strong ambivalence about abortion, or had negative cultural/religious attitudes. After surveying the experience of 32 Los Angeles psychiatrists who averaged 12 years of professional practice, Kummer (1963) reported that 75 percent of these physicians did not recall seeing a single patient with moderate or severe psychiatric sequelae from either illegal or therapeutic abortions. The other 25 percent had encountered significant sequelae only rarely. Not surprisingly, Kummer titled his report "Post-abortion psychiatric illness: A myth?"

Postliberalization Studies

Studies of psychological effects of abortion conducted during the immediate era after liberalization have been catalogued by Gunn (1976), reviewed by the Osofskys (1973, 1975), and summarized by the Institute of Medicine (1975). Current publications are regularly cited in Abortion Research Notes (IRCAR, 1977). A particularly unfortunate example of ventilating personal views and ignoring methodological considerations is Denes' (1976) dramatic presentation of psychological trauma occasionally associated with second trimester abortions (David, 1977a). Other illustrative papers include, for example, a case study of the development of an obsessive compulsive neurosis after viewing the fetus during a second trimester saline abortion (Lipper & Feigenbaum, 1976) and a carefully delineated follow-up study of emotional responses after first trimester abortion, suggesting that current sampling techniques may result in an underestimation of negative sequelae (Adler, 1975). Athanasiou et al. (1973) reported an unusual matched control study of women seeking either term deliveries or first or second trimester abortions; they noted that "induced abortion appears to be a benign procedure compared to term birth, psychologically and physically."

It is seldom realized that post-abortion psychosis is practically unknown (Jansson, 1965). There are about 4,000 documented postpartum psychoses requiring hospitalization in the United States per year (between 10-20 per 10,000 deliveries); there should be a sizable number of hospitalized post-abortion psychoses if abortion were as traumatic for some women as term delivery (Fleck, 1970). It would appear unlikely that a significant number of hospitalized psychoses related to abortion could be "hidden" in the record. Yet there is hardly any mention of post-abortion psychosis in the literature (David, 1973a; David & Friedman, 1973). Similarly, although "postpartum blues" are well known as typical depressive stress reactions to the end of pregnancy, post-abortion "blues" have been observed to be generally brief and mild unless a serious mental disturbance was present before abortion (Osofsky, Osofsky, & Rajan, 1973).

An early report on the psychiatric complication rate of abortion was compiled by the Joint Program for the Study of Abortion (Tietze & Lewit, 1972). From July 1, 1970, to June 30, 1971, the 66 participating institutions reported a total of 16 major psychiatric complications from a pool of 72,988 abortions, including two suicides and five depressive reactions associated with major hemorrhage or protracted fever. One of the two women committing suicide had a history of psychiatric hospitalization before and after the abortion; the procedure itself was not the cause of death. The second suicide was of a young woman who was falsely diagnosed as pregnant and who committed suicide before that information could be conveyed to her after the surgical procedure (Tietze, 1974b). The complications recorded in the JPSA data yield a psychiatric complication rate of two per 10,000 abortions (without other concurrent surgeries), and four per 10,000 abortions for local women later seen for follow-up evaluations. In a prospective study of abortion psychosis in the United Kingdom, Brewer (1977) found an incidence of three per 10,000 legal abortions compared with postpartum psychosis of 17 per 10,000 deliveries.

Particularly reflective of the professional judgments involved in rating psychological sequelae of abortion was a unique experience reported by Fingerer (1973). When the same psychological test protocols (e.g., Spielberger's State-Trait Anxiety Inventory, Zuckerman's Affective Adjective Check List, and a measure of depressive symptomatology) were given to five groups, highest indications for anxiety and depression were obtained (in decreasing order) by (a) psychoanalytic post-doctoral students answering the way they believed theory would predict an aborting woman would feel the day after her procedure; (b) graduate and undergraduate students, role playing as if they were about to obtain an abortion; (c) persons accompanying the abortion patient to the clinic; (d) women before their abortions; and (e) the same women the day after the procedure. Concludes Fingerer: "the psychological aftereffects of abortion seem to reside in psychoanalytic theory and societal myths."

Assuming that psychiatric or psychological morbidity is a real and measurable phenomenon, the explanation for the wide range of opinions still expressed in the psychiatric literature and in public debates may well lie in the inadequacy of much of the published work, including (a) overemphasis on clinical case histories that ignore the large majority of aborting women who never seek postoperative psychiatric consultation, (b) the lack of psychological assessment prior to the unwanted pregnancy or abortion, and (c) the absence of standardized follow-up procedures and anchored psychiatric diagnoses. Unless the pre-abortion psychiatric condition of the woman is examined, it is impossible to draw conclusions concerning the post-abortion condition presumed to be caused by the procedure. An effort is currently in progress in Denmark, where the unique Danish population registration system makes it feasible to compare the incidence of post-abortion hospitalization for mental disorder with postpartum admissions to psychiatric hospitals, while also controlling for prior mental disorder (David & Wagner, 1977).

When interpreting alleged psychological sequelae of abortion, it is wise to consider the checklist of cautions devised by Moore (1974), which summarizes most of the points already stated in this chapter. A review of the diverse literature leads to the conclusion that legal induced abortion does not carry a significant risk of psychiatric trauma, and that whatever psychological risk exists is less than that associated with carrying a pregnancy to term. Although the risk of psychological sequelae is greater in second trimester abortions, especially for the very young who find it difficult to cope with delivering a recognizable fetus, sensitive counseling can greatly reduce the momentary trauma. In those rare instances where post-abortion psychiatric disturbances appear, they are more likely to relate to the degree of adjustment existing before the pregnancy than to the abortion procedure (Belsey et al., 1977). Feelings of guilt and depression, when noted, are usually mild and transient. It seems reasonable to conclude that for the vast majority of women abortion engenders a sense of relief and represents a maturing experience of successful coping and crisis resolution.

CURRENT CONCERNS

The Doctor's Dilemma

Medical and allied health personnel are central to the equitable and effective provision of abortion services. As "gatekeepers," they control access to abortion and are involved in virtually every phase, from early referral and the decision to abort to post-abortion counseling and follow-up care. Their attitudes are increasingly the subject of psychosocial research in fertility regulation, as noted in Part V of this volume.

For many physicians and nursing staff, performing abortions represents a personal, ethical, and moral dilemma, posing conflicts between the commitment to save lives and the decision to terminate unwanted pregnancies (Char & McDermott, 1972; Bourne, 1972; Kessler & Weiss, 1974; McCormick, 1975; Nathanson & Becker, 1977). Conditions of practice, perceptions of professional roles, and socioeconomic status of the woman seem to be interrelated. Women with greater economic resources historically have had far fewer difficulties in obtaining abortions from qualified physicians than have economically disadvantaged women, whether the abortion sought was legal or illegal (Gordon, 1976). Non-university-affiliated physicians practicing primarily among low income groups often tend to express more conservative attitudes (LoSciuto et al., 1972). Inequity is increased in those areas where private prejudice is permitted to become public policy because physicians and hospital administrators refuse to perform, or to permit, legal abortions.

The medical staff dilemma is particularly apparent in the choice of procedure for a second trimester abortion. If a woman requests termination during the 14th week, should the physician wait until week 16 or 17, relying on intra-amniotic installation of saline, or proceed immediately with the newer dilatation and evacuation (D&E) procedure? Although the saline technique is psychologically easier for the attending staff it can be difficult for the woman requiring a 12-36 hour hospital stay including pseudo labor and the trauma of delivering a dead fetus with recognizable features. Recent experience with the D&E method suggests that it is significantly safer than saline, far less time-consuming, and can be administered in the "grey zone" of the 13-16th week gestational interval (CDC, 1976). Although D&E suction greatly reduces the risk of psychological trauma for the woman, the psychological burden is much greater for the operating room staff, who perceive themselves as far more involved in the act

of abortion (Burnhill, 1977). It has been estimated that less
than one percent of all abortions in the United States would
be performed by instillation at 17 weeks or later if all women
presenting at 16 weeks or earlier had D&E performed as soon as
they sought medical care (Cates, 1977).

The most recent available study of the influence of
physicians' attitudes on abortion performance, patient management, and professional fees was conducted by Nathanson and
Becker (1977) among all obstetrician-gynecologists with any
private practice in Maryland during 1975. Religion was found
to be the most powerful predictor of abortion performance:
only 15 percent of Catholic physicians performed any abortions.
Conservative values about current questions of bioethics, provision of reproductive health services, and women's roles are
also negatively associated with performing abortions. More
liberal attitudes are positively related to numbers of abortions performed. Such physicians are less likely to insist on
spousal or parental consent, but charge relatively higher fees
and are more likely to request advance payment.

Physicians who report feeling satisfaction with their
patients are less likely to request parental consent for unmarried adolescent women; charge lower fees; do not accept
Medicaid; and do not ask for advance payment. They tend to
have predominantly white middle-class practices, providing
abortion as an accommodation to women of their own social
status with whom they have had a prior professional relationship. Physicians emotionally uncomfortable with abortion as
an operative procedure perform fewer terminations and are
more likely to insist on spousal or parental consent, but
charge lower fees and are more likely to accept Medicaid patients. They seem reluctant to profit from a personally dis-
agreeable practice (Nathanson & Becker, 1977).

Within this context of personal dilemma it must be
recognized that courses in human sexuality and mention of contraception and abortion are a relatively recent phenomenon in
medical and nursing schools (Lief, 1963; Lief & Karlan, 1976;
Woods, 1977). Even now many physicians and/or nurses decline
to staff abortion services, protected by conscience clauses
in prevailing statutes. As one consequence, eight out of ten
US counties did not have a single abortion facility in 1975
(Sullivan, Tietze, & Dryfoos, 1977). As long as obstetrician-
gynecologists and allied health professionals remain ambivalent about legal/moral issues, it is not surprising that personal feelings about the patients and the procedure become
major determinants of health gatekeeper responses to women's
requests for terminating unwanted pregnancies.

Menstrual Regulation

The availability of menstrual regulation techniques (the process of removing the contents of the uterus by suction within days of a missed period) has added a new dimension to the perception of pregnancy and abortion (van der Vlugt & Piotrow, 1974; Potts, 1976). Whether or not the woman wishes to wait for positive proof of pregnancy before requesting menstrual regulation (MR) is a decision she will have to make. Some women prefer not to know.

In speculating on future developments, consideration should be given to such menses-inducing or menses-regulating agents as prostaglandins and their analogs. Although many hurdles remain, it is not too early to envisage the social and societal impact of the potential availability of medicated tampons or tablets, offering women (if they choose) the freedom to regulate their monthly cycles or induce menses within days after a period has been "missed" and the prospect of a possible unwanted pregnancy becomes apparent.

A review of available literature suggests that the psychosocial aspects of normal menstruation, cycle regulation, and delayed menses have received relatively little attention from behavioral scientists (David, 1973b; Weideger, 1976; DeLaney et al., 1976). With increasing availability of menses-regulating agents or procedures, there may well be a concomitant need to develop research strategies to enhance understanding of perceptions of the menstrual cycle and femininity, the search for culturally acceptable fertility-regulating methods, and the complex choice behaviors and couple communication process in fertility regulation.

Public Policy and Private Decisions

Fertility regulation, whether by pre- or post-conceptive means, is neither a socially progressive nor a reactionary idea when viewed in historical perspective (David, 1978a). Although many individual physicians have made outstanding contributions and consistently championed the rights of women, organized medicine has often been reluctant to advocate family planning services unless established under medical control. It is rarely mentioned that fertility regulation per se is not a symptom of illness and seldom a medical issue. Abortion does involve medical skills but may come under increasingly individual control if technology continues to advance safely toward envisaged goals.

The decision to practice or not to practice effective
fertility regulation, or how to resolve an unwanted pregnancy,
is essentially a private matter. The gap between policy
choices and the conflict between public acceptability and private usefulness are well delineated by Potts in chapter 15.
As this chapter has attempted to indicate, such decisions are
the end products of complex interaction processes, including
psychosocial and socioeconomic determinants, couple communication, and cultural environmental influences, which are gradually receiving increasing research and policy recognition.

CONCLUSION

Review of the vast literature on abortion is hardly
conducive to maintaining scientific detachment. As Callahan
(1970) phrased it nearly a decade ago, "Abortion is a source
of social and legal discord, moral uncertainty, medical and
psychiatric confusion, and personal anguish." How many colleagues in the behavioral and medical sciences, and in the
mental health professions, think of abortion in one way and
speak and write of it in another? How closely does actual
practice conform to expressed beliefs? Although 80 percent
of Maryland gynecologists supported the drive for liberalization of the Maryland abortion law, fewer than 20 percent actually performed one abortion during the first year of practice
under the reform statute (Cushner, 1970).

There is little mention in the research literature of
the right of women to determine for themselves how many children they wish to have and when they want to have them. The
right to legal and safe abortion in the United States, although
affirmed by the January 1973 Supreme Court Decision, is in actual practice severely limited by economic realities and lack
of facilities outside major metropolitan centers for reasons
that are primarily related to sociopolitical considerations.

When society has reached the state in which all pregnancies are planned and wanted, and children are born to parents sufficiently mature to provide adequate care, then abortion
services may well become obsolete. Until that time access to
abortion, as well as to other pregnancy-related services, must
be regarded as a basic human right, a moral choice a woman
should be free to make and implement without undue restrictions
imposed by a still largely male-dominated governing structure.

REFERENCES

Abernathy, V. The abortion constellation: Early history and present relationships. Archives of General Psychiatry, 1973, 29, 346-350.

Adler, N. E. Emotional responses of women following therapeutic abortion. American Journal of Orthopsychiatry, 1975, 43, 446-454.

Adler, N. E. Sample attrition in studies of psychosocial sequelae of abortion: How great a problem? Journal of Applied Social Psychology, 1976, 6, 240-259.

Alan Guttmacher Institute. Eleven Million Teenagers. New York: Author, 1976.

Alan Guttmacher Institute. Planned births, the future of the family, and the quality of American life. New York: Author, 1977. (a)

Alan Guttmacher Institute. Washington Memo, June 24, July 1, July 15, 1977. (b)

Alan Guttmacher Institute. Washington Memo, August 3, 1977. (c)

Alan Guttmacher Institute. Washington Memo, January 13, January 27, 1978.

Arnold, C. B. The sexual behavior of inner city adolescent condom users. Journal of Sex Research, 1972, 8, 298-309.

Arnold, C. B., & Slagle, S. J. Who's at risk of having unwanted conceptions? A causal analysis of psychosocial data on 625 young, middle-class women with low fertility. Paper presented at Workshop on Psychosocial Aspects of Fertility, Montreal, 1976.

Athanasiou, R. et al. Psychiatric sequelae to term birth and induced early and late abortion: A longitudinal study. Family Planning Perspectives, 1973, 5, 227-231.

Baldwin, W. H. Adolescent pregnancy and childbearing. Population Bulletin, 1976, 31, No. 2.

Baldwin, W. H. Update 1975: Adolescent childbearing. Intercom, 1977, 5(2), 11-12.

Belsey, E. M., Greer, H. S., Lal, S., Lewis, S. C., & Beard, R. W. Predictive factors in emotional response to abortion: King's termination study. Social Science and Medicine, 1977, 11, 71-82.

Blumberg, R. Fairy tales and facts: Economy, family, fertility, and the female. In I. Tinker & M. B. Bramsen (Eds.), Women and world development. Washington: Overseas Development Council, 1976.

Bolter, S. The psychiatrist's role in therapeutic abortion: The unwitting accomplice. American Journal of Psychiatry, 1962, 119, 312-316.

Bourne, J. P. Abortion: Influences on health professionals' attitudes. Hospitals, 1972, 46, 80-83.

Bracken, M. B., Hachamovitch, M., & Grossman, G. Correlates of repeat induced abortions. Obstetrics and Gynecology, 1972, 40, 816-825.

Bracken, M. B., & Kasl, S. V. First and repeat abortions: A study of decision-making and delay. Journal of Biosocial Science, 1975, 7, 473-491. (a)

Bracken, M. B., & Kasl, S. V. Denial of pregnancy, conflict, and delayed decisions to abort. Proceedings of the International Congress of Psychosomatic Obstetrics and Gyecology. Basel: Karger, 1975. (b)

Bracken, M. B., & Kasl, S. V. Delay in seeking induced abortion: A review and theoretical analysis. American Journal of Obstetrics and Gynecology, 1975, 121, 1008-1019. (c)

Bracken, M. B., & Kasl, S. V. Psychosocial correlates of delayed decisions to abort. Health Education Monographs, 1976, 4, 6-44.

Bracken, M. B., & Swigar, M. E. Factors associated with delay in seeking induced abortions. American Journal of Obstetrics and Gynecology, 1972, 113, 301-309.

Burnhill, M. S. Vaginal techniques for second trimester induced abortion. Unpublished paper. Washington: Preterm, 1977.

Brewer, C. "Incidence of post-abortion psychosis:" A prospective study. British Medical Journal, 1977, 1(6059), 476-477.

Byrne, D. A pregnant pause in the sexual revolution. Psy-
    chology Today, 1977, 11(2), 67-68.

Cahn, J. Adolescents' needs regarding family planning services.
    Unpublished paper presented to the World Population Society,
    November 1975.

Cahn, J. Fertility management for teenagers. Planned Parent-
    hood of New York City, unpublished paper, January 1976. (a)

Cahn, J. Correlates of repeat abortions. Unpublished paper
    presented at the Annual Meeting of the Planned Parenthood
    Federation of America, October 1976. (b)

Callahan, D. Abortion: Law, choice, and morality. New York:
    Macmillan, 1970.

Carter, J. Excerpts from July 12, 1977, presidential press
    conference. Washington Post, July 13, 1977.

Cates, W. Personal communication, 1977.

Center for Disease Control. Comparative risks of three methods
    of midtrimester abortion. Morbidity and Mortality Weekly
    Report, 1976, 25, No. 46.

Center for Disease Control. Abortion surveillance, annual
    summary, 1975. Atlanta: Author, 1977.

Char, W. G., & McDermott, J. F. Abortions and acute identity
    crisis in nurses. American Journal of Psychiatry, 1972,
    128, 66-71.

Cobliner, W. G., Schulman, H., & Smith, V. Patterns of contra-
    ceptive failures. Journal of Biosocial Science, 1975, 7,
    307-318.

Cobliner, W. G., Schulman, H., & Smith, V. Dynamics of con-
    traceptive failures. The Journal of Psychology, 1976, 94,
    153-162.

Cvetkovich, G., Grote, B., Bjorseth, A., & Sarkissian, J. On
    the psychology of adolescents' use of contraception.
    Journal of Sex Research, 1975, 11, 256-271.

Cushner, I. Report in American Medical News, June 8, 1970.

David, H. P. Unwanted pregnancies: Costs and alternatives.
    In C. F. Westoff & P. Parke, Jr. (Eds.), Demographic and
    social aspects of population growth. Vol. 1 of the Com-
    mission on Population Growth and the American Future
    Research Reports. Washington: U.S. Government Printing
    Office, 1972.

David, H. P. Psychological studies in abortion. In J. T. Fawcett (Ed.), Psychological perspectives on population. New York: Basic Books, 1973. (a)

David, H. P. Psychosocial aspects of menstrual cycles and menses regulation. In P. A. van Keep & P. Freebody (Eds.), The menstrual cycle and missing menstruation. Geneva: International Health Foundation, 1973. (b)

David, H. P. Abortion and family planning in the Soviet Union: Public policies and private behavior. Journal of Biosocial Science, 1974, 6, 417-426.

David, H. P. Acceptability of fertility-regulating methods in cross cultural perspective. Paper presented at invitational session of National Council on Family Relations, New York City, October 22, 1976. Populi, 1977, 4(4), 18-24.

David, H. P. Review of M. Denes, "In necessity and sorrow: Life and death in an abortion hospital." Contemporary Psychology, 1977, 22, 388-389. (a)

David, H. P. Healthy family functioning: An overview. Geneva: World Health Organization, 1977. (Document MNH/77.7) (b)

David, H. P. International abortion legislation and practices in historical perspective. In P. J. Huntingford (Ed.), Techniques of abortion and sterilization. London: Academic Press, forthcoming. (a)

David, H. P. Healthy family functioning: Cross-cultural perspectives. In P. Ahmed & G. Coelho (Eds.), Toward a new definition of health. New York: Plenum, forthcoming. (b)

David, H. P., & Friedman, H. L. Psychosocial research in abortion: A transnational perspective. In H. J. Osofsky & J. D. Osofsky (Eds.), The abortion experience: Psychological and medical impact. Hagerstown, Md.: Harper & Row Medical Division, 1973.

David, H. P., & Johnson, R. L. Fertility regulation in early childbearing years: Psychosocial and psychoeconomic aspects. Preventive Medicine, 1977, 6, 52-64.

David, H. P., & Wagner, M. G. Danish experience with effects of liberalized abortion. (HD 09739) Personal communication on research in progress, 1977.

Day, N., Brady, L., Faerstein, M., Stone, D., Radford, J., & Potts, L. Improving family planning services for teenagers. San Francisco: Urban and Rural Assistance Associates, 1976.

DeLaney, J., Lupton, M. J., & Toth, E. The curse: A cultural history of menstruation. New York: Dutton, 1976.

Denes, M. In necessity and sorrow: Life and death in an abortion hospital. New York: Basic Books, 1976.

Diamond, M., Steinhoff, P. G., Palmore, J. A., & Smith, R. G. Sexuality, birth control and abortion: A decision-making sequence. Journal of Biosocial Science, 1973, 5, 347-362.

Fingerer, M. E. Psychological sequelae of abortion. Journal of Community Psychology, 1973, 1, 221-225.

Fleck, S. Some psychiatric aspects of abortion. Journal of Nervous and Mental Disease, 1970, 151, 42-50.

Friedman, H. L. Fertility choice behavior--some recommendations for research design. Family Planning Perspectives, 1974, 6, 184-185.

Friedman, H. L., Johnson, R. L., & David, H. P. Dynamics of fertility choice behavior: A pattern for research. In S. H. Newman & V. D. Thompson (Eds.), Population psychology: Research and educational issues. Washington: DHEW, Center for Population Research, 1976. Publication No. (NIH) 76-574.

Galdston, I. Abortion in the United States. New York: Hoeber, 1958.

Gebhard, P. H., Pomeroy, W. B., Martin, C. E., & Christensen, C. V. Prengnancy, birth, and abortion. New York: Hoeber, 1958; Greenwood, 1976.

Goldsmith, S., Gabrielson, M. O., Gabrielson, I., Mathews, V., & Potts, L. Teenagers, sex, and contraception. Family Planning Perspectives, 1972, 4, 32-38.

Gordon, L. Woman's body; woman's right. New York: Grossman/ Viking, 1976.

Graves, W. L. Unwanted pregnancy: Sequelae of abortion vs. delivery. Unpublished report. Atlanta: Emory University School of Medicine, 1975.

Gunn, A. E. Bibliography of abortion research, 1973-74. In A. R. Omran (Ed.), Liberalization of abortion laws: Implications. Chapel Hill: Carolina Population Center, 1976.

Guttmacher, A. F. Abortion: Yesterday, today, and tomorrow, the case for legalized abortion now. Berkeley, Calif.: Diablo Press, 1967.

Hardin, G. Abortion or compulsory pregnancy? Journal of Marriage and the Family, 1968, 30, 246-251.

Hass, P. H. Maternal role incompatibility and fertility in urban Latin America. Journal of Social Issues, 1972, 28, 111-127.

Hiatt, F. Mother was surprised. The Washingtonian, December 1976.

Hoffman, L. The employment of women, education, and fertility. Merrill-Palmer Quarterly, 1974, 20, 99-119.

Hogue, C. Low birth weight subsequent to induced abortion: A historical prospective study of 948 women in Skopje, Yugoslavia. American Journal of Obstetrics and Gynecology, 1975, 123, 675-681.

Illsley, R., & Hall, M. H. Psychosocial aspects of abortion: A review of issues and needed research. Bulletin of the World Health Organization, 1976, 53, 83-106.

Institute of Medicine. Legalized abortion and the public health. Washington: National Academy of Sciences, 1975.

International Reference Center for Abortion Research. Guide to the 1968-1972 international abortion research literature. Washington: Transnational Family Research Institute, 1973.

International Reference Center for Abortion Research. Abortion Research Notes, 1972-   Bethesda, Md.: Transnational Family Research Institute, 1977.

Jaffe, F. S., & Dryfoos, J. Fertility control services for adolescents: Access and utilization. Family Planning Perspectives, 1976, 8, 167-175.

Jansson, B. Mental disorders after abortion. Acta Psychiatrica Scandinavia, 1965, 41, 87-110.

Jekel, J. F., Tyler, N. C., & Klerman, L. V. Induced abortion and sterilization among women who became mothers as adolescents. American Journal of Public Health, 1977, 67, 621-625.

Juhasz, A. M. Changing patterns of premarital sexual behavior. Intellect, 1976, 104, 511-514.

Kantner, J. F., & Zelnik, M. Sexual experience of young unmarried women in the United States. Family Planning Perspectives, 1972, 4, 9-18.

Kantner, J. F., & Zelnik, M. Contraception and pregnancy: Experiences of young unmarried women in the United States. Family Planning Perspectives, 1973, 5, 21-35.

Kantner, J., & Zelnik, M. Sex and reproduction among U.S. teenage women. Draper World Population Fund Report No. 1 Autumn, 1975.

Kasarda, J. Economic structure and fertility; A comparative analysis. Demography, 1971, 8, 307-317.

Kellerhals, J. Personal communication, 1977.

Kerenyi, T. D., Glascock, E. L., & Horowitz, M. L. Reasons for delayed abortion results of 400 interviews. American Journal of Obstetrics and Gynecology, 1973, 117, 299-311.

Kessler, K., & Weiss, T. Ward staff problems with abortion. International Journal of Psychiatry in Medicine, 1974, 5, 97-103.

Kirkendall, L. A., & McDermott, R. J. Premarital intercourse. In J. P. Semmens & K. E. Krantz (Eds.), The adolescent experience. London: Macmillan, 1970.

Kretzschmar, R., & Norris, A. Psychiatric implications of therapeutic abortion. American Journal of Obstetrics and Gynecology, 1967, 198, 367-373.

Kummer, J. Post-abortion psychiatric illness: A myth? American Journal of Psychiatry, 1963, 119, 980-983,

Lee, N. H. The search for an abortionist. Chicago: University of Chicago Press, 1969.

Lief, H. I. What medical schools teach about sex. Bulletin of Tulane University Medical Faculty, 1963, 22, 161-168.

Lief, H. I., & Karlen, A. (Eds.), Sex education in medicine. New York: Halsted, 1976.

Lipper, S., & Feigenbaum, W. M. Obsessive compulsive neurosis after viewing the fetus during therapeutic abortion. American Journal of Psychotherapy, 1976, 30, 666-674.

LoSciuto, L. A., Balin, H,, & Zahn, M, A. Physicians' attitudes toward abortion. The Journal of Reproductive Medicine, 1972, 9, 70-74.

Luker, K. Taking chances; abortion and the decision not to
contracept. Berkeley: University of California Press,
1975.

Luker, K. Contraceptive risk taking and abortion: Results
and implications of a San Francisco Bay area study.
Studies in Family Planning, 1977, 8, 190-196.

Maccoby, N., & Farquhar, J. W. Communication for health:
Unselling heart disease. Journal of Communication, 1975,
25, 114-126.

Mandy, A. J. Reflections of a gynecologist. In H. Rosen (Ed.),
Therapeutic abortion. New York: Julian Press, 1954.

McCormick, E. P. Abortion attitudes of medical and paramedical personnel. Unpublished paper. Washington: Transnational Family Research Institute, 1975.

McCormick, E. P., Johnson, R. L., Friedman, H, L., & David,
H. P. Psychosocial aspects of fertility regulation. In
J. Money & H. Musaph (Eds.), Handbook of sexology. Am-
sterdam: Excerpta Medica, 1977.

Meyerowitz, S., Satloff, A., & Romano, J. Induced abortion
for psychiatric indication. American Journal of Psychiatry, 1971, 127, 1153-1160.

Miller, W. B. Personality and ego factors relative to family
planning and population control. Conference proceedings:
Psychological measurement in the study of population problems. Berkeley: University of California, Institute of
Personality Assessment and Research, 1972,

Miller, W. B. Psychological vulnerability to unwanted pregnancy. Family Planning Perspectives, 1973, 5, 199-201.

Miller, W. B. Sexual and contraceptive behavior in young
women. Primary Care, 1976, 3, 427-453,

Miller, W. B. Personal communication, 1977.

Miller, W. B., & Godwin, R. K. Psyche and demos. New York:
Oxford University Press, 1977.

Misra, B. Correlates of male attitude toward family planning.
     In D. Bogue (Ed.), Sociological contributions to family
     planning research. Chicago: University of Chicago Press,
     1966.

Mohr, J. C. Abortion in America. New York: Oxford Univer-
     sity Press, 1978.

Moore, E. C. Induced abortion and contraception: Sociologi-
     cal aspects. In S. H. Newman, M. B. Beck, & S. Lewit
     (Eds.), Abortion obtained and denied: Research approaches.
     New York: Population Council, 1971.

Moore, E. C. International inventory of information on in-
     duced abortion. New York: International Institute for
     the Study of Human Reproduction, Columbia University,
     1974.

Moore, E. C. Fertility regulation: Friend or foe of the fe-
     male. In J. Money & H. Musaph (Eds.), Handbook of sex-
     ology. Amsterdam: Excerpta Medica, 1977.

Nathanson, C. A., & Becker, M. H. The influence of physicians'
     attitudes on abortion performance, patient management,
     and professional fees. Family Planning Perspectives,
     1977, 9, 158-163.

National Center for Health Statistics. Advance report, final
     natality statistics, 1975. Monthly Vital Statistics Re-
     port, 1976, 25, No. 10, Supplement.

Niswander, K., & Patterson, R. Psychologic reaction to thera-
     peutic abortion. Obstetrics and Gynecology, 1967, 29,
     702-706.

Niswander, K., Singer, J., & Singer, M. Psychological re-
     action to therapeutic abortion. II. Objective response.
     American Journal of Obstetrics and Gynecology, 1972, 114,
     29-33.

Osofsky, J. D., & Osofsky, H. J. The psychological reaction
     of patients to legalized abortion. American Journal of
     Orthopsychiatry, 1972, 42, 48-59.

Osofsky, J. D., Osofsky, H. J., Rajan, R., & Fox, M. R.
     Psychologic effects of legal abortion. Clinical Obstetrics
     and Gynecology, 1971, 14, 215-234.

Osofsky, J. D., Osofsky, H. J., & Rajan, R. Psychological ef-
     fects of abortion: With emphasis upon immediate reactions
     and follow-up. In H. J. Osofsky & J. D. Osofsky (Eds.),

The abortion experience. Hagerstown, Md.: Harper & Row
Medical Division, 1973.

Osofsky, J. D., Osofsky, H. J., Rajan, R., & Spitz, D. Psychosocial aspects of abortion in the United States. The
Mount Sinai Journal of Medicine, 1975, 42, 456-468.

Patt, S., Rappaport, R., & Barglow, P. Follow-up of therapeutic abortion. Archives of General Psychiatry, 1969,
20, 408-414.

Payne, E. C., Kravitz, A. R., Notman, M. T., & Anderson, J. V.
Outcome following therapeutic abortion. Archives of
General Psychiatry, 1976, 33, 725-733.

Peck, A., & Marcus, H. Psychiatric sequelae of therapeutic
interruption of pregnancy. Journal of Nervous and Mental
Disease, 1966, 143, 417-425.

Pohlman, E. Psychology of birth planning. Cambridge, Mass.:
Schenkman, 1969.

Potts, M. The physician's responsibility in the provision of
menstrual induction/early abortion. In H. R. Holtrop,
R. S. Waife, W. Bustamante, & A. Rizo (Eds.), New developments in fertility regulation. Boston: Pathfinder Fund,
1976.

Potts, M., Diggory, P., & Peel, J. Abortion. Cambridge:
Cambridge University Press, 1977.

Reiss, I. L., Banwart, A., & Foreman, H. Premarital contraceptive usage: A study of some theoretical explorations.
Journal of Marriage and the Family, 1975, 37, 619-630.

Rosen, H. (Ed.). Therapeutic abortion. New York: Julian
Press, 1954.

Rosen, H. (Ed.). Abortion in America. Boston: Beacon Press,
1967.

Ross, S. Population Institute teen values project. Unpublished paper. Cited in Intercom, 1977, 5(6), 14.

Rovinsky, J. Abortion recidivism. Obstetrics and Gynecology,
1972, 39, 649-659.

Ryder, N. Contraceptive failure in the United States. Family
Planning Perspectives, 1973, 5, 133-142.

Salaff, J. Institutionalized motivation for birth limitation
  in China. Population Studies, 1976, 26, 233-262.

Scales, P. Males and morals: Teenage contraceptive behavior
  amid the double standard. The Family Coordinator, 1977,
  26, 211-222.

Scales, P., Etelis, R., & Levitz, N. Birth control counselors'
  involvement of young males in contraceptive decision making.
  Journal of Community Health, 1977, 3, 54-60.

Schneider, S. M., & Thompson, D. S. Repeat aborters. American Journal of Obstetrics and Gynecology, 1976, 126, 316-
  320.

Seeley, O. Personality style and family planning behavior:
  Use of traditional questionnaires versus standardized personality measures. Paper presented at Workshop on Psychosocial Aspects of Fertility, Montreal, 1976.

Shah, F., Zelnik, M., & Kantner, J. F. Unprotected intercourse among unwed teenagers. Family Planning Perspectives, 1975, 7, 39-45.

Shelton, J. D. Very young adolescent women in Georgia: Has
  abortion or contraception lowered their fertility?
  American Journal of Public Health, 1977, 67, 616-620.

Simmons, A. B. The VOC approach in population policies: New
  hope or false promise? Paper presented at the IUSSP International Population Conference, Mexico City, August
  1977.

Simon, N., & Senturia, A. Psychiatric sequelae of abortion.
  Archives of General Psychiatry, 1966, 15, 378-389.

Simon, N., Senturia, A., & Rothman, D. Psychiatric illness following therapeutic abortion. American Journal of Psychiatry, 1967, 124, 59-65.

Sklar, J., & Berkov, B. Teenage family formations in postwar
  America. Family Planning Perspectives, 1974, 6, 80-90.

Sloane, B. The unwanted pregnancy. New England Journal of
  Medicine, 1969, 280, 1206-1213.

Smith, B. A social-psychological view of fertility. In J. T.
  Fawcett (Ed.), Psychological perspectives on population.
  New York: Basic Books, 1973.

Steinhoff, P. G. Personal communication, 1977.

Steinhoff, P. G., Smith, R. G., & Diamond, M. The Hawaii pregnancy, birth control, and abortion study: Social-psychological aspects. Proceedings of Conference on Psychological Measurement in the Study of Population Problems. Berkeley: University of California, Institute of Personality Assessment and Research, 1972.

Stycos, J. M., Back, K. W., & Hill, R. Problems of communication between husband and wife on matters relating to family limitation. Human Relations, 1956, 9, 207-215.

Sullivan, E., Tietze, C., & Dryfoos, J. G. Legal abortion in the United States, 1975-1976. Family Planning Perspectives, 1977, 9, 116-129.

Swigar, M. E., Breslin, R., Pouzzner, M. G., Quinlan, D., & Blum, M. Interview follow-up on abortion applicant dropouts. Social Psychiatry, 1976, 11, 135-143.

Swigar, M. E., Quinlan, D. M., & Wexler, S. D. Abortion applicants: Characteristics distinguishing dropouts remaining pregnant and those having abortion. American Journal of Public Health, 1977, 67, 142-146.

Tietze, C. The "problem" of repeat abortions. Family Planning Perspectives, 1974, 6, 148-150. (a)

Tietze, C. Personal communication, September 13, 1974, to the Institute of Medicine. (b)

Tietze, C. Contraceptive practice in the context of a non-restrictive abortion law: Age-specific pregnancy rates in New York City, 1971-1973. Family Planning Perspectives, 1975, 7, 197-202.

Tietze, C. Legal abortions in the United States: Rates and ratios by race and age, 1972-1974. Family Planning Perspectives, 1977, 9, 12-15. (a)

Tietze, C. Abortion and contraception. Family Planning Perspectives, 1977, 9, 297. (b)

Tietze, C. Induced abortion: 1977 supplement. Reports on Population/Family Planning, 1977, No. 14 (2nd edition). (c)

Tietze, C. Personal communication, 1977. (d)

Tietze, C., & Lewit, S. Joint program for the study of abortion: Early medical complications of legal abortion. Studies in Family Planning, 1972, 3, 97-122.

Tietze, C., & Lewit, S. All about abortion. Workmen's Circle Call, May 1977. (a)

Tietze, C., & Lewit, S. Mortality and fertility control. Paper presented at the First National Medical Conference on the Safety of Fertility Control, Chicago, March 1977. (b)

Tietze, C., & Murstein, M. C. Induced abortion: 1975 fact-book. Reports on Population/Family Planning, December 1975, No. 14 (2nd edition).

Trost, J. Personal communication, 1977.

van der Vlugt, T., & Piotrow, P. Menstrual regulation update. Population Report, 1974, Series F, No. 4.

Walter, G. Psychologic and emotional consequences of elective abortion: A review. Obstetrics and Gynecology, 1970, 36, 482-491.

Weideger, P. Menstruation and menopause. New York: Knopf, 1976.

Weinstock, E., Tietze, C., Jaffe, F. S., & Dryfoos, J. G. Abortion need and services in the United States, 1974-1975. Family Planning Perspectives, 1976, 8, 58-69.

Weller, R. The employment of wives, dominance and fertility. Journal of Marriage and the Family, 1968, 33, 437-442.

Westoff, C. F., & Jones, E. F. Contraception and sterilization in the United States, 1965-1975. Family Planning Perspectives, 1977, 9, 153-157.

Whittemore, K. The availability of nonhospital abortions. In R. E. Hall (Ed.), Abortion in a changing world. Vol. 1. New York: Columbia University Press, 1970.

Whittington, H. G. Evaluation of therapeutic abortion as an element of preventive psychiatry. American Journal of Psychiatry, 1970, 126, 1224-1229.

Woods, S. M. Sex education in medical schools. In J. Money & H. Musaph (Eds.), Handbook of sexology. Amsterdam: Excerpta Medica, 1977.

Wyatt, F. Clinical notes on the motives of reproduction. Journal of Social Issues, 1967, 23, 29-56.

Zelnik, M., & Kantner, J. Attitudes of American teenagers to abortion. Family Planning Perspectives, 1975, 7, 89-91.

Zelnik, M., & Kantner, J. F. The resolution of teenage first pregnancies. Family Planning Perspectives, 1974, 6, 74-90.

Zelnik, M., & Kantner, J. F. Sexual and contraceptive experience of young unmarried women in the United States, 1976 and 1971. Family Planning Perspectives, 1977, 9, 55-71.

Zelnik, M., & Kantner, J. F. First pregnancies to women aged 15-19: 1976 and 1971. Family Planning Perspectives, 1978, 10, 11-20.

PART THREE

CHOICE BEHAVIOR

6

Studies in Choice Behavior
in Yugoslavia*

Nila Kapor-Stanulovic and Herbert L. Friedman

Editors' Note: Abortion legislation, including
approval on sociomedical grounds, was adopted
in Yugoslavia in 1952 and further liberalized
in 1960. The introduction of modern contraceptives is of more recent origin. In 1974 the
Federal Constitution reaffirmed "the right to
decide freely on childbirth." The two studies
reported in this chapter explore determinants
of choice in Novi Sad, where both abortion and
modern contraceptives are equally available
and accessible at virtually no cost. The research method included an Abortion Index, concepts of Psychological Costs and Personal Efficacy, abortion and contraception belief
measures, and separate but simultaneous interviews with marital partners. The findings are
discussed in terms of differences between aborting and contracepting women, and implications
for reducing reliance on abortion to terminate
unwanted pregnancies.

INTRODUCTION

The Clinic of Obstetrics and Gynecology of the University of Novi Sad Medical School serves both the rural population of the northern province of Vojvodina and the people
living in the urban capital of Novi Sad. Induced abortion is

*The studies reported were joint projects of the De-
partment of Obstetrics and Gynecology, School of Medicine,
University of Novi Sad and the Transnational Family Research
Institute. They were supported, in part, by a grant from the
Ford Foundation. We are pleased to acknowledge the contribu-
tions of Professor Berislav Beric in faciliting the studies.

usually performed on an outpatient basis, using the vacuum aspiration method in the first trimester of pregnancy. Contraceptive counseling accompanies the abortion and there is a
separate contraception clinic located in the same grounds. Induced abortion is a widespread, safe, and socially acceptable
practice in this region. Modern contraceptives are only gradually beginning to be used despite efforts of encouragement.
In the Novi Sad setting, both abortion and modern contraception are easily available, virtually free, and equally accessible. It was in this setting that the basic questions of
the two studies (1973 and 1974) reported here were posed:
What are the psychological aspects and consequences to couples
of the choice of abortion as a fertility-regulating method?
What are the reasons for the predominance of abortion over
modern contraceptives? What measures might be warranted and
taken to increase the successful use of modern contraceptives?

Before the research began, the records of both abortion and contraception clinics for the year 1971 were examined.
In that year, 6,022 women had abortions. For 2,114 of them
(35 percent), it was the first abortion; the remaining 64 percent had had between 1 and 27 previous abortions, with an average of 1.8 previous abortions. Nine hundred twenty-seven
(15 percent) were single, less than 1 percent were divorced
or widowed, and the remainder were married. Fifteen percent
were childless, 31 percent had one child, 40 percent had two
children, and the rest had more than two. Only 18 of the
more than 6,000 women were beyond the first trimester of pregnancy at the time of the abortion. Ages ranged from 14-45,
with approximately 10 percent under 20, 25 percent from 20-24,
20 percent from 25-29, 23 percent from 30-34, and the remainder over 35. Approximately 58 percent came from the urban
area, 42 percent from rural ones. In the same year, 3,423
visits were paid to the contraception clinic. Of the 493
women (15 percent) who came for the first time, some 202 (or
41 percent) did not adopt a method.

STUDY ONE: PERCEPTIONS AND CONSEQUENCES

The research plan for this study entailed interviewing a sample of abortion-seeking couples shortly after the
woman had had an abortion and before her next ovulation, that
is, eight to ten days after the abortion. This is the time
when the decision-making process concerning the pregnancy
terminated in abortion is still fresh in the woman's mind, and
when the problem of future fertility regulation becomes acute.
The design required simultaneous but separate interviews of
the woman and her spouse, using a specially constructed 70-
item questionnaire encompassing a wide range of social factors

based in part on Bogue (1970). The interview lasted about 45 minutes and was conducted by a team of male and female interviewers.

The Sample

Of the 75 married couples initially approached, 48 consented to be interviewed. Of those who refused to participate, the main reason given was the unwillingness of the husband to cooperate in the investigation. Thus it may be that the sample represents somewhat more concordant couples. The mean age of the wives was 28.1; the youngest was 16, the oldest 52. The mean number of living children was 1.7, ranging from 1-6. The mean number of previous abortions was 3.4, ranging from 0-20.

Measures Employed

Abortion Index. In studying abortion, a key problem is how to treat the variable "number of abortions." The number itself is not a good indicator of repeated abortion-seeking behavior. Five abortions in three years represents a very different kind of behavior than five abortions over a period of twenty years. In order to obtain a more objective comparison of women with multiple abortions, the absolute number of abortions has been replaced by an abortion index, which measures the frequency of abortions over a fixed period of time of exposure. Because all the respondents in this study are married, the following formula has been used:

$$\frac{\text{number of abortions}}{\text{years of marriage - 1 year for each full term pregnancy}}$$

Psychological Cost. Every action has its price, its psychological "cost." We consider it one of the basic determinants of some forms of behavior. It is based more on an affective than a rational principle, and is manifest as the realization of how unpleasant an experience is, or how difficult it is to bear, or what is lost by undergoing it. Psychological cost is particularly important if one wishes to examine ambivalence, or explain the choice of behavior in situations where other solutions might appear more logical. In this study, the psychological costs of abortions and contraception were measured and compared; the measure was comprised of total scores on a series of rating scales.

Abortion and Contraception Belief Measures. Despite differences in terminology, the "expectancy X value" behavior theorists concerned with decision making hold that "the strength of the tendency to act in a certain way depends upon the expectancy that the act will be followed by a given consequence (or goal) and the values of that consequence (or goal) to the individual" (Atkinson, 1964). The "expectancy X value" theories seem to suggest that respondents who perceive abortion (or contraception) as leading to positive goals and preventing negative consequences will be more likely to abort frequently (or use reliable contraceptives). Beliefs about abortion and contraception were assessed with a series of questions based upon a procedure developed by Rosenberg and Oltman (1962) and further used by Crawford (1971). Respondents were asked what they believed were the consequences of abortion, how important these consequences were to them, and how certain they were that abortion would lead to these consequences. After asking for the perceived advantages, the same series of questions regarding the consequences, their importance, and expectancies was asked concerning the perceived disadvantages of abortion. For each perceived consequence mentioned, the importance of the consequence was multiplied by the strength of the expectancy or "belief certainty" measure. The algebraic sum of the importance belief certainty products for the advantages and disadvantages was then used as the summary belief measure. The same procedure was repeated for the perceived advantages and disadvantages of contraception. Hereafter, the phrases "abortion belief measure" and "contraception belief measure" will be used to designate these assessments.

Findings of Interview One

The data obtained were analyzed for each couple individually. The concordance of the answers of husband and wife—the extent to which they chose the same options on each question—was established by the method of significance of proportions (Brunning & Kintz, 1968).

The first topic of the interview dealt with the process of deciding on the abortion that had just been performed. The couples agree markedly in their answers about who reached the decision to terminate the pregnancy and how it was reached. The concordance of husband/wife responses was highly significant, (p < .01). The answers are in concordance also on questions of whether there was any ambivalence in reaching the decision on the latest abortion (p < .01), in estimating the reaction of the marriage partner to that pregnancy (p < .01), and who, in principle, ought to decide on the fate of a pregnancy (p < .01).

Qualitative analysis reveals that most commonly the decision was reached after discussion with the marriage partner (85.4 percent of wives and 83.3 percent of husbands) and that the decision was made immediately upon the discovery that the wife was pregnant (79.2 percent of wives and 72.9 percent of husbands). Only 12.5 percent of wives and 20.8 percent of husbands had welcomed the pregnancy. For the rest, it was an unpleasant and unexpected happening. Generally speaking, couples believed that the fate of the pregnancy should be decided by both partners (87.5 percent of women and 95.8 percent of men).

However, there is no agreement on the question of what they would do if the wife became pregnant again. The husbands are equally inclined to choose abortion again, to accept the pregnancy, or to leave the decision to the wife. The wives are much more resolute: 70.8 percent would again decide on abortion.

Conversations on topics dealing with the regulation of reproduction in marriage were relatively infrequent. When started, usually by the wife, the conversation was short. Descriptions of the frequency and quality of communications about abortion and contraception are quite similar for husbands and wives. Indices of concordance are high and are statistically significant. Nevertheless, both husband and wife agree ($p < .01$) that they communicate about abortion and contraception more easily among themselves than with acquaintances and friends. That may be the reason the couples interviewed do not know much about how others regulate their fertility. In this respect, both husband and wife are equally uniformed ($p < .01$).

Communication is much better when it comes to routine everyday problems and cares. Such conversations are frequent. Eighty-three percent of women and 93.5 percent of men state that they regularly talk about current problems and that they are content with these discussions. However, when it is a matter of personal cares and problems, the percentage of those who keep a great deal to themselves increases. Twenty-seven percent of the wives and 31.3 percent of the husbands are selective in what they confide to their spouses. Concordance of these answers is great ($p < .01$), which means that if one partner is reticent the other also becomes selective about what to confide to the spouse. The opposite condition holds.

There is a relatively high degree of satisfaction with marriage. Ninety-two percent of the women and 98 percent of the men state that they are either satisfied or very satisfied

with their marital situation and that they do not want any
major alterations in the relationship. However, the extent to
which couples choose the identical options shows considerable
divergence. The views on the marriage and the quality of the
marital relationship only rarely correspond. Concordance of
the answers here does not approach statistically significant
levels. The opinions diverge about who makes a greater number
of decisions, or who makes them more often--in other words,
which partner is dominant. There is a tendency to let the
wife take the leading role in running the household and bringing up the children. The husband decides on all major expend-
itures and "more important" issues in life. It is interesting
to note, however, that the husbands and wives in our sample
are greatly satisfied with the existing division of duties and
responsibilities (p < .01).

We were particularly interested in the status of the
wife as she evaluates it and as it is viewed by the husband.
There is no agreement between husband and wife as to whose
life is "harder." Although the wives tend to believe that
life is harder for them, the husbands are inclined to say that
life is equally hard for men and women. Neither is there
agreement on the question of whether or not it is better for
the marriage if the wife does not work. Men show the traditional attitude of wanting the women to stay at home and maintain their customary roles as wives and mothers.

Marriage partners agree that the burden of raising
children rests mainly on the mother (p < .05). Child care may
also be undertaken by various other persons, but not by the
father, who is spared the major duties concerning children.
The conclusion of the interviewees that the role of mother
makes it difficult for a woman to be professionally active is
in accordance with these findings. Both men and women agree
that a conflict of roles exists for the woman (p < .05). If
the question is asked whether professional activity is more
important than children, marriage, and husband, both marriage
partners agree (p < .05) that for the woman the profession
ought to be secondary.

Husband and wife strongly agree about the desire for
another child (p < .01). Forty-two percent of both men and
women want another child; 54.2 percent of the women and 50.0
percent of the men definitely do not want another child. The
remainder are ambivalent.

Whether the specific number of abortions a woman has
had will be perceived as "few" or "many" depends on different
factors. At times, even one abortion is too many. Such estimates were, as expected, very uneven. The same number of

abortions was estimated as "many" by one woman and as "few" by another. What is of interest is that husband and wife agree (p < .05) with respect to such estimates, which relates to their view of abortion and its role in their marriage.

Plans for the Future

Both husband and wife have, in the majority of cases, already thought of what to do in the future in order to regulate their fertility (p < .01). However, the differences are rather great with regard to what they have decided, or whether they have come to a specific decision. Each partner tends to think that a decision has been reached jointly (p < .05) and that his or her choice is the one the partner agrees to. In fact, however, the decision of husbands and wives are markedly different.

What are these decisions? In 87.5 percent of the cases the husbands have decided that a certain contraceptive, not previously used, should be tried. Only 6.2 percent have not yet decided what to do. Among the women, however, the situation is different. Only 37.5 percent have decided to start using a particular contraceptive; 47.9 percent do not as yet know how they will regulate their fertility. It should be remembered that these are the answers immediately given preceding the first ovulation after the abortion. We maintain, therefore, that this postponing of the decision to start using some contraceptive is of considerable significance, especially in the light of other findings discussed later.

When deciding on a specific contraceptive, men rely frequently on the opinion and advice of others and not on their own assessment of the method. Women more often rely on their own judgment and information. Even though women believe in the use of contraceptives in principle, they are inclined to postpone or delay the decision to start using some form of fertility regulation for several reasons. In justifying their choice of method, women tend to give such subjective reasons as, "It is more convenient," "It is a simpler method," "I got used to it," and the like; the men mostly give such objective explanations as, "It is safer," and "It was recommended as good."

Advantages and Disadvantages of
Abortion and Contraception

Husband and wife also show considerable concordance on perceived advantages and disadvantages of abortion and on the advantages of contraception, p < .05 and < .01, respectively. Opinions are divided regarding the disadvantages associated with contraceptives, however.

What are the advantages and disadvantages of abortion?
All advantages of abortion cited could be reduced to the fact
that abortion makes both the number and timing of children
possible. It prevents the inconvenience of having a child
when the parents are either too young or too old, or when they
are suffering from financial or housing uncertainties. The
unfavorable aspects of abortion included "danger to the woman's
health," cited by 81.2 percent of the women and 93.7 percent
of the men, and "the physical pain of abortion," mentioned by
8.2 percent of the women and 4.2 percent of the men. Only
one married couple stated that abortion is murder.

Contraception, like abortion, is perceived as providing
the possibility of family planning. There were also frequent
replies that contraception increases enjoyment in sexual relations because it removes the fear of unwanted pregnancy and
the need for abortion.

Women list among the disadvantages of contraceptives
the various side effects that occur during their use, as well
as the potential long-term danger in using them. Men often
mention that contraceptives are not foolproof protection
against pregnancy. Only in regard to the disadvantages of
contraceptives do answers of women and men vary to such an extent that indices of concordance do not reach statistically
significant values.

Results of Special Measures
The mean values for measures of abortion cost, contraception cost, abortion belief, and contraception belief for
our sample of 48 couples are given in Table 6-1.

Table 6-1

Mean Values for Measures of Abortion and Contraception
Cost and Belief

	Male	Female
Cost		
Abortion	19.98	19.50
Contraception	8.27	12.58
Belief		
Abortion	0.77	-0.06
Contraception	3.29	2.85

Women perceive abortion as being more costly than contraception (t = 6.93, p < .01) and have more positive beliefs about the consequences of contraception than of abortion (t = 3.59, p < .01). Similarly, men perceive abortion as being more costly than contraception (t = 13.15, p < .01) and they too have more positive beliefs about the consequences of contraception than those of abortion (t = 3.27, p < .01).

A comparison of their responses shows no significant mean differences on abortion cost, nor on abortion and contraception belief measures. They do differ on contraceptive cost, however. Although both men and women perceive contraception cost to be lower than abortion cost, women perceive contraception as significantly more costly than do men. There is much greater variability on the contraceptive responses for both men and women, suggesting much less familiarity with the subject.

It is clear that more women focus on the advantages rather than the disadvantages of abortion. Using the means as the dividing line, there were significantly more wives (34) with high abortion belief scores than those with low scores (14), x^2 = 8.34, p < .01. The men viewed abortion differently. Only 17 scored high on this measure; 31 expressed low abortion belief, x^2 = 4.08, p < .05.

The mean value of the abortion index was .77, i.e., somewhat less than an average of one abortion per year. No significantly high correlation was found between the abortion index and any of the following variables for women: abortion cost, contraceptive cost, abortion belief, contraceptive belief, abortion attitude, contraceptive attitude. The conclusion reached was that, with women, the frequency of abortion had no influence on the formation of the above variables.

With men, the picture is rather different. There is a negative correlation between the abortion index and the measure of abortion belief (r = -.067) and a strong positive correlation with the perception of abortion cost (r = 0.80). Thus, for the men, the more frequently their wives undergo the expenses of abortion, the lower the belief in the advantages of abortion and the more costly it is perceived to be.

Findings of Interview Two

The second part of the longitudinal investigation was conducted 14 months after the first interview. On this occasion, only the wives in the sample were reinterviewed. The major purpose of this second interview was to establish the

fertility-regulating behavior which actually took place during
the time elapsed since the initial interview. For this purpose,
it was not considered necessary to interview the husbands as
well, and it would have added considerably to the cost and difficulty of the procedure.

Interviews were conducted at home. Seven couples could
not be reached because of address changes, so the final sample
for this part of the investigation is comprised of 41 couples.

In the period elapsed, 22.9 percent of the women
started using modern contraceptives and were still using them
successfully at the time of the interview. An equal number of
women started using modern contraceptives but, for various reasons, very soon discontinued use. These women, those who relied on coitus interruptus and those who did nothing to prevent
another pregnancy, make up the 62.5 percent of the women who,
after having undergone at least one abortion, still form a
group at great risk of repeated pregnancies and probable
abortions.

Of this group six had, in fact, undergone another induced abortion in the year elapsed. It was characteristic of
these women that they had scored low on the psychological cost
of abortion scales at the initial interview, suggesting that
they did not consider abortion to be unpleasant or difficult.
Their average abortion index was 1.1, higher than the mean for
the original 48 women (.77). It appears that women who start
their fertility careers with frequent abortions are likely to
continue this behavior.

Among the remainder of the group, it was found that
one woman had, in the meantime, given birth to a child; one
was pregnant at the time of the interview and intended to have
the child; and one was hoping to become pregnant. Thus, three
women (6.3 percent) were expressing or had already realized
their desire to have another child 14 months after the termination of an unwanted pregnancy.

It is interesting to note that the values for psychological cost of abortion and contraception had not changed
significantly in the past 14 months. This supports the idea
that psychological cost is not easily changed. The high contraception cost scores proved to be good predictors of future
contraceptive use. Women with high contraception cost scores
either had not started using contraceptives or had stopped using them after a short time (x^2 = 7.34, p < .01),

The general conclusion drawn from the first half of
the investigation of 48 married couples was that prospects of

their changing their manner of regulating reproduction were slight. Indecision and resistance of the women to modern contraceptive methods was considered considerable and communication between partners on topics connected with regulating reproduction was too minimal for the investigators to expect major changes in behavior.

Longitudinal investigation after a 14-month lapse confirmed such conclusions. Most of the couples behaviorally demonstrated their unreadiness to regulate their fertility by methods other than those that had, in their own experience, proved inadequate to prevent impregnantion.

Discussion

For most of the post-abortion couples interviewed in this study, it is clear that a joint decision for abortion was made on becoming aware of the unwanted pregnancy. It is also characteristic of these couples that they rarely discuss fertility regulation with each other, and even more rarely with persons outside the family who might be knowledgeable about modern contraception. It is also rather startling to find that although both husband and wife indicate that they have thought about future fertility regulation, and those who have come to a decision say that it was a joint one, in actual fact there is very low concordance on both the extent to which a decision has been made and the specific method itself, if one was chosen.

The vast majority of men favor trying a new method of contraception. The women, on whom the burden would fall, are much less resolute. The postponement of the decision by the woman at a time when she is once again vulnerable to conception, combined with the illusion that she and her husband are in agreement, increases the likelihood of another unwanted pregnancy in these families. Although they indicate that thought has been given to future birth prevention, the follow-up interview confirms the hypothesis that, in fact, their fertility-regulating behavior did not change.

It is also significant that although there is agreement between husbands and wives on the utility and costliness of abortion, and on the general advantages of contraception, they do not agree on the disadvantages of contraception--women finding it significantly more costly. This undoubtedly accounts for part of the indecision to begin and reluctance to continue using a modern contraceptive among the majority of women in this sample. Induced abortion is not considered a highly traumatic event in Novi Sad, but it is, nevertheless, perceived as

significantly more costly than contraception by both men and
women. It is used in spite of its higher cost because great
value is placed on its effectiveness at a time when the desired timing (and number) of childbirths in the family is
threatened.

        Many couples in this study are thus faced with a situ-
ation in which their desire for controlling family size over-
rides the psychological costliness of the abortion procedure
to them, but does not alter their behavior sufficiently so
that effective contraception takes place. In all such cases
one must rule out lack of information about the existing contraceptives as a possible cause for the nonuse of contraceptives. In fact all these couples were given full and individual information on contraceptive methods at the end of the
first interview. Fourteen months later the majority of women
(62 percent) were not using modern contraception in spite of
the information and support given. This situation is quite
likely to result in another unwanted pregnancy, and a repeat
abortion. The questions thus raised were: Why are women reluctant to use effective contraceptives? What makes modern
contraceptive methods unacceptable to a large portion of
women in this region?

                STUDY TWO: THE DETERMINANTS OF CHOICE

        In this second study, an attempt is made to understand
the nature of the forces that ultimately lead the majority of
women using the Novi Sad clinics to choose abortion over contraception, and to examine the possibilities of altering the
behavior pattern of the aborting women to the pattern exhibited
by those women successfully employing contraception. Several
methodological innovations are reported.

        The main objectives of the study were to examine the
differences in experience, behavior, attitudes, and beliefs of
the two groups of women coming to the same clinic for two different kinds of fertility-regulating services: abortion and
contraception. Because the two services are virtually equally
accessible, legal, and inexpensive, it was felt that the differences between the two groups would provide important information about the basic determinants of choice between the two
methods. A knowledge of these determinants can, in turn, both
help to predict events in other countries and help to turn
women in this part of Yugoslavia toward more modern methods of
contraception, replacing abortion as a method of fertility
regulation.

The Sample

In order to examine the differences between aborting and contracepting women, 144 subjects were randomly selected-- 72 women whose abortion request had been approved and who were waiting at the clinic for the procedure to be performed and 72 women who had come to the contraceptive clinic (regardless of their prior fertility-regulating experience). Two experienced female interviewers fluent in the local language gathered the information through individual interviews at the clinic sites.

Measurement

Precoded interviews of some 72 items were the main means of data gathering. Included in the interview schedules were three composite measures: an abortion cost scale, a contraception cost scale, and a measure of personal efficacy or locus of control (after Rotter, 1975). The composite measure of the psychosocial cost attributed to abortion by the respondent was derived from ten questions, six of which concerned the procedure of abortion itself and four of which related to the acquisition of the service. The options to such questions were on a 3-point scale: 1 for "not at all"; 2 for "a little"; and 3 for "very much." Thus, the higher the composite score in the possible range from 10-30, the more negatively were the attributes evaluated. The contraception cost scale was designed in exactly the same way, the sole difference being that the questions were addressed to contraception rather than abortion. Both scales had previously been used on the Novi Sad population. The measure of "personal efficacy" consisted of seven questions regarding the degree to which the respondent felt she had control over her own fate. Three options were provided: "don't know," "it doesn't depend on me," and "it's a result of my own efforts"; scored, respectively, 1, 2, and 3.

Also employed was the abortion index (AI) described earlier. For the unmarried women in this study an arbitrary measure of the abortion index was used. An AI of one was assigned for each induced abortion, on the rough reckoning that there will have been about one year of exposure to sexual intercourse for each induced abortion experienced. Finally, the fertility histories of the respondents were examined in terms of the pattern of the first three major events, i.e., the order in which delivery, induced abortion, and/or contraception appeared in the respondent's history.

Data Analysis

The results of the interviews were coded, key punched, and processed by computer. In addition to the derivation of the composite scores mentioned above and the frequency of analysis, a number of statistical tests were employed, including t tests, chi squares, biserial correlations, and Spearman's rho, according to specific needs.

The Findings

Experience and Behavioral Characteristics

In terms of their fertility characteristics, the two groups--aborting women (Group A) and contracepting women (Group C)--show some major differences. Group A tends to be younger, and includes more unmarried women and a greater number of women who are childless. Forty-five percent of Group A are under 25, as against 28 percent of Group C. Thirty percent of Group A are unmarried, as compared with 10 percent of Group C; 24 percent have no living children, as compared with 12.5 percent of Group C. For those in Group A who are married, however, none (as compared to 8 percent in the other group) has been married less than one year. Although 39 percent of Group A had never had an induced abortion prior to the current one, 21 percent of Group C had never had an induced abortion (see Table 6-2).

Table 6-2

Previous Induced Abortions

Number of Abortions	Abortion Group (N=72)	Contraception Group (N=72)
0	38.9%	20.8%
1	29.2%	13.9%
2-4	22.2%	47.2%
5+	9.7%	18.1%

The rate of induced abortion, as expressed by the respective abortion indices of Groups A and C of 0.8 (s.d. .62) and 0.4 (s.d. .51), shows a statistically significant

difference (t = 3.48 df 142, p < ,001). The abortion group,
in other words, is having abortions at about double the frequency of the contraceptive group when exposure to risk is
taken into account. In terms of fertility histories (see
Tables 6-3 and 6-4), women in both groups tended to have a
child born prior to using either contraception or abortion--
69 percent of Group A and 74 percent of Group C. For those
62 women in Group A who record a second event, 42 percent of
them followed the first delivery with a second one, whereas
this was true for only 27 percent of Group C women. Group C
women, on the other hand, followed their first delivery with
either abortion or contraception more frequently than Group A
did. It appears that the Group A women have been experiencing
both deliveries and abortions at a higher rate. A discussion
of fertility behavior and abortion-seeking patterns is more
fully discussed in a paper by Kapor-Stanulovic and Beric (1974).

The two groups are somewhat different in their sociodemographic characteristics, although not strongly so. Group
A women were more often rural (43 percent) than Group C women
(32 percent). About half the women in each group are housewives without other employment; among those who do work, Group
C includes more office workers relative to unskilled laborers
(25 percent vs. 18 percent). In Group A the reverse relationship obtains (17 percent vs. 18 percent). There is a larger
absolute number of students in Group A than in Group C (9 vs.
7), but not in proportion to what one might expect given the
greater numbers of younger women. In terms of completed education, Group C is a bit stronger than Group A. Four percent
of Group C have some college (against none in Group A); 11
percent of Group A have never had any formal education (against
7 percent of Group C). Overall, the tendency is for Group C
women to be somewhat better educated and employed and more
urban, although the differences are not statistically
significant.

Contraceptive Practices

The contraceptive practices of the two groups differ
markedly. In response to the question as to whether any attempt had been made to avert the current pregnancy, 51 Group A
women (72 percent) said that they had; 21 (29 percent) had not.
For those 51 respondents who had attempted any method of contraception, some 30 (58 percent) had relied on coitus interruptus, whereas this method was not used at all by Group C
women (see Table 6-5). None in Group A had had an IUD, compared with 38 percent of Group C. Eighteen percent of the
women in Group A and 38 percent of Group C stated that they
had been using the pill. Group C women were also using injec-
tables (17 percent) and vaginal methods (6 percent). Since
the Group A women were selected on the basis of their need for

Table 6-3

Order of Fertility Events

	Delivery	Abortion	Contraception
First Fertility Event			
Group A (N=72)	69.4%	27.8%	2.8%
Group C (N=72)	73.6%	15.3%	11.1%
Second Fertility Event			
Group A (N=62)	48.4%	38.7%	12.9%
Group C (N=71)	29.6%	47.9%	22.5%
Third Fertility Event			
Group A (N=54)	37.0%	61.1%	1.9%
Group C (N=65)	24.6%	53.9%	21.5%

Table 6-4

First Two Fertility Events

	Group A (N=62)	Group C (N=71)
Delivery-Delivery	41.9%	26.8%
Delivery-Abortion	30.7%	39.4%
Delivery-Contraception	9.7%	14.1%
Abortion-Delivery	6.5%	7.0%
Abortion-Abortion	4.8%	4.2%
Abortion-Contraception	3.2%	1.4%
Contraception-Delivery	0.0%	0.0%
Contraception-Abortion	3.2%	0.0%
Contraception-Contraception	0.0%	7.0%

an abortion, it is to be expected that poor methods, combined with no method, would predominate. However, it is perhaps surprising that a full 72 percent of the group considered that they had tried to avert this birth by contraceptive means and had failed. When they were asked why they had failed, a

majority (51 percent) said that they didn't know, 41 percent
blamed it on irregular use, and only 8 percent blamed it on
the method itself.

Table 6-5

Methods of Contraception Recently Used

	Group A (N=72)	Group C (N=68)
Oral	18.1%	38.2%
IUD	0.0%	38.2%
Vaginal	5.5%	5.9%
Injections	0.0%	16.7%
Coitus Interruptus	41.7%	0.0%
Other	5.5%	0.0%
None	29.2%	0.0%

Attitudes and Beliefs

The differential contraceptive experience of the two
groups is matched by different perceptions of their husbands'
attitudes. Seventy-eight percent of the women of Group C
stated that their husbands would be in favor of using a contraceptive method, against only 46 percent of the women in
Group A. Of the husbands in Group A, 16 percent were believed
to be definitely against contraception (against only 2 percent
of the Group C husbands). The contracepting women were also
asked how their husbands felt about their current contraceptive
method. Of the 64 women responding to this question, 50 percent said their husbands were indifferent, 31 percent said that
they favored the current method, and 5 percent did not know.
An additional 6 percent of the group said that their husbands
would prefer that they use no method.

Although 76 percent of the women in this group intended to continue with their contraceptive method and only 18
percent wished to change or stop altogether (the remainder were
first-time visitors), it was often some problem with the method
which brought the women to the clinic. Despite this, some 80
percent indicated general satisfaction. Most of the women in
this group were contracepting either to postpone the next child
(29 percent) or not to have any more children (64 percent). An
additional 4 percent gave not being married as their reason,
and 3 percent had other reasons.

ABORTION IN PSYCHOSOCIAL PERSPECTIVE

Both groups of women were asked whether they wanted to have a child in the future. In Group C, 31 percent said "yes," 56 percent said "no," and 14 percent said "maybe." Group A women showed a similar pattern--39 percent "yes," 55 percent "no," and 6 percent "maybe." The same question was asked with respect to a future abortion. To this question the aborting women showed a preponderance of uncertainty; 71 percent of them said "maybe," 4 percent "yes," and 25 percent "no." The contracepting group was a bit more certain about the likelihood of a future abortion, although even in this group 47 percent were unsure. Although 10 percent said "yes," a much larger proportion (43 percent) said "no." It can be seen, however, that a majority in both groups would not rule out a future abortion.

Contraceptive Attitudes

The attitudes toward contraception in general, as measured by the composite score of psychosocial cost, also show differences between the two groups. As noted earlier, the scores can range from 10-30. The higher the score the greater the negative subjective assessment. Group A shows a mean score of 14.00 (s.d. 2.99) and Group C a mean of 11.21 (s.d. 1.74). These means are statistically significantly different at the .01 level of probability (t = 1.67, df 142). This is also reflected in the mean ranks assigned separately to each of the aspects of the use and acquisition of contraceptive means (see Table 6-6). In each case, the mean rank is higher for the abortion group than for the contraception group. The largest differences appear in Group A's judgment that contraception is more unpleasant, harmful to health, and conflict-producing. It should be noted, however, that all the ranks assigned by Group C are closer to a mean of 1, which represents a judgment of "not at all," than they are to 2, which signifies "a little." Group A follows this pattern to some extent, except in stronger negative judgments that contraception makes one nervous, is unpleasant, and is harmful to health. Nevertheless, even for this group, none of the mean ranks is significantly above 2.

Abortion Attitudes

The situation with respect to the abortion cost scale is somewhat more negative for both groups, although again it is Group A that has the more negative attitude. The mean composite score from Group A is 20.57 (s.d. 3.62), and from Group C is 19.58 (s.d. 3.54). The difference between the two means, however, falls short of significance at the 5 percent level (t = 1.67, df 142, p < .10). An examination of the mean ranks assigned to each of the 10 descriptors also shows the differences to be small between the two groups, except in regard to the time required to be absent from the home, which Group A

Table 6-6

Mean Ranks

	Abortion Cost Scale		Contraception Cost Scale	
	Group A	Group C	Group A	Group C
Use of Method				
Unpleasant	2.69	2.83	1.79	1.20
Painful	2.58	2.78	1.10	1.03
Harmful	2.66	2.81	2.10	1.42
Shameful	2.08	1.97	1.17	1.01
Nervous-making	2.55	2.58	1.71	1.14
Conflict-producing	1.90	1.75	1.47	1.04
Mean	2.41	2.43	1.55	1.14
S.D.	0.33	0.39	0.32	0.15
Obtaining Product/Service				
Complicated	1.53	1.54	1.27	1.09
Time-consuming	1.53	1.37	1.11	1.11
Expensive	1.24	1.05	1.04	1.00
Absence from home	1.82	1.36	1.24	1.14
Mean	1.53	1.33	1.17	1.12
S.D.	0.24	0.20	0.32	0.12
Overall mean	2.06	2.00	1.40	1.12
S.D.	0.53	0.69	0.36	0.12

considers to be much more costly (see Table 6-6). With respect to abortion, both groups show an overall mean rank of 2,
thus considering it to be "a little costly." On certain individual items, however, the mean rank is closer to 3 ("very
much"). This is true for both groups, particularly with regard to the degree of unpleasantness, pain, and harm to health
that they believe to be involved.

Use vs. Service

A comparison of ranks assigned to the experience of a
method itself, as opposed to its acquisition as a service or
product, shows that both groups clearly assign greater costs
to the experience than to the acquisition. Thus, for Group A
the mean rank assigned to the abortion procedure is 2.4, but
only 1.5 for acquiring the service; similarly, contraception

itself is assigned a mean rank of 1.5, but acquiring the means is ranked as 1.2. Group C shows a similar pattern in regard to abortion, assigning mean ranks of 2.4 to the experience and 1.3 for the acquisition. In the case of contraception, use and acquisition are ranked equally; however, both are given mean ranks of 1, which effectively indicates that neither one is considered costly.

In sum, both groups show a significantly higher cost attached to abortion than to contraception, the respective mean ranks being 2.1 and 1.4 for Group A and 2.0 and 1.1 for Group C, with Group C showing a greater difference in subjective assessments of the costs of the two methods.

Further Service Assessments

Both groups were asked how much time they were taking for the procedures at the clinic and how long they thought abortion or contraception (the alternative method for each group) would take them. The contracepting women thought that abortion would take less time than the aborting women did; conversely, the aborting women though that contraception would take less time than contracepting women did (see Table 6-7). For both groups, however, neither procedure was considered to require very much time. When asked whether the procedure they were then undergoing was "time-consuming" (without further qualification), a majority in each group (54 percent of Group A and 67 percent of Group C) did not consider it so; the remainder did.

Table 6-7

Hours Needed/Spent for Abortion and Contraception

Hours Needed/Spent	Group A (N=72)	Group C (N=72)
Abortion		
0-9	31.9%	45.8%
10-19	50.0%	41.7%
20+	18.1%	12.5%
Contraception		
0-1	45.8%	29.2%
2-4	43.1%	62.5%
5+	11.1%	8.3%

Another question was posed to examine the subjective
costs of the services to the women. The women were asked
whether the clinic was "far" from their homes. As noted earlier, 57 percent of the aborting women and 68 percent of the
contracepting women resided in Novi Sad, so it was to be expected that a greater proportion of Group A would indicate
"far"--although it should be remembered that this is a subjective matter. The Group A women did indeed consider the clinic
to be "far" in larger measure than Group C. Fifty-three percent of aborting women considered it "far," 26 percent "not
far," and 21 percent indicated "not very far." In Group C,
43 percent said "far," 49 percent "not far," and 8 percent
"not very far." However, when the women were asked whether it
was difficult for them to come to the hospital, the vast majority in both groups (83 percent of Group A and 89 percent of
Group C) said "no." An additional 8 percent in Group A said
"not very" (none did in Group C), so that for both groups only
a small number considered it difficult (8 percent in Group A
and 11 percent in Group C). Bearing in mind that both groups
laid less stress on the procedures of obtaining abortion or
contraception than on the actual experiences of the methods
themselves, and noting that aborting women not only had to
come further more often (by reason of their addresses) but
also more often considered it far from home, the overall evidence suggests that motivation for abortion is strong enough
to diminish any importance that might be attached to the subjective notion that it is "difficult" to come to the clinic.

Personal Efficacy

The composite measure of "personal efficacy" indicated
some important differences between the two groups. On seven
major topics related to marriage, health, economics, and social life, the women were asked to assess whether success or
failure in these areas would be a result of their own efforts
or whether it was really not dependent on them, but a matter
of fate. On all seven items, the mean rank for Group C is
higher (i.e., believed to be more under their own control)
than for Group A (see Table 6-8). The overall mean for Group
C is 2.69; for Group A, 2.47. Furthermore, if one looks at
the numbers in each group of 72 respondents who positively responded with the statement "my own efforts," the pattern re-
peats itself and the differences are statistically significant
(t = 3.05, df 6, p < .01).

In looking at the ranks assigned to each aspect by
the two groups, some differences emerge (see Table 6-9). There
is a correlation (Spearman's rho) of .47 between the two
orders; however, that is not statistically significant for

seven rankings. The largest difference between the two groups
is the variable of whether the individual has control over
having a happy marriage. Group C gives that variable its
second-strongest response; for Group A it ranks sixth, or next-
to-last. Interestingly, both groups place control over the

Table 6-8

Personal Efficacy Measure

	Mean Ranks		Number of Positive Responses	
	Group A	Group C	Group A	Group C
Control Over:				
Who you marry	2.72	2.81	54	61
Happy marriage	2.34	2.82	37	63
Acquiring money	2.67	2.94	51	70
Health/sickness	2.46	2.71	45	60
Friends/enemies	2.19	2.33	32	42
Number of children	2.37	2.68	44	59
Behavior of children as adults	2.54	2.57	49	52
Mean	2.47	2.69	44.6	58.1
S.D.	0.18	0.19	7.80	8.89

Table 6-9

Order of Rankings

	Group A	Group C
Control Over:		
Who you marry	1	3
Happy marriage	6	2
Acquiring money	2	1
Health/sickness	4	4
Friends/enemies	7	7
Number of children	5	5
Behavior of children as adults	3	6

number of children they will have in the fifth position out of
seven rankings; but for Group C, as in all other aspects save
one, their rank is closer to 3 than to 2. For Group A, this
is only true for two of the aspects--whom they marry and
whether they acquire money.

In sum, on this important characteristic there is a
significant difference between the two groups in the extent to
which they believe they have control over certain major life
experiences, with the women of Group C showing the more active
view.

Discussion

The findings reported above tend to show a pattern of
differences between the two groups which suggests a greater
degree of control, planning, and husband-wife agreement in the
group of contracepting women. Although the women of Group C
are somewhat older than Group A, they have about the same number of children (on average, 1.4) and 20 percent of them have
never had an abortion. Because Group A contains a larger percentage of unmarried and childless women, and in view of the
fertility patterns (which show a greater tendency to follow
one delivery with another without an intervening period of
contraception or abortion), it is clear that the women of
Group A, when they do begin to have children, have them at a
higher rate. Group C women, on the other hand, show the tendency to regulate their fertility much earlier in their fertility careers.

The heavier reliance on abortion of Group A women (the
abortion index of Group A is double that of Group C) appears
to be not so much a result of a preference for abortion as it
is a major failure to contracept successfully. Fully 72 percent of the women of Group A indicate that they tried to prevent the pregnancy they have come to abort. The predominant
method of use, however, was coitus interruptus, a method not
used at all by Group C. Abortion was used to a large extent
to back up contraceptive failure. A far greater proportion of
women in Group A are unsure about whether or not they will
have another abortion.

The women of Group A have a lower sense of their own
personal efficacy than the women of Group C. Although there
is a somewhat larger number of rural and less well-educated
women in the Group A sample, the differences are not significant; the beliefs they hold about the extent of their own personal influence over their fates is statistically significant
for the two groups. This difference may account for the
choice of contraceptive methods through which women of Group
A tried to prevent the pregnancy. The existing modern

contraceptives are "female" ones, requiring the initiative and responsibility of the woman. Having a low sense of their personal efficacy, these women found the use of modern contraceptives incompatible with their personalities. Following the same reasoning, it is obvious why women of Group C, with their higher sense of personal efficacy, made attempts to regulate their fertility much earlier in their fertility histories.

For both groups, contraception is perceived as a less costly method than abortion on every criterion measured; however, the women of Group A have a more negative view of contraception than do the women of Group C. This also in large measure may be due to their low sense of personal efficacy. The active role required by women when using modern contraceptive methods makes the use of these methods appear more difficult to them. Contraception is, then, perceived as having more disadvantages, and the general view of contraceptives becomes a more negative one.

There are also similarities as well as differences between the two groups. Neither group considers either the procedure of acquiring an abortion or that of obtaining a contraceptive means to be subjectively costly. Service appears not to be a serious problem to either group. It is further evident that abortion is viewed as more costly than contraception by both Group A and Group C women. The women of both groups are similar in their wish to control their fertility; the differences occur in the choice of a fertility-regulating method.

Implications

This project was designed primarily to study the differences between contracepting and aborting women when both methods were equally accessible. It is clear that both methods are, in fact, equally accessible, at least to the extent that acquiring them is not seen as a problem. It is also clear, however, that abortion is considered more costly than contraception by both groups of women. Although the aborting women in this study tend to use abortion more frequently, they also indicate a strong desire to contracept. The methods they use, however, are relatively primitive. It is clear from their requests for abortions that these women want to control their fertility, and it is clear both from the greater negative value they place on abortion relative to contraception and to their efforts to contracept that the women in the abortion group would like to be successful contraceptors.

Perhaps what is needed is a program of contraceptive education in which the husband as well as the wife is involved and, perhaps, a greater concentration on an effective male method of contraception. These aborting women have less faith

in their control over their own destinies and believe themselves to be less in agreement with their husbands about the
need for contraception than the contracepting women. This may
be a projection of their own problems in the use of modern female contraceptive methods. The aborting women are to some
extent more rural and less well educated, but not greatly so.
Because it is likely that they play a more traditional and
perhaps subservient role in the family, a good contraceptive
program should probably attempt to elicit the husband's interest and support and to improve couple communication on
topics related to human reproduction. Although the contracepting women are less in need of assistance, the data suggest
that they may, nevertheless, also be vulnerable to future
abortions. It is likely that their contraceptive success
would also benefit from education directed to both husband
and wife.

It is also clear that no change can be expected either
from an increase in the awareness of the aborting women of modern contraceptives or from an improvement in the service. The
problem appears to be more closely related to a low sense of
personal efficacy in the sphere of sex and human reproduction.
The modern contraceptives are "female" ones, which require
the initiative and responsibility of the woman. Alternative
methods for these women might include (1) a post-conception
method requiring only that the woman decide whether to accept
the pregnancy or not and not requiring her to consider the
risks or take any action in advance; (2) a long-term contraceptive, requiring only a single decision and entailing a
second decision only when a child is wanted; and (3) a safe
and efficient contraceptive for the man to use, relieving the
woman of the burden of initiative and responsibility in this
sphere of the couple's life.

The findings and methodology of this project suggest
that it is possible to identify early in the fertility careers
of couples their particular vulnerability to the likelihood of
repeat abortions. The early pattern of the order of fertility
and fertility-regulating events, the abortion index (which
shows behavior over period of risk), the sense of couple concordance, and the sense of personal efficacy appear to be good
predictors of future behavior. Through such a process of
early identification optimal approaches may be utilized to
help families prevent both unwanted pregnancy and unwanted
pregnancy terminations.

REFERENCES

Atkinson, J. W. *An induction to motivation*. Princeton: Van
    Nostrand, 1964.

Bogue, D. J.   A model interview for fertility research and
     family planning evaluation. Family Planning Research and
     Evaluation Manual No. 3. Chicago: Community and Family
     Study Center, University of Chicago, 1970.

Brunning, S. L., & Kintz, B. L.   Computational handbook of
     statistics. Glenview, Ill.: Scott, Foresman, 1968.

Crawford, T. J.   Beliefs about birth control and their rela-
     tionship to attitudes and reported behavior. In Confer-
     ence Proceedings: Psychological Measurement in the Study
     of Population Problems. Berkeley: University of Cali-
     fornia, Institute of Personality Assessment and Research,
     1971.

Kapor-Stanulovic, N., & Beric, B.   Fertility behavior and
     abortion seekers--patterns of events. Paper presented at
     the International Congress of Medical Sexology, Paris,
     1974.

Rosenberg, M. J., & Oltman, P. K.   Consistency between atti-
     tudinal effect and spontaneous cognitions. Journal of
     Psychology, 1962, 54, 485-490.

Rotter, J. B.   Some problems and misconceptions related to the
     construct of internal vs external control of reinforcement.
     Journal of Consulting and Clinical Psychology, 1975, 43,
     56-67.

7

From Abortion to Contraception—
the Japanese Experience*

Minoru Muramatsu and Jean van der Tak

Editors' Note: The Japanese experience in
family planning represents one of the most
rapid and successful voluntary efforts in
history. It is also very much a private matter. Psychosocial research on fertility behavior continues to be a greatly neglected
area among Japanese behavioral scientists.
This chapter speculates on possible reasons
for the shift from abortion to contraception
as the chief means of fertility regulation,
despite unrestricted access to relatively inexpensive legal abortions and official re-
straints on use of oral contraceptives.

INTRODUCTION

The outstanding feature of Japanese fertility in recent years has been the unmistakable shift from abortion to
contraception as the chief means of fertility regulation. In
the absence of specific psychosocial research our explanations
will be largely conjectural, based on tangential studies plus
observations published in English by the Japanese Organizations
for International Cooperation in Family Planning (Kunii & Katagiri, 1976; JOICFP, 1977a). The need for research in fertility-
regulating behavior has not seemed compelling so long as Japanese couples are smoothly adjusting family size to current

*We are pleased to acknowledge the considerable assist-
ance rendered to us by the availability in Japanese and English
of the biennial family planning surveys conducted by the Mainichi Newspapers, as well as related publications prepared under
the auspices of the Japanese Organization for International
Cooperation in Family Planning.

personal and societal circumstances. There also appears to
be a continuing reluctance to probe in scientifically acceptable depth what is still regarded as primarily a private and
somewhat taboo area of human behavior (Iritani, 1974).

Psychosocial research into Japanese attitudes towards
childbearing and children was initiated in surveys of the Statistical Office of the Ministry of Health and Welfare (1970,
cited in Muramatsu, 1972) and of the Institute of Population
Studies (Sixth Fertility Survey of 1972, and the recently completed Value of Children Study, part of a cross-cultural project coordinated by the East-West Center of Hawaii, both cited
in Iritani, 1974). Contraception/abortion practices and attitudes remain to be researched in depth. Circumstantial evidence, however, suggests reasons for the shift in deep-seated
attitudes towards abortion and contraception--and thus in
fertility-regulating behavior (Muramatsu, 1977). Foremost
among these has been the unrivaled recent promotion and acceptance of what Potts (1974) has termed "the glorious Japanese condom."

BACKGROUND

Family planning as an important social movement
gained adherents in Japan in the period after World War I.
Margaret Sanger visited Japan in 1922. By the 1930s, the Japanese crude birthrate had fallen to about 32 per 1,000 population, indicating that births were already being controlled
far below the feasible physiological maximum of about 50 per
1,000, despite government opposition to birth control and an
official policy of population expansion. The leading means
of control then were increasingly delayed marriage, out-
migration, induced (illegal) abortion, and traditional contra-
ception--particularly the condom and the rhythm method. Following World War II, the flood of returning servicemen and
expatriates and natural postwar fertility boom pushed the
birthrate to a high of 34 per 1,000 in 1947. This was universally perceived to be causing population pressure intolerable
in the light of the country's devastated postwar situation.
Within a decade, the birthrate had been halved to 17 (1957).
After a slow rise to 18-19, and a dramatic drop to 13.7 in
the Fiery Horse Year of 1966 (discussed below), the birthrate
is again at about 16-17 per 1,000 population. In some years
the net reproduction rate has dropped below unity,* giving
rise to some concern about future replenishment of labor force
supplies.

---

*The net reproduction rate indicates the number of
daughters a cohort of women would bear during their lifetime,

THEORETICAL RESEARCH IN ABORTION-CONTRACEPTION

There is no doubt that the initial sharp postwar drop
in birthrates was due primarily to induced abortion, which in
practice--if not entirely in theory--became legally available
on request following the 1948-1952 Diet repeal of the 1940
National Eugenic Law with its severe strictures on induced
abortion. Under this so-called Eugenic Protection Law, recorded numbers of abortions rose from 246,000 in 1949 to a
peak of 1.17 million in 1955, but have since declined to
around 700,000 annually. From this alone, it would appear that
there has been a shift from abortion to contraception in maintaining the relatively stable levels of annual birthrates in
the past two decades. However, as is well know, there is reason to believe that officially recorded abortions underestimate the true incidence of abortion in Japan. This has been
attributed to underreporting by "designated" physicians authorized to perform abortions, over 80 percent of which take
place in such physicians' private clinics (Roht & Aoyama,
1973), and also to nonreporting by those other than designated
physicians performing abortions. Unless a physician reports
an abortion as performed for health reasons so that a client
may benefit from a private health insurance policy, a fee is
charged that in 1967 reportedly ranged from US $10-$15 (Muramatsu, 1967) and in 1971 from $30-$50 (Roht & Aoyama, 1973).
Japanese National Health Insurance does not cover elective induced abortion.

The apparent discrepancy between recorded and actual
numbers of annual abortions has prompted considerable research,
summarized in Muramatsu (1973b). Two researchers, Aoki and
Muramatsu, based their approaches on the computed differences
between actually recorded numbers of live births and the numbers that theoretically could be expected in the absence of
deliberate fertility control. The difference is divided into
portions prevented by abortion and contraception in a given
year, setting aside couples protected by sterilization (considered to provide permanent contraception). Basic data used
for these calculations have included census data on numbers
of married women by age-group from 15-49 (ignoring small numbers of extra-marital births), data on current contraceptive
practice among Japanese couples gathered in the biennial family planning surveys of the Mainichi Newspapers (described

---

assuming continuation of a fixed set of the age-specific fertility and mortality rates current in one year. An NRR below
unity indicates that on these assumptions a population would
not replace itself in the long run.

below), and past research on numbers of pregnancies to be expected in the year following abandonment of contraception at
a level of effectiveness corresponding to that observed in
these survey years, taking into account theoretical fecunda-
bility by age, etc. The results can be seen in Table 7-1.

Table 7-1

Shifts in the Contraception:Abortion Ratio
in Controlling Numbers of Births

	Aoki	Murumatsu
1955	3:7	100:257
1960	5:5	100:180
1965	7:3	100:103
1970	7:3	100: 85

Note. The data in column 1 are from Aoki, 1972. The data in
column 2 are from Muramatsu, 1973a.

Muramatsu's calculations indicate a lesser degree of shift
than those of Aoki, but the direction is certain. This research also indicates that abortion use probably peaked around
1960, rather than 1955 as suggested by the official data.

    Prime factors in the increasing weight of contracep-
tion in Japanese fertility control have been (1) an increase
in the proportion of contraceptors and (2) an improvement in
the effectiveness with which contraception is practiced.

INCREASE IN THE PROPORTION OF CONTRACEPTORS

    The proportionate increase in contraceptors has been
documented in a 27-year series of biennial family planning
surveys conducted from 1950-1977 by the Mainichi Newspapers,
based on interviews with national samples of about 3,000-3,800
currently married women under age 50 selected by stratified
random sampling. Table 7-2 shows the 1950-1977 percentage
distribution of these interviewed wives by status of contraceptive practice. It can be seen that the combined proportion
of current and past contraceptors--"ever-users"--increased
from 29 percent in 1950 to 63 percent in 1959. In the latter

half of the 1960s, this proportion stabilized at about 72 percent. In 1975, in reached a high of 82 percent. The proportion of never-users was as high as 64 percent in 1950, but dropped below 30 percent in 1963 and has continued to decline to a low of 13.3 percent in 1975 and 1977.

Adjusting for misreporting, Tietze and Dawson (1973) estimate the 1971 percentage of current contraceptors among fertile-aged Japanese wives as 59 rather than the 53 percent reported. This is close to the comparable 65 percent reported by currently married women (aged 15-44) in the US National Fertility Survey of 1970 (Westoff, 1972).

Table 7-2

Percentage Distribution of Wives by Status
of Contraceptive Practice: 1950-1977

	1950	1955	1959	1963	1967	1971	1975	1977
Current users	19.5	33.6	42.5	44.0	53.0	52.6	60.5	60.4
Past users	9.6	18.8	20.2	19.0	19.2	20.2	21.0	19.4
Never-users	63.6	41.6	33.0	29.8	23.1	16.8	13.3	13.3
Others & NA	7.3	6.0	4.3	7.2	4.7	10.4	5.2	6.9
Total	100.0	100.0	100.0	100.0	100.0	100.0	100.0	100.0

Note.   From Population Problems Research Council, The Mainichi Newspapers. Reports of Thirteenth and Fourteenth National Survey on Family Planning.

Decline in Proportions Resorting to Abortion

The Mainichi surveys also show a rise in the percentage of respondents admitting to having had at least one abortion from 15 percent in 1952 to 41 percent in 1961, a drop to 32 percent from 1963-1967, followed by a lesser rise to around 37-38 percent from 1969-1975. The Mainichi survey data indicate that abortion usage probably peaked about 1960 and has since declined, particularly among younger women.

That data collected by interview, as in the Mainichi surveys, probably yield underestimates of abortion experience is suggested by results of a combined mail questionnaire and

interview survey of both married and single women aged 20-45
conducted in the Hochi prefecture in 1971 by Roht. Lower reporting of abortion was obtained by interview (40.3 percent)
than by mail questionnaire (46.6 percent), which the researchers attribute to the inhibiting presence of the interviewer
(Roht & Aoyama, 1973).

Timing of Starting Contraception as a
Factor in Increasing Proficiency

In earlier years in Japan, contraception, like abortion, meant for the most part the ultimate discontinuation of
childbearing. It was first adopted by relatively older women
who had already achieved their desired number of children.
Thus, family planning was synonomous with "having no more
children," and young married women tended to pay little attention to the subject. With expansion of family planning education campaigns, more women--particularly the young--began to
appreciate its importance not only for stopping births but
also for child spacing. As time went on, women began to initiate contraception much earlier in marital life than did previous generations, as can be seen in Table 7-3 (also derived
from Mainichi survey data). By 1973, 20 percent of respondents reported having begun contraception immediately after
marriage, in contrast to only 5.9 percent in 1950; the largest
proportion (35 percent) began after the birth of a first child.
In the surveys of 1950, 1955, and 1961, most respondents reported having delayed contraception until they had borne at
least two children. Since 1971 there has been a slight decline after the first birth and increase after the second
birth. (It should be noted that these changes in timing according to birth intervals may be due to declining numbers of
higher order births or earlier actual use of contraception.)

This earlier initiation of contraception has not only
increased the overall proportion of contraceptors among married women, but probably also enhanced proficiency, With
earlier exposure to contraception, many couples acquire skills
enough to practice it more successfully by the time they have
achieved their desired family size. Another result of the
shift to earlier start of contraception in the family life
cycle is that some women have come to avoid induced abortion
even when contraception has failed. When contraception is
practiced for the purpose of discontinuation of childbearing,
contraceptive failures almost invariably lead to abortion;
when family planning is practiced for spacing of births, failures are not necessarily followed by induced abortion. Ar-
rival of the second child a little earlier than planned may
not matter so much. Although this consideration was not taken

Table 7-3

Percent Distribution of Current Users by Time of
Starting Contraception: 1970-1977

Starting Time	1950	1955	1961	1965	1971	1975	1977
Immediately after marriage	5.9	9.0	5.3	13.6	18.0	19.8	20.9
After 1st birth	18.9	19.3	16.7	31.0	36.0	34.0	33.0
After 2nd birth	21.4	23.3	33.9	26.9	26.7	27.7	29.4
After 3rd birth	19.7	21.5	25.2	18.1	13.8	12.1	12.0
After 4th or more births	27.2	?	?	?	2.2	2.4	1.3
NA	6.9	?	?	?	3.3	4.0	3.4
Total	100.0	100.0	100.0	100.0	100.0	100.0	100.0

Note. From Population Problems Research Council, The Mainichi
Newspapers, Summary of Eleventh National Survey on Family
Planning, Tokyo: 1972, Table 2-4-1, p. 23; and Report of
Thirteenth National Survey on Family Planning, Tokyo: 1975,
p. 27, plus findings from Fourteenth Survey,

into account in our theoretical analysis of the shift from
abortion to contraception in the overall suppression of Japanese fertility, it could have been one of the many factors involved in the actual situation.

In the fourteenth Mainichi Newspapers survey, conducted in 1977, the modal number of "two children" viewed as
"ideal," as well as actually born, continued as the dominant
trend in the most reproductive age group. Among younger subjects 20-24 years of age, however, 4 percent cited "no children" as ideal and another 11 percent preferred only one child.
The corresponding figures for 1975 were 1.3 and 5 percent, respectively. This change in attitude among younger wives may
foreshadow lower future fertility (JOICFP, 1977b).

Changing Reasons for Practicing Fertility
Control as a Factor in Method Choice

Abortion is the most infallible of reversible methods
for controlling family size, This may have been one reason

for its choice over the then-available contraceptive methods
during the postwar period of economic recovery (until about
1955). Suggestive evidence is available from Aso (1972), which
shows that the highest rate of (recorded) abortions and lowest
level of living index (as computed by the author) occurred
about 1953-1954, and that the rapid economic development since
1954 has corresponded with a constant decline in the abortion
rate. Thus, the behavior of Japanese women faced with a poor
economic situation in the early 1950s can perhaps be compared
with that of their forebears in the latter half of the Tokugawa
Shogunate (1603-1867), when abortion and infanticide were apparently common among peasants at times of critical economic
distress, such as crop failures (Muramatsu, 1967). A Japanese
Population Association survey of 1952 (cited in Aso, 1972, p.
13) indicated that main reasons for having a first abortion at
that time were economic-related (80 percent), although reasons
for subsequent abortions were said to be physical (76 percent).
Abortions then were relatively cheap (approximately US $6.10),
readily available in every community, and certain of preventing birth. When economic conditions improved and couples
could afford the risk of having an "extra" child, contraception
increased.

Suggestive evidence on this point also comes from
Mainichi survey data, which indicate trends in abortion experience and contraceptive practice by rural-urban residence and by
education, as seen in Table 7-4. Abortion experience was
higher among married women in major cities and better educated
women (at least women with 10-12 years of schooling) at all
four dates shown--1952, 1955, 1959, and 1965--but fell off
more rapidly from 1959 to 1965 in major cities than in rural
areas (43.2 percent to 37.4 percent, compared to 32.4 to 30.5
percent) and among those with 10-12 years' education (40.9 to
33.8 percent), while continuing to increase among the less educated (30.5 to 31.9 percent). Meanwhile, contraceptive practice rose in all these population segments. Apart from the
factor of probable earlier exposure to and greater accessibility of contraception in urban areas and among the better educated, these trends could indicate that higher socioeconomic
groups were more constrained to limit fertility during times
of less-than-adequate economic conditions, and also more determined to profit from improving conditions thereafter. Thus,
they were likely to react more sharply to economic conditions
by first resorting to the sure method of abortion and then
hazarding the shift to contraception when the economic pressure
eased. In this connection, it should be pointed out that the
overall shift to contraception is undoubtedly associated with
rises in the overall level of education (by 1969, 87 percent
of Japanese girls aged 12-17 were enrolled in secondary
schools [UNESCO, 1972, Table 2.7]) and urbanized proportion of

Table 7-4

Trends in Abortion Experience and Contraceptive
Practice in Japan, 1952-1965

	1952	1955	1959	1965
Percent of Women with Experience of Induced Abortion, by Area				
Major cities	18.7	30.3	43.2	37.4
Other urban	20.0	27.0	35.5	31.5
Rural	12.6	24.8	32.4	30.5
Percent of Women with Abortion Experience by Educational Level				
9 years or less	12.2	22.2	30.5	31.9
10-12 years	20.9	36.0	40.9	33.8
13+ years	36.6	26.8	29.3	32.1
Percent of Women Using a Contraceptive Method, by Area				
Major cities	52.0	56.6	66.7	68.6
Other urban	46.0	52.9	64.0	67.5
Rural	34.6	50.8	58.1	66.1
Percent of Women with Contraceptive Experience, by Educational Level				
9 years or less	20.1	28.2	35.0	39.3
10-12 years	38.7	46.1	51.6	54.9
13+ years	47.0	48.8	51.9	56.2

Note. From I. Figa-Talamanca. The effects of programs of
birth control education on the practice of induced abortion in
Japan, Genus, 1970, 26(3-4), Tables 8, 9, 7, and 10, respectively, pp. 247-250, adapted from Population Problems Research
Council, The Mainichi Newspapers, Summaries of National Surveys
on Family Planning, various years.

the population (72 percent by 1970 [UN, 1972, Table 5]), although class differentials in contraceptive and abortion use are narrowing.

Similar shifts in motives for controlling fertility can be seen in responses to survey questions on reasons for practicing contraception, asked of current and past contraceptors. In 1957 and 1961, "economic insecurity" was given as the leading reason. By 1965, this was foremost with only 16 percent of contraceptors (and 18 percent in 1975), with preservation of maternal health and "giving children a good education by limiting their number" being now most important (Muramatsu, 1967, p. 55; Population Problems Research Council, 13th Mainichi survey, pp. 28-29).

Attitudes Toward Contraception and Abortion

The percentage of Mainichi respondents who "think that contraception is a good thing" increased from 60.7 percent in 1950 to 67.4 percent in 1955. "Family planning" was substituted for "contraception" in 1963, when 88 percent agreed with this statement (most of the remainder had "never thought of it' and the approving proportion has stabilized at 85-87 percent since then (Population Problems Research Council, 13th Mainichi survey, p. 26). Thus, it is evident that family planning, or contraception, became widely supported in Japan in the 1960s.

The Japanese, in general, have seldom viewed abortion as commendable. On pragmatic grounds they tend to be more tolerant than certain social leaders who have called for amendments to the abortion law on the grounds of moral unwholesomeness and health hazards, in addition to fear of a diminishing population (Muramatsu, 1971, 1977). Japanese women do not necessarily associate induced abortion with a sense of religious sin, but tend to evaluate it in relation to its health hazards or what others may say about it (Muramatsu, 1967, pp. 78-79). Roht and Aoyama (1973) note that many women travel to neighboring towns or use false names when seeking an abortion. "While abortion is easily obtained, it is a private matter and women do not wish to be the subject of gossip" (Muramatsu, 1967, p. 104). In the 1965 Mainichi survey, only 18 percent of women with experience of abortion had no "guilt" feelings; more than 60 percent admitted some regretful or remorseful feelings.

Recent Mainichi data suggest that disapproval of unrestricted abortion may be increasing. Respondents who approved of abortion without qualification dropped from 11.5 percent to 8.6 percent between the surveys of 1967 and 1971, although the proportion rose slightly to 9.2 percent in 1975.

From 1967-1975 the percentage of women approving of abortion
only "under certain conditions" (to protect the mother's life
or health, in cases of rape, to prevent hereditary illness, or
"when living conditions are difficult and contraception fails")
rose from 61.7 percent to 68.2 percent (Population Problems
Research Council, 9th and 13th Mainichi surveys, pp. 58 and
31). However, the data also suggest that when personally con-
fronted with an unwanted pregnancy, a substantial proportion
of Japanese wives would still resort to abortion under any
circumstances. When current contraceptors were asked what they
would do in case of contraceptive failure, the proportion re-
plying that they would carry the pregnancy to term rose from
43.0 percent to 46.3 percent between the surveys of 1969 and
1973, but dropped back to 38.4 percent in 1975. Meanwhile,
the proportion who would "accept" an induced abortion fell
from 37.6 percent to 32.7 percent between the first two dates,
but was again up to 37.5 percent in 1975 (Population Problems
Research Council, 10th and 13th Mainichi surveys, pp. 57 and
29).

Sources of Family Planning (Contraceptive) Knowledge

In 1951, alarmed by the sharp increase in abortion,
the Japanese Cabinet issued a statement to the effect that contraception was to be recommended as a far more reasonable method of family limitation than abortion, and that official programs to promote family planning should be strengthened. In
1952 the Ministry of Health and Welfare compiled a scheme for
a national family planning program covering the whole range
from public education to individual technical guidance. Health
centers, midwives, local communities, and voluntary organizations participated (Muramatsu, 1971) in a program that undoubtedly influenced the gradual shift from abortion to contraception. However, budgetary appropriations allocated by
national government and local communities declined in the 1960s
compared to the 1950s. Although the government-sponsored family planning program is still in existence, its scope and coverage have diminished (Muramatsu & Kuroda, 1974). In recent
years the budget has increased, but the increase is not remarkable when compared to the rise in the cost of living. The
estimated total for 1976 is around one million dollars, or
about one cent per capita (Muramatsu, 1977). The practice of
family planning in Japan is largely a private affair. (It is
suspected that until 1960 the real emphasis of the government
program was on limitation of births. After 1960, and especially during the late 1960s, the stress shifted to promoting
family planning not as birth limitation but as a means to allow each couple to have the number of children desired. A
similar shift in fertility attitudes from public to private

concerns is revealed by a drop from 36 percent to 15 percent in the Mainichi respondents favoring a population slowdown for Japan between the surveys of 1950 and 1969 [Muramatsu & Kuroda, 1974]).

In the 1971 survey, for instance, the most common source of contraceptive information among personal contacts was the "husband" (22.8 percent), followed by physicians and friends (16.1 percent and 15.1 percent, respectively). This was especially true in urban areas and among younger women under age 30 (where friends rated above doctors as information sources). In rural areas, however, "nurses and public health nurses" were somewhat more important than husbands as personal sources of information (19.3 percent compared to 15.5 percent), perhaps because of the active family planning program of rural community services and the Agricultural Cooperative mentioned below. Among mass media sources magazines were by far the largest source of information, far outranking health centers, training courses, women's club meetings, etc. (Population Problems Research Council, 11th Mainichi survey, pp. 29-31). Japanese women's magazines have been active for many years in promoting contraception.

INCREASING AVAILABILITY AND EFFECTIVENESS OF CONTRACEPTION

Although abortion was the dominant method of controlling births in the first postwar years, Mainichi data indicate that it became increasingly used and viewed as a supplementary method in cases of contraceptive failure. In Table 7-5 it can be seen that the proportion of women experiencing both abortion and contraception increased over the years from 31.5 percent in 1952 to 50.6 percent in 1959, with a drop thereafter to 44.1 percent in 1967. (The percentage of respondents who had had an abortion but never practiced contraception also rose, but in 1967 was just over one-tenth.) Probably a prime reason for reduction in abortion is the decline in contraceptive failures, which in turn can be attributed to the increasing availability and more effective use of contraceptive methods.

The Condom

Improved contraceptive practice in Japan can be equated with the increased availability, acceptability, and effectiveness of the condom. It is by far the most common contraceptive method, with a rate of usage that towers above that of every other country in the world. Matsumoto et al. (1972) observe

Table 7-5

Percent of Women Reporting Abortion Experience
with or without Contraceptive Practice

	1952	1955	1959	1965	1967
With contraceptive practice	31.5	44.9	50.6	47.4	44.1
Without contraceptive practice	4.8	6.9	10.5	9.4	12.2

Note. From I. Figa-Talamanca, 1970, Table 11, and Population
Problems Research Council, 9th Mainichi survey, Table III-4,
p. 55 (1967).

that in the first Mainichi survey of 1950 the percentage of
condom users among contracepting couples was 35.6. A substantial increase to 55.8 percent was reported in the second survey, indicating that by 1952 the majority of Japanese contracepting couples utilized condoms. The percentage increased
steadily with each survey and in 1977 stood at 78.9 percent.
In 1968, Japan accounted for over a third of the total world
condom production of 15.16 million gross (1 gross = 12 dozen =
144), only slightly surpassed by the United States, with Britain
producing 13 percent. Condom production increased twelvefold
in the two decades from 1951 to 1970.

Why the overwhelming popularity of condoms in Japan?
Matsumoto and his colleagues in 1972 felt that simply to state
that IUDs and oral contraceptives lacked official government
or medical approval seemed an inadequate explanation. Ota and
Yusei rings were approved by the government as intrauterine
contraceptive devices in August 1974. Until that time, IUDs
were prohibited by a 1936 addition to the 1931 Regulations for
the Control of Harmful Contraceptive Devices. In practice, a
saving clause was attached to the prohibition to the effect
that the IUD might be used under proper medical supervision
for experimental purposes. Thus, the proportion of contraceptors reporting use of Ota rings doubled from 4.3 percent in
the 1965 Mainichi survey to 9.1 percent in 1977.

As of July 1977, the Ministry of Health still has not
officially sanctioned the use of pills for contraceptive purposes. Fear of possible harmful effects after long-term use

and of improper handling if dispensed through the loose Japanese system of drug sales are said to be the major reasons for this disapproval. It is permitted to use medicines similar to oral contraceptives for the treatment of menstrual disorders and cycle regulation; the physician may prescribe the pills at his own discretion. By 1977, 3.3 percent of contraceptors reported use of pills.

In addition to official barriers to IUD and pill use as contraceptives, Matsumoto et al. (1972) noted that in the Japanese cultural tradition "there is a strong resistance to the insertion of a foreign object into the body, to injury or scarring of the body, or to the disturbances of bodily hormonal balances (harmony) by drugs or chemicals" (Mainichi Population Problems Research Council, Demographic Revolution in Japan, 1970, quoted in Matsumoto et al., 1972, p. 254).

Another reason for the popularity of condoms after World War I may be that the condom habit learned by males during their military years carried over into later family life. (Condoms to prevent venereal disease have been stressed by the Japanese army and navy since at least the late 19th century.) However, younger husbands now of fertile age have had no army experience. "Also, American soldiers appear not to have perpetuated the condom use learned in the US army upon returning to civilian life" (Matsumoto et al., 1972, p. 254). Crowded Japanese housing conditions with only sliding doors between rooms are also said to make other methods such as spermicide, diaphragm, or douching difficult to practice.

The safe period (rhythm) method invariably ranks second in all reports of contraceptive practice. Widespread use derives from its long history in Japan following discovery of its basic principle by the Janpanese physician Ogino in 1924. Women's magazines have provided ample explanations--often more than necessary for the lay public (Muramatsu, 1967). Reported usage declined from 38.8 percent to 29.9 percent of contraceptors between 1965 and 1975. However, there is evidently more use of the basal body temperature method, which may have improved the efficiency of rhythm. In addition, the practice of combining two or more methods--usually the condom and rhythm-- is increasing. In a 1954 survey, 32 percent of couples were using a combination of two or more methods (Muramatsu, 1967). By 1969, approximately 44 percent of contraceptors combined use of the condom and safe period (Matsumoto et al., 1972, p. 254). In general, combined methods result in fewer failures than does reliance on a single method.

Male Orientation of Condoms as
Factor in Acceptability

It is apparent that the popularity and effectiveness
of condoms in Japan could only be achieved with male understanding and cooperation. Matsumoto et al. (1972) suggest
that Japanese husbands seem as highly motivated for family
limitation as their wives. However, evidence from a 1970 survey of the Statistical Office of the Ministry of Health and
Welfare somewhat weakens this supposition. Among 4,403 couples with two children, 63 percent of wives reported wanting
no more children, but only 49 percent of husbands. Among the
3,128 surveyed couples with three children, the figures were
85 and 76 percent, respectively.

Because male reluctance to use the condom has been reported from many countries, and because traditional male dominance continues to play a major role in Japanese society, it
seems appropriate to speculate about possible reasons for the
decided preference for male rather than female methods of contraception in Japan. Condom use has proliferated under a variety of social, economic, and historical circumstances. One
reason may be the high quality and easy availability of condoms relative to pills and IUDs. For example, Matsumoto et al.
(1972) note Harvey's observation that preference for the condom, rather than arising from any inexplicable difference between the Japanese and other peoples, may simply be due to the
thinness and lightness of the product, which minimize loss of
satisfaction in use. The Japanese condom is described as "a
better product in a better package with better promotion"
(Matsumoto et al., 1972).

It may also be speculated that Japanese husbands have
increasingly recognized the economic costs of raising and educating children, and assumed the concomitant responsibility
for more effective family planning, thus reducing reliance on
abortion. As Professor Kuroda notes in his summary to the
1977 Mainichi Newspapers report, "The survey was characterized
both by a Western trend of fertility control and by the dominant status of the condom, a traditional method of contraception among the Japanese; in other words, the coexistence of
the Western style with the Japanese one" (JOICFP, 1977b).

Manufacturing, Promotion, and Sales Techniques
as Factors in Acceptability and Effectiveness

Japanese manufacturers compete vigorously for control
of the condom market. Four companies produced 95 percent
of condoms in 1972, trailed by a dozen smaller companies. Technically, their product--subjected to testing procedures often
more rigorous than those of the official supervisory agent

(Pharmaceutical and Supply Bureau, Ministry of Health and Welfare)--is nearly flawless. However, as emphasized in a report of the Population Information Program (May 1974), technical efficiency is no longer a problem with today's condoms. They rarely have holes or rupture during use. Pregnancy rates measured strictly in terms of method failure are less than five pregnancies per 100 couple-years of exposure. On the other hand, use effectiveness is dependent upon consistent use. As the PIP report observes, based on US surveys, most condom users occasionally take chances that can lead to pregnancy, particularly younger fecund couples using condoms for delaying rather than preventing births. To increase the contraceptive effectiveness of condoms therefore means to increase consistent use (i.e., at every coitus). Increasing consistent use means, in turn, increasing both the availability and acceptability of condoms, especially among younger, more fecund couples.

It is here that Japan has led the way. As related by Matsumoto et al. (1972) and others, Japanese manufacturers have pioneered new models, new packaging, and new sales techniques. A Japanese firm was the first to introduce colored condoms in 1949. Popular pastel colors are stressed with such advertising slogans as: "Opal color invites sweet dreams; pink, delectable moods." Eight percent of Japanese condoms are lubricated. (Spermicides are not used because that would place condoms under stricter medical-pharmaceutical supervision.) Thickness is usually 0.03 mm., compared to 0.045 mm.-0.05 mm. in the United States. Currently, one company is promoting a plastic condom that receives ten dippings in contrast to two for Latex condoms (and is therefore stronger), but is a sheer 0.02 mm. thick and thus better fitting. Included in packages are disposal bags, napkins, "finger sacks," and simple reordering cards that can be handed to a druggist without a word. The modern designs for condom wrappers and box packaging are "works of leading Tokyo commercial artists known for their talents in cosmetic packaging and advertising" (Matsumoto, 1972).

Neighborhood drugstores featuring "skin corners" are reported as the major sales outlets for condoms. Recently women--who tend to buy in larger bulk quantities than men-- have constituted approximately half the buyers, indicating the importance of attractive packaging. Larger supermarkets stock condoms beside feminine napkins and tampons. Condom vending machines have been legalized, though strongly opposed by women's organizations because children tend to mistake them at times for chewing gum dispensers.

Since 1955, public health workers and many midwives and field workers of the Japanese Family Planning Association

have worked as promotional agents for condoms. During the
1960s strong efforts were made to reach families of middle and
lower socioeconomic levels with reasonably priced condoms.
Profit margins for these workers rose from 50 yen for one
dozen condoms selling at 100 yen in 1955 to 200-300 yen for
condoms selling at 1000 yen per twelve in recent years (Matsumoto et al., 1972).* Door-to-door selling by saleswomen
to housewives--promoted by private companies since 1967--ac-
counts for 15-20 percent of Japanese condom sales (Population
Information Program, December 1973). Reportedly, by 1972 an
experienced saleswoman earned from 200,000-500,000 yen a
month--far above that year's average earnings of males. According to Matsumoto et al. (1972), saleswomen report that
about one out of every five housewives will invite them into
their homes. In one sales region an ingenious system has
been devised to guard customer privacy. Saleswomen work in
teams on a schedule that prevents any one from calling twice
at the same household, therefore sparing customers the embarrassment of revealing how many condoms a couple uses (Population Information Program, December 1973).

A recent law protects consumers against overly aggressive condom promotion tactics, such as the tendency of some
women sales teams to high-pressure young wives into purchasing
a dozen gross or more at one time. Promotion has gradually
shifted to stressing the erotic enjoyment of condoms--plus
birth (and VD) control. An early example was the postwar advertisement that resulted in soaring sales for one pharmaceutical company's CCC (for "contra-ceptive cream") brand of condoms: "1--Hime; 2--Taro; 3c's." Translation would be: first
a princess; second a Taro (a common boy's name); then the use
of CCCs. In contrast, a recent advertisement for a brand
named "Zero-0" depicts a masked and black-caped Captain Zero
waving his saber in one hand with a white-gowned damsel em-
braced in the other, exclaiming, "Your extraordinary Knight
[night] Zero!" Such approaches play on the ancient Japanese
tradition of sex toys. The authors conclude that, "present
condoms are not actually effective in sex stimulation, but the
various 'accessories' help to make them seem so" (Matsumoto
et al., 1972, p. 255). However, recent research by the World
Health Organization Task Force on Acceptability of Fertility-
Regulating Methods suggests that many Japanese perceive the
condom in itself as sexually stimulating. As described by
Marshall (1974, p. 6), "one of the attributes of the condom--
that it is coitus-connected--is considered unattractive among
many Westerners who feel it detracts from the spontaneity of
sex, but it is considered attractive by many Japanese who feel

---

*1 yen = 1/3 cent in 1974.

that putting on the condom is an integral part of erotic
foreplay."

Costs

Condom costs in 1972 ranged from 300-1500 yen per
dozen, depending upon extras. Reportedly, those priced about
500 yen per dozen, which reduces to about 42 yen per condom,
are best sellers. On this basis, a rough estimate of average
annual costs of condom usage can be made. An average of two
coital acts each week yields 105 per year. At 42 yen per time,
this amounts to 4,368 yen, or approximately US $14.56 for a
year's average supply of condoms. As already noted, costs of
private abortions (1971) ranged between $30 and $50. Thus in
Japan today complete contraceptive coverage would seem to be
a cheaper method of birth control than abortion.

Use Effectiveness

Firm data on use effectiveness of condoms are few.
Matsumoto et al. unearthed only one 1956-1958 survey, of a
mining community by the Institute of Public Health, which indicated a failure rate of 3.6 percent (cited in Matsumoto et
al., 1972, p. 255). This is very low compared to a Population
Information Program compilation of international studies revealing rates ranging from 3-36 percent, with most concentrated at 10 percent and upward (Population Information Program, May 1974, Table 4).

Differential Practice Rates

In the 1971 Mainichi survey, condom practice among
contraceptors was still highest in largest cities (76.9 percent), compared to 69.6 percent in rural areas (a larger gap
than in 1969 when the respective percentages were 69.3 and
68.2, which may be due to increasingly aggressive marketing in
urban areas since 1970). Matsumoto et al. state that the im-
pressive rural rate reflects the recent active role of the
powerful Nokyo (Agricultural Cooperative) in the family planning movement in villages. Each farmhouse is reached systematically through circulation of the Ai no kobako (The Love
Box), containing condoms and a sealed piggy bank for customers
to pay for purchases anonymously. Also, the Mainichi surveys
have consistently shown greater condom use by couples in which
wives have higher educational attainment.

In short, thanks to commercial ingenuity contraception
in Japan (for which read: condom use) has become attractive
to both males and females, easily available without embarrass-

ment, relatively cheap, entirely free of health hazards, even fun, and perhaps sexually stimulating. Thus, in all likelihood it is practiced more consistently and therefore effectively. This, in turn, has reduced failure rates and the need to resort to abortion.

Sterilization

Sterilization has yet to be popularized in Japan, although permitted on eugenic indications and for "protection of mother's life and health" under the same law legalizing abortion. As with induced abortion, reported numbers are considered an underestimate of the true incidence, which is perhaps five to ten times higher. A total of 11,737 sterilizations was reported in 1973, of which only 2 percent were vasectomies. The percentage of contraceptors reporting sterilization of either husband or wife in the Mainichi surveys has fluctuated at a low level--5.7 in 1965, 3.6 in 1967, 5.4 in 1969, and 4.7 in 1975. A clue to the relative unpopularity of sterilization may be the conservatism of family planning educators who view the finality of sterilization as a bar to its use other than as an extreme last resort. This attitude might change if a reliable reversible method were developed. In addition, a deep-rooted fear of unsexing or bodily change through such "maiming" may still be at work, especially among men, as evidenced by the low percentage of vasectomies noted.

SUMMARY

Although widespread abortion was largely responsible for the initial dramatic decline of birthrates in postwar Japan, theoretical and survey research reveals that beginning about 1960 the balance in maintaining the relatively stable birthrates of the past two decades has increasingly shifted in favor of contraception. The proportion of contraceptors and effectiveness of contraceptive practice have steadily increased among married women, with a concomitant decline in abortion-- now used chiefly in cases of contraceptive failure. Younger couples initiate contraception earlier in marriage for birth spacing, whereas formerly contraception (and abortion) was adopted only after attainment of desired family size (currently two-to-three children). Timing failures that occur when contraception is used for birth spacing may not lead to abortion so inevitably as failures when contraception is being practiced for birth limitation.

No psychosocial research has yet probed deep-seated personal reasons for the shift from abortion to contraception, but clues as to the probable nature of such reasons can be gleaned from indirect evidence. During the first economically depressed postwar years, the infallibility (and relative cheapness) of abortion as a birth control method was perhaps a reason for its preponderance over then-available methods of contraception, despite theoretical disapproval. When economic conditions improved and the risk of an "extra" child could be afforded, contraception increased. Officially organized family planning programs launched in 1952 have had some influence, but family planning in Japan is now generally a private affair, except for successful programs of local community services and the Agricultural Cooperative in rural areas. Husbands and women's magazines are cited as leading sources of contraceptive information by survey respondents.

The decline in contraceptive failure, and hence the need to resort to abortion, is associated with the increasing availability, effectiveness, and acceptability of contraception. In Japan, this can be equated with the development and aggressive promotion of condoms by commercial firms. Medical and government restrictions still hamper use of pills for contraception, and IUDs were approved only in 1974. Pioneering techniques of manufacturing, packaging, distribution, and promotion have resulted in a high-quality condom, attractive and easily available to both males and females, with resulting practice rates far above those of any other nation and probably more consistent (and hence effective) use. Sterilization still meets with considerable resistance among the Japanese, particularly among the men.

Concluding Note

The Japanese crude birthrate dropped precipitously to 13.7 per 1,000 population in 1966--a Year of the Fiery Horse (occurring once every 60 years), which is traditionally believed to be inauspicious for the birth of girls, who are said to grow up to be bad-natured and, hence, difficult to marry off. Although Aso (1972) cites evidence that some girls actually born in that year were misreported, there was undoubtedly a drop in births. Tietze and Lewit (1969) attribute this to a probable large upswing in unreported abortions (recorded abortions showed no trend change). They reason that the segment likely to be so superstitious would be most conservative and least inclined to use contraception. Aso, however, points out that the Mainichi survey shows a peak of current contraceptive practice in 1965 (56 percent) and a drop to 53 percent in 1967 (when the birthrate surged up to 19.4), from which he concludes that a swell in contraception rather than abortion produced the desired birth avoidance. Insufficient evidence

is available to decide which argument is correct. The Fiery
Horse Year phenomenon is an example of the strong psychological or cultural influence found in Japanese fertility-regulating
behavior, which is, as yet, insufficiently studied.

REFERENCES

Aoki, H. On as estimation of effects of fertility control in
Japan. Tokyo: Ministry of Health and Welfare, Institute
of Population Problems, 1972. English Pamphlet Series
No. 79.

Aso, T. Fertility control transition from abortion to contraceptives in Japan since 1948. Paper prepared for Population Association of America meeting, Toronto, April 1972.

Figa-Talamanca, I. The effects of programs of birth control
education on the practice of induced abortion in Japan.
Genus, 1970, 26(3-4), 237-258.

Iritani, T. The recent bibliography of family planning and
fertility behavior in Japan. Paper presented at UN ECAFE
Expert Group Meeting on Social and Psychological Aspects
of Fertility Behaviour, Bangkok, June 1974.

Japanese Organization for International Cooperation in Family
Planning (Eds.). Fertility and family planning in Japan.
Tokyo: Author, 1977. (a)

Japanese Organization for International Cooperation in Family
Planning. JOICFP News, August 1977, No. 38. (b)

Kunii, C., & Katagiri, T. (Eds.). Basic readings on population
and family planning in Japan. Tokyo: Japanese Organization for International Cooperation in Family Planning,
1976.

Marshall, J. F. Perceptions and attitudes towards fertility-
regulating methods and services. Paper presented at the
United Nations ECAFE Group Meeting on Social and Psychological Aspects of Fertility Behaviour, Bangkok, June 1974.

Matsumoto, Y. S., Koizumi, A., & Nohara, T. Condom use in
Japan. Studies in Family Planning, 1972, 3, 251-255.

Muramatsu, M. (Ed.). Japan's experience in family planning--
past and present. Tokyo: Family Planning Federation of
Japan, 1967.

Muramatsu, M. Japan, Country Profile, March 1971.

Muramatsu, M. Psychological research in family planning: A view from Asia. Paper presented at the Symposium on Psychological Research in Family Planning, XXth International Congress of Psychology, Tokyo, 1972.

Muramatsu, M. An analysis of factors in fertility control in Japan: An updated and revised version. Bulletin of the Institute of Public Health, 1973, 22, 228-236. (a)

Muramatsu, M. Incidence of abortion in Japan: Analyses and results. In International Union for the Scientific Study of Population, International Population Conference, Liège, 1973 (Vol. 2). Liège: Author, 1973. (b)

Muramatsu, M. Family planning: History, programs, and practice. In JOICFP (Eds.). Fertility and family planning in Japan. Tokyo: JOICFP, 1977.

Muramatsu, M., & Kuroda, T. Japan. In N. Berelson (Ed.), Population policy in developed countries. New York: McGraw-Hill, 1974.

Population Information Program. Condom--an old method meets a new social need. Population Reports, Series H, No. 1, December 1973.

Population Information Program. The modern condom--a quality product for effective contraception. Population Reports, Series H, No. 2, May 1974.

Population Problems Research Council, The Mainichi Newspapers. Summaries of ninth (1967), tenth (1969), eleventh (1971), twelfth (1973), and thirteenth (1975) surveys. Tokyo: Author, 1968, 1971, 1972, 1974.

Potts, M. The glorious Japanese condom. Paper presented at the UN ECAFE Expert Group Meeting on Social and Psychological Aspects of Fertility, Bangkok, June 1974.

Roht, L. H., & Aoyama, H. Induced abortion and its sequelae: Prevalence and associations with the outcome of pregnancy. International Journal of Epidemiology, 1973, 2, 103-113.

Tietze, C., & Dawson, D. Induced abortion: A factbook. Reports on Population/Family Planning, December 1973.

Tietze, C., & Lewit, S. Abortion. Scientific American, 1969, 220, 21-27.

United Nations. <u>Demographic Yearbook 1971.</u> New York: Author, 1972.

UNESCO. <u>Statistical Yearbook 1971.</u> Paris: Author, 1972.

Westoff, C. F. The modernization of U.S. contraceptive practice. <u>Family Planning Perspectives,</u> 1972, <u>3</u>(3), 8-12.

8

Patterns of Abortion
and Contraceptive Practice
in Hungary*

András Klinger and Egon Szabady

Editors' Note: The series of surveys on fertility intentions, contraceptive practices,
and abortion seeking conducted by the Hungarian Central Statistical Office since the late
1950s have yielded a continuing flow of infor-
mative findings on demographic, socioeconomic,
health, and psychosocial factors. Of particular importance are the changes in patterns of
fertility regulation noted after the implementation of the October 1973 population policy decisions, which restricted availability
of elective abortions, increased financial
aid to families with children, and introduced
organized programs on health and family planning for newly married couples.

INTRODUCTION

In Hungary, as in other industrialized countries, the
birthrate has declined significantly over the past 25 years,
falling below replacement levels in the 1960s and early 1970s.
As one result, the present aim of Hungarian population policy
is a gradual increase in the number of births, at least to ensure replacement of the population, which would otherwise become skewed toward the old. Figures for 1975 show increases
in the major indicators of population growth, but analysis of

*The Transnational Family Research Institute consulted
with Hungarian colleagues on the design and analysis of the
1970-1971 pilot surveys of psychological factors in repeated
abortion seeking, and assisted in drafting questions designed
to explore behavioral differences between aborting and contracepting women for the April 1974 TCS Survey.

of available preliminary data for 1976 suggests that this
growth may not be permanent (Klinger, 1977).

It is the purpose of this chapter to review changing
patterns in abortion and contraceptive practices as reflected
in the continuing surveys conducted by the Hungarian Central
Statistical Office since the late 1950s. Although content,
sampling, and survey techniques have varied to a certain extent, the data from these studies permit a comparison of
changes over nearly two decades (Klinger, 1977). To the extent possible, consideration will be given to socioeconomic,
psychosocial, and health implications of the findings, and to
special studies on repeated abortion-seeking behavior.

In 1960, the Hungarian crude birthrate of 15 per 1,000
population and the general fertility rate of 59 per 1,000
women of reproductive age (15-49) were both about one-third of
those registered at the start of regular data collection in
the 1880s. Contraception accounts for most of this evident
increase in birth control. It is estimated that of 1,000
women of reproductive age, the numbers becoming pregnant annually dropped from about 200-230 in the 1880s to 130-140 in the
second half of the 1960s. However, the important role of induced abortion is evidenced in the decline in the proportion
of pregnancies ending in birth, from an estimated two-thirds
to three-quarters 80 years ago to 43 percent by 1960. In 1976,
induced abortions still comprised 51 percent of all registered
obstetrical events (see Table 8-1).

ABORTION TRENDS

Abortion virtually on request became legal in Hungary
on June 3, 1956. Although the medical commissions established
to authorize abortions were expected to try to dissuade women
from apparently unjustifiable abortions, in practice the commissions generally granted permission if applicants insisted.
From a medical point of view, this law change proved beneficial to some extent. Pregnancy interruptions in hospitals or
maternity homes replaced the estimated 100,000-150,000 annual
abortions formerly performed illegally in poor sanitary conditions. Abortion-related mortality and morbidity were reduced to new low levels. Legalization also encouraged recourse
to abortion among those women who otherwise would have been
deterred by its high cost and illegality. Legal abortions rose
to a peak of 206,800 in 1969, while annual births fell to a low
of 130,100 in 1962 and rose again to about 154,300 in 1969
(see Table 8-1). For some women repeated abortions--often several in one year--became the major means of birth control. According to surveys of the late 1960s and early 1970s, these

Table 8-1

Total Live Births and Incidence of Induced
Abortion in Hungary, 1955-1976

Year	Live Births	Incidence of Induced Abortion			
		Number	Per 1,000 Women Aged 15-49	Per 1,000 Live Births	Per 1,000 Total Obstetrical Events
1955	210,400	35,400	14	168	120
1956[a]	192,800	82,500	33	428	260
1957	167,200	123,400	49	738	370
1958	158,400	145,600	58	919	420
1959	151,200	152,400	61	1,008	450
1960	146,500	162,200	65	1,108	470
1961	140,400	170,000	69	1,211	490
1962	130,100	163,700	66	1,259	500
1963	132,300	173,800	70	1,313	510
1964	132,100	184,400	74	1,396	520
1965	133,100	180,300	72	1,356	520
1966	138,500	186,800	73	1,349	520
1967	148,900	187,500	72	1,259	500
1968	154,400	201,100	76	1,302	510
1969	154,300	206,800	78	1,340	520
1970	151,800	192,300	72	1,268	510
1971	150,600	187,400	69	1,244	510
1972	153,300	179,400	67	1,168	490
1973	156,200	169,700	63	1,086	480
1974[b]	186,300	102,000	38	548	318
1975	194,200	96,200	36	495	300
1976	185,400	94,700	36	511	308

Note. Annual statistics provided by Central Hungarian Statistical Office, Budapest.
[a]Abortion on request legalized June 3, 1956.
[b]Population policy measures instituted January 1, 1974.

D&C abortions increased the chances of prematurity and, hence, perinatal deaths among subsequent births.

Since 1970, the level of induced abortions has declined with the increasing use of oral contraceptives--a decline made more significant by the relative increase in the number of women of reproductive age in this period. Between 1969 and 1976, the ratio of legal abortions per 1,000 live births dropped from 1,340 to 511, and the legal abortion rate per 1,000 women aged 15-49 declined from 78 to 36 (see Table 8-1).

Abortion was a mass phenomenon with unfavorable implications for the health of women and their subsequently-born infants. For instance, the proportion of women aborting their first pregnancies--which can be considered especially harmful for the outcome of later pregnancies--amounted to 18 percent among legal abortors in 1976. It was estimated in a 1966 survey of women 15-49 years old that 67 percent of those who had ever experienced abortion had terminated their first pregnancies. Seventy-five percent of women having repeat abortions in 1975 reported that their most recent obstetrical event also had been an induced abortion, with one-third of these events occurring no more than one year previously. Although the large majority of abortions in Hungary are performed before the thirteenth week of pregnancy, a less salutary statistic is that in 1975 over 80 percent of women left the health institution on the day of the abortion. The potential danger of this practice lies in the fact that 62 percent of Hungary's economically active women are manual workers who, having not taken sick leave, probably would return to work on the following day.

Of the women having induced abortions in 1975, about 59 percent reported not having used contraception previous to pregnancy. A further 15 percent used birth control only irregularly. Of those who had contracepted regularly before becoming pregnant, 43 percent took oral pills. Thirty percent had used the pill during the previous year, but a large proportion had stopped contracepting for reasons other than the desire to become pregnant--presumably because of side effects.

POPULATION POLICY MEASURES

The situation regarding abortion, contraception, and fertility in Hungary changed markedly as a result of the October 1973 Decision of the Council of Ministers on the Tasks of Population Policy. Coming into effect in January 1974, this decision introduced a sweeping range of measures designed to raise average family size to 2.3-2.5 children (to keep fertility above replacement level), to promote the use of effective contraception, and to lower the incidence of induced abortion "in order to decrease significantly its harmful impact on the health of mother and descendants." Pregnancy termination is still permitted in cases of potential danger to a woman's health or life, risk of a deformed fetus, rape, incest, age of woman over 40 (under December 31, 1978, authorization may be given to women over 35) and in such "reasonable" circumstances as unmarried status, lack of proper housing, husband's military service or imprisonment, and for "serious social reasons." Abortion is now more difficult to obtain for married women with less than three living children. The fees for abortions performed for other than medical reasons (medical abortions continue to be free) have been raised from the former 300 FT (about US $13) to 600-1,000 FT, "to cover completely the actual costs"--but after pregnancy termination working women must receive two days sick leave (with social security benefit).

To encourage the substitution of effective contraception for abortion, the decree empowers most general practitioners to prescribe oral contraceptives (formerly limited to gynecologists in clinics or hospitals); stipulates that marriage licences may be issued to couples under age 35 only after they present proof that they have received contraceptive training and supplies from a physician; greatly extends the network of family planning consultation and supply; and calls for introduction of courses on sex, family life, family planning, and contraception at all school levels, including university, and as part of military training.

In a 1974 nationwide public opinion survey conducted by district nurses visiting 2,000 households selected at random, the majority of the 3,837 interviewees were well informed about the new population policy measures. The greater availability of modern contraceptives is viewed by most women as compensating for the restrictions placed on authorized pregnancy termination. There was also nearly universal endorsement of sex education, at the latest in early adolescence.

The immediate results of these measures (and simultaneous increases in family and child welfare payments and other fertility incentives) are evident in the 45 percent drop in legal abortions, from 169,700 in 1973 to 94,700 in 1976; an increase from 11 percent to about 20 percent in the proportion of women aged 17-49 using oral contraceptives; and a rise in the crude birthrate from 15-18 per 1,000 population. It should be noted, however, that the proportion of spontaneous abortions treated in hospitals rose to 22 percent of all registered abortions, from an average of 13-14 percent for the preceding three years.

SOURCES OF DATA ON ABORTION

With pregnancy terminations performed legally in
health institutions since 1956 and the more recent spread of
contraception requiring medical control (and thus registration),
data have become available for extensive study of the prevalence and characteristics of abortion in Hungary and of its
health effects on women and their subsequently-born children.
Such studies have been based on data collected jointly by the
Hungarian Central Statistical Office and the Ministry of
Health, drawn from the following sources:

1. Abortion Registration

Continuous, overall information on abortion is available from the summary reports submitted by health institutions
from 1956 to 1970 and, since 1971, from obligatory individual
records on induced and spontaneous abortions, incorporated
within the "accounting system" for the whole country and sent
monthly to the Central Statistical Office. For induced abortions, these individual records include reports by both the
abortion committees (covering denied as well as authorized
abortion applications since 1974) and by the obstetrical facilities performing the abortions. These data facilitate analysis of the demographic, health, social, and other characteristics of all women having induced and spontaneous abortions,
as well as continuous monitoring of abortion totals.

2. Sample Surveys of Women Experiencing an Obstetrical Event

Data for more probing analyses of the correlates of
abortion have come from a series of sample surveys conducted
under the auspices of the Hungarian Central Statistical Office.
The first type has been based on samples drawn from groups of
women who have just undergone an obstetrical event, such as a
live or stillbirth or induced abortion, or who have received
pregnancy-related treatment in an authorized health institution. Surveys of this type include the following:

1958 TCS. As part of a pilot KAP study (designated TCS, the
abbreviation for fertility, family planning, and birth control
in Hungarian), data were collected during 1957-1958 and 1959
from case histories, questionnaires, and interviews of some
2,000 women having abortions at 12 hospitals throughout the
country.

*October 1960 and April 1964--One-Month Patient Statistics on
Abortion.* Case histories were collected and interviews conducted for all women having abortions, giving birth, or being

treated for spontaneous abortion (or ectopic pregnancy in
1960) in authorized facilities during October 1960 and again
during April 1964: 26,157 in 1960 and 27,915 in 1964. This
provided information on the characteristics of abortors as opposed to women choosing to carry pregnancy to term, but excluded those giving birth at home (5.4 percent of total births
in 1963), successful contraceptors, and the sterile.

Sample Surveys of 1968, 1970-1971. Studies on the possible
association between abortion and premature births and perinatal
mortality have been based on data covering 20 percent of all
institutionalized obstetrical events (live and stillbirths,
induced and spontaneous abortions) in 1968, and on all premature births (weight under 2,500 grams), stillbirths, deaths
up to six days; and, as a control group, every fifth full-
term delivery (2,500 grams and over) from individual records
for July 1970 to December 1971 at obstetrical clinics and de-
partments of Budapest and leading country hospitals.

1970-1971 Pilot Surveys of Repeated Abortion Seeking. Pilot
surveys to probe the psychological aspects of repeated abortion seeking involved in-depth interviews of 279 women hospitalized for delivery, abortion, or gynecological treatment at
six health institutions in March 1970 and 218 similar patients
at three hospitals and three outpatient clinics in winter
1970-1971. A segment of the 1974 TCS survey was also concerned
with psychological aspects of abortion.

3. Representative Retrospective Family Planning and
Contraceptive Surveys

        Data derived from survey samples of women not selected
on the basis of having just undergone an obstetrical event
serve for the analysis of other aspects of induced abortion:

1966 TCS. In this first full-scale KAP study in Hungary,
nurses conducted home interviews with 8,800 married women aged
15-49, drawn from a two-stage random sample of 0.5 percent of
the country's households.

1974 TCS. This April 1974 survey, similarly based on a random
national sample of dwellings, covered 3,142 married women under the age of 35 and subsamples of women who had used oral
contraceptives continuously throughout 1972 (1,142), or had an
induced abortion in 1972 (1,117), with special questions designed to examine behavioral differences between aborting and
contracepting women. Another TCS survey was conducted in 1977.

4. Longitudinal Prospective Surveys of Married Couples

        The Hungarian TCS surveys, to date, have employed the
traditional KAP retrospective survey methodology of

investigating past and current fertility and birth control attitudes and behavior based on a one-time interview of a representative cross section of women of childbearing age. Although this method gives an overall picture of trends up to and at the time of the survey, it also contains the possibility for bias in the data collected. Asked to report on past fertility and birth control history and attitudes (e.g., number of children planned at the time of marriage) at varying times after the events, respondents may tend to forget or to rationalize "after the fact." This is particularly serious in the case of reporting on fetal wastage, through either spontaneous or induced abortion. To obviate this potential source of data bias, and to complement the findings of the TCS surveys, two prospective surveys of fertility/family planning behavior and attitudes in Hungary are currently being conducted. Based on the marriage cohorts of 1966 and 1974, findings from these surveys can give a picture of trends only during the period covered by the investigation and limited to the subpopulation from which the sample is selected, which is necessarily much smaller, owing to the costs involved in tracing individual respondents for reinterview. However, such continuous, prospective observation yields much more accurate information.

1966 HL Longitudinal Survey of Couples Marrying in 1966. Separate interviews with each spouse were conducted on the day of registering the intention to marry, by marriage registrars, of a random national sample of 5.2 percent of all couples marrying during 1966 (4,822). In 1969, in 1972, and in 1975, district nurses reinterviewed all women from the original sample who could be traced and who were available and willing to respond. The follow-up rate was high, with 96 percent of the original women respondents accounted for in the 1969 data collection and 92 percent in 1972. Because the aim of this survey is to describe changes in fertility behavior and attitudes occurring with increasing marital duration, questions on family planning were asked and/or processed only for women still living with their husbands, born in 1927 or later, and for whom questionnaires were fully completed on each occasion. In 1969, this constituted 82 percent of the original 1966 sample of women. The number declined to approximately 75 percent in 1972 and to 70 percent in 1975.

1974 HL Longitudinal Survey of Couples Marrying in 1974. Taking advantage of the compulsory premarital counseling introduced in 1974, a random sample of 10 percent of couples registered for such consultations in the latter half of 1974 (5 percent of the 1974 marriage cohort), in which the woman was less than 35 (92 percent of women entering into marriage), was interviewed by local health visitors and medical doctors: a total sample of 5,540. As in the 1966 longitudinal survey,

women will be reinterviewed at three-year intervals for information on fertility-relevant experience in these intervals.

5. Sample Surveys of Women Using Oral Contraceptives

Some information on the relationship of induced abortion and the practice of modern contraception in Hungary was
gleaned from two surveys designed primarily to study the demographic and health characteristics of women using oral contra-
ceptives--efficacy and possible side effects. In a survey
conducted by the Demographic Research Institute of the Central
Statistical Office, retrospective data were collected for some
50,000 women using the oral contraceptive Infecundin between
May 1, 1967, and March 31, 1969, and on April 15, 1969. Three-
year follow-up data have been collected for all women reques-
ing Infecundin or Bisecurin oral pills since August 1970 at
about 50 consultation centers throughout the country.

PSYCHOSOCIAL ASPECTS OF ABORTION
SEEKING IN HUNGARY

The data sources enumerated have permitted extensive
analysis of the demographic, socioeconomic, and health aspects
of abortion in Hungary. However, psychosocial aspects of
abortion--the topic of this volume--have been specifically investigated only in the 1970-1971 pilot surveys of repeated
abortion seeking (Szabady & Klinger, 1970) and in subsamples
of the 1974 TCS survey. Inferences about probable psychological determinants of abortion seeking can be drawn from these
studies. As a first step, we trace the development of the
predominant two-child family in Hungary, which implies a compelling need for effective birth control by whatever means may
be available.

The Two-Child Family

Statistics available since the 1880s from censuses and
vital registration show that in the last decades of the nine-
teenth century, the average family size in Hungary was close
to six. As seen in Table 8-2 (column 3), this average, or
total, fertility rate, based on annual age-specific fertility
rates, dropped below three by 1940. The average order of
birth, a truer measure of actual family size, remained a little
higher (column 4), indicating that the three-child family was
most characteristic of the period immediately preceding World
War II. Following World War II, annual fertility rates rose
somewhat--particularly in 1954, as a result of a temporary increase in births following strict enforcement of existing laws

Table 8-2

Measures of Fertility, Hungary, 1940-1974

Year	Live Births		Total Fertility Rate[a]	Average Order of Birth[b]
	Per 1,000 Population	Per 1,000 Women Aged 15-49		
	(1)	(2)	(3)	(4)
1940	20	70	2.45	2.89
1950	21	77	2.57	2.51
1952	20	74	2.47	2.46
1954	23	88	2.97	2.50
1960	15	59	2.02	2.18
1962	13	53	1.80	2.15
1970	15	57	1.96	1.88
1973	15	58	1.95	1.86
1974	18	70	2.32	1.89
1975	18	73	2.38	1.87
1976	17	70	2.26	1.84

[a]Average number of children a woman would bear if she survived to the end of her childbearing years exposed to the age-specific fertility rates of the year in question

[b]Calculated from annual order-specific birthrates

against illegal abortion in 1953. In 1962, the total fertility rate dropped to a low of 1.8. Although this sharp decline was facilitated by legalization of abortion in 1956, it was ultimately motivated by rapidly changing social and economic conditions, which depressed family size goals.

Socioeconomic Changes

In 1949, Hungary was predominantly an agricultural, rural country as it had been for 1,000 years. Over half the

labor force worked in agriculture and 62 percent of the population lived in rural villages. By 1972, only 17 percent of
the labor force were in agriculture and nearly 70 percent in
industry or construction. The proportion of population living in rural areas dropped to 52 percent. These radical
changes in social and residential mobility raised educational
levels and, in turn, the cultural and economic aspirations of
the population, particularly among women. By 1970, 70 percent
of women aged 15-54 were employed outside the home, including
81 percent of those aged 20-24 and 77 percent of those aged
20-39. Educational attainment grew more rapidly among women
than men. Four times as many women completed secondary school
in 1970 as did 20 years earlier, compared to a doubling of
this level among men. Reinforced by a drastic decline in in-
fant mortality, from about 100 per 1,000 live births in 1948
to 30 in 1976, and the increased cost of raising children,
these dramatic shifts inevitably altered family life patterns
and family size desires.

Recent Fertility Trends

        Annual fertility rates began to rise again about 1967
from the low levels of 1962-1965. This was partly due to a
growing proportion of women of childbearing age, but more in
response to a wide range of pronatalist measures instituted
by the government in the late 1960s. For instance, child care
leave for working women was introduced in 1967, ensuring a
partly-paid leave until a child's third birthday. At the end
of 1976, 287,000 women were on child care leave; live births
to working women as a percent of total live births rose from
59 percent in 1967 to 88 percent in 1976. As seen in Table
8-2, average family size, or the total fertility rate, just under two before 1973, jumped to 2.3 in 1976. The 1974 increase
in births was caused primarily by the increase in the number
of second-borns, which accounted for 59 percent of the gain
over 1973 births. The continuing low level of birth order
suggests that this resulted from a shift to earlier timing of
second births in response to the new population measures of
January 1974, and that average completed family size will remain at two for women able to realize their family size desires (Klinger, 1977). First-born births also rose in 1974
because of the proportionate increase in youngest, most fertile
age groups among women of childbearing age--those women born
during the "baby boom" of 1953-1954.

        The convergence on the two-child family is also demon-
strated by changes in the percentage distribution of live
births by birth order. The proportion of first and second order births generally increased steadily between 1954 and 1976,
while the proportion of third and higher order births declined

or stagnated. In 1974, only second-born births markedly increased their share of total births. Further, the convergence is in no way due to an increase in childless marriages. In fact, the proportion of childless women of reproductive age dropped from 18 percent in 1949 to 14 percent in 1970.

Family Size Plans and Desires

That this convergence on the two-child family in actual practice well reflects current fertility attitudes in Hungary is evident from findings of the various family planning surveys on the number of children planned at marriage and desired and ideal family size. The similarity of questionnaire content and concept from survey to survey permits reasonable comparison of such findings, despite the differences noted in survey methodology and sample population.

As seen in Table 8-3, the average number of children planned at marriage for women marrying under age 35 was 2.25 among respondents in the 1958 TCS. By 1966, this had dropped to 2.05 according to the TCS survey of that year, and to 1.89 among respondents interviewed on the day of their marriage (1966 HL). The average rose again to 2.18 among women about to be married, queried in the 1974 HL; the proportion of women planning three children had increased while those planning one child had decreased compared to eight years earlier. However, the data clearly show the growing predominance of the two-child family in the plans of newlyweds, from 64 percent in 1958 to 73 percent in 1974. The married women in the 1974 TCS survey reported an average of 2.09 children planned at the beginning of the marriage, with 74 percent preferring a two-child family. By 1977 there was a slight decrease to 2.05 children, with an increase among those preferring a one-child family from 10 percent to 12 percent.

A better indication of family size ideas than the number planned at marriage, which can change considerably, is the number of children desired altogether, shown for the different survey dates in the lower part of Table 8-3. This is derived from the sum of the respondent's children living at the time of the interview and the number desired additionally. The trend here is similar, if less marked. Between 1958 and 1972, the proportion of couples desiring two children grew from 49 percent to 71 percent, while those wanting three or more fell from 29 percent to 12 percent. Since 1972, this process has been reversed. Nevertheless, relatively more respondents queried in the TCS of 1977 desire two children (65 percent) than did those of 1966 or 1958 (56 percent and 49 percent, respectively), and fewer prefer three or more (14 percent) than at the earlier dates (23 percent in 1966 and 29 percent in 1958).

Table 8-3

Percentage Distribution of Married Women under Age 35 by
Number of Children Planned at Marriage and Desired
Subsequently: Hungary, 1958-1975

	Percentage Distribution of Women Planning/Desiring					Average Number of Children Planned
	0	1	2	3	4 or more	
			Children			
Number of children planned at marriage						
1958/TCS-58	1	13	64	17	5	2.25
1966/TCS-66	1	14	70	12	3	2.05
1966/HL-66	1	20	70	8	1	1.89
1974/HL-74	0	6	73	19	2	2.18
1974/TCS-74	0	10	74	14	2	2.09
1977/TCS-77	0	12	75	13	2	2.05
Total number of children desired						
1958/TCS-58	4	18	49	18	11	2.33
1966/TCS-66	1	20	56	16	7	2.10
1972/HL-66	1	16	71	10	2	1.97
1974/TCS-74	1	18	63	14	4	2.06
1975/HL-66	3	20	60	13	4	1.97
1977/TCS-77	2	17	65	14	3	2.02

The two-child convergence is further confirmed by data
from the 1966 TCS and 1974 TCS on the family size considered
"ideal," independently of couples' personal plans or desires.
In these eight years, the proportion of respondents considering two children as ideal rose from 60 percent to 68 percent.
The three-child family ideal dropped from 30 percent to 22
percent, and the one-child ideal doubled from 3 percent to 6
percent.

Abortion Trends by Number of Living
Children and Marital Status

The two-child norm is strongly reflected in the national series of annual abortion ratios per 1,000 live births
by number of living children (see Table 8-4).

Table 8-4

Legal Abortions Per 1,000 Live Births by
Number of Living Children:
Hungary, 1964-1975

Number of Living Children	Legal Abortions Per 1,000 Live Births								
	1964	1968	1969	1970	1971	1972	1973	1974	1975
0	420	400	450	430	450	450	430	290	270
1	1,470	1,290	1,350	1,240	1,180	1,080	960	340	280
2	4,300	4,870	5,120	5,090	5,010	4,660	4,090	1,870	1,760
3	3,770	4,150	4,340	3,910	3,680	3,420	3,260	1,970	1,950
4 or more	2,210	2,040	2,110	2,070	1,830	1,690	1,590	1,040	1,010

Since 1964, abortion ratios generally have been highest among
women with two living children, which suggests that two is the
number of children beyond which additional births are generally
most unacceptable to Hungarian women. The much lower abortion
ratios at zero and one parities relative to those at two, three,
and four or more further suggest that most Hungarian women
prefer to have at least two children. However, it can be seen
that the ratio of induced abortions to live births was relatively stable among childless women until the advent of the new
population policy measures in 1974. The proportion of childless women among all legal abortors in Hungary has risen
steadily in recent years, from 16.7 percent in 1969 to over 24
percent in 1975. This is perhaps associated with the trend in
abortion by marital status.

Since liberalization of abortion in 1956, the overwhelming majority of legal abortors in Hungary have been

married women. However, the proportion of unmarried women
among all those obtaining legal abortions has risen steadily
and in 1976 amounted to nearly one-third. This, in turn, is
perhaps associated with trends in age-specific legal abortion
rates. As seen in Table 8-5, before 1972 annual abortions
per 1,000 women continued to increase among Hungarian women
aged 19 or less (with the exception of 1971), while rates for
older women, at least to age 35, reached a peak in 1971 and
declined steadily thereafter. The continuing rise in legal
abortions among unmarried and teenage women may, of course,
reflect increasing sexual activity among such women. However,
the data also suggest that, while the availability of effective contraception, particularly orals, since 1968-1970 has
served increasingly to supplant abortion among married women
wishing to control their fertility (after two children), this
alternative was, at least initially, not as accessible to
young, unmarried women.

Table 8-5

Legal Abortions Per 1,000 Women by Age of Women:
Hungary, 1957-1975

Year	19 or less	20-24	25-29	30-34	35-39	40 or more
1957	15.2	76.2	94.7	77.1	57.9	17.2
1965	31.7	114.7	139.6	113.3	67.9	23.7
1969	39.2	137.6	156.3	123.8	74.7	24.0
1970	40.6	120.7	140.3	113.7	71.6	24.1
1971	37.1	118.6	127.0	109.4	75.1	29.6
1972	55.4	112.3	111.5	94.2	63.1	9.4
1973	38.3	98.3	105.6	95.1	68.5	14.0
1974	26.6	52.5	54.6	55.8	50.1	11.3
1975	26.5	50.0	51.6	51.7	47.1	10.7

There is some evidence that among oral contraceptors
the proportion of those 19 years and younger increased from
2.5 percent in 1970 to 6.4 percent in 1975. Within this group
of teenage women, the proportion of unmarried females grew
from 1.4 percent in 1970 to 5.5 percent by 1975. It is a

positive phenomenon that 80 percent of the teenage oral contraceptors in 1975 had no record of a previously induced abortion, compared to 66 percent in 1970. This trend contributed
to the observation that among teenagers the proportion of induced abortions per 1,000 females, after having gradually increased to 42 by 1972, declined to 27 by 1975.

Abortion and Contraception

Given the increasing concentration in actual practice
and desire on a family of no more than, if at least, two children, it is to be expected that findings from the series of
family planning surveys would reveal a concomitant increase in
the practice of birth control, whether by induced abortion or
contraception. And, indeed, these findings indicate that the
percentage of Hungarian married women of reproductive age currently practicing birth control rose from 76 percent in 1958
to 84 percent in 1966, and in 1974 could be estimated at
around 90 percent.

Decline in Abortion

The findings also indicate that until the mid-1960s
more women tended to combine contracpetion and induced abortion
than to rely exclusively on one or the other approach to fertility control, but that there is now an increasing shift from
abortion to contraception. In the 1958 TCS, 37 percent of all
respondents surveyed reported combined use of abortion and
contraception. This increased to 44 percent in the 1966 TCS,
probably as a result of abortion legalization in 1956, but
dropped to 26 percent in the 1969 reinterview of the 1966 longitudinal marriage sample. Concurrently, the proportion of
all respondents who reported induced abortion as their only
means of birth control dropped from 18 percent in 1958 to 14
percent in 1966 and 4 percent in 1969. A comparable drop in
abortion practice is evident from data on the percentage of
survey respondents having ever had an abortion, independently
of whether or not they also use contraception. More reliably
to compare such findings from the various populations sampled,
this trend is best noted among women aged 30-34 at the time of
the interview. Among women of this age, 66 percent in 1959
had had at least one induced abortion. There was a drop to 63
percent in the 1966 TCS and to 46 percent in the 1972 reinterview of the 1966 marriage sample.

Contraceptive Practice

The drop in abortion practice is clearly due to the
growing practice of contraception. More important, in recent
years there has been a shift to more reliable methods of modern

contraception, thus reducing the incidence of unplanned pregnancies and the need for abortion. Among TCS respondents aged
under 35 at the time, the percentage reporting current use of
contraception increased from 58 percent in 1958 to 75 percent
in 1977. About 76 percent of the 1966 marriage cohort were
contraceptors in 1975, nine years after marriage (see Table
8-6, left-hand panel). This table also portrays the even
greater shift in methods used.

The natural methods listed include rhythm, coitus interruptus, douching, and "others," such as prolonged breastfeeding and abstinence. Mechanical methods are the condom
(used since the beginning of the century), the diaphragm (introduced in 1949), and the intrauterine device (IUD). Available since 1971, the IUD is limited to women who have already
delivered a child or to women aged over 18 who should not become pregnant for medical reasons. Medical examination is required following the first menstrual period after insertion
and every six months thereafter. IUD use has not yet become
sufficiently widespread to have a measurable impact on the
abortion rate. The chemical methods of spermicidal jelly and
foam were first made available in 1954. Oral contraceptives
were introduced in 1967 with the Hungarian product Infecundin,
followed by Bisecurin in 1971 and Continuin in 1974. These
combination pills are available to all women over age 18 (and
to younger women who are married or have had a child or an induced abortion) by prescription only; a prior physical examination is required. At one time such examinations could be
done only by gynecologists at a specialized outpatient clinic
or hospital; laboratory tests were also required. Following
the 1973 Population Planning decree, district industrial plant
physicians, most of whom are general practitioners, were empowered to prescribe the pill and to decide whether laboratory
tests were necessary. Social insurance covers 85 percent of
the cost of pills, currently 3 Ft. (US $0.15) for a month's
supply. Although there are no laws prohibiting sterilization,
the operation is usually performed only for health reasons.

As can be seen in the right-hand panel of Table 8-6,
natural methods predominated before the introduction of pills,
and even increased from 67 percent to 70 percent between 1958
and 1966 as the primary method used by the contraceptors aged
under 35 interviewed in TCS surveys. In 1966 coitus interruptus was by far the most popular--62 percent of contracepting
couples employed this method--followed by condoms (17 percent).
In 1966 natural methods were most popular in rural areas; mechanical and chemical methods were more favored in urban areas.
This pattern of contraceptive use indicates that prior to the
introduction of oral contraceptives Hungarian couples wishing
to limit their fertility were forced to resort to induced

Table 8-6

Percentage Distribution of Married Women Aged under 35 Practicing Contraception, by Primary Method Used

Primary method of contraception	Primary contraceptive methods of 100 married women aged under 35							Primary contraceptive methods of 100 married women aged under 35 using contraception						
	1958 TCS	1966 TCS	1966 HL in 1969	1966 HL in 1972	1966 HL in 1975	1974 TCS	1977 TCS	1958 TCS	1966 TCS	1966 HL in 1969	1966 HL in 1972	1966 HL in 1975	1974 TCS	1977 TCS
Natural														
Rhythm	4	2	4	4	4	3	3	7	3	7	6	5	4	4
Coitus interruptus	30	42	28	26	19	26	17	52	62	42	35	25	35	23
Douching	4	3	3	1	1	1	0	7	5	4	1	1	2	1
Other	0	0	1	0	0	0	0	1	0	1	0	1	0	0
Together	38	47	36	31	24	30	20	67	70	54	42	32	41	28
Mechanical														
Condom	12	12	9	7	6	7	4	21	17	13	9	8	10	6
Diaphragm	3	4	2	1	1	2	1	5	6	3	2	1	2	2
IUD[a]	-	-	1	4	8	6	10	-	-	1	5	10	8	13
Other	0	0	1[b]	0	0	0	0	0	0	2[b]	1	0	0	0
Together	15	16	13	12	15	15	15	26	23	19	17	19	20	21
Chemical	3	3	1	1	1	1	1	5	4	2	2	1	2	1
Oral[a]	-	0	17	26	36	27	36	-	0	25	36	47	36	49
Sterilization[a]	-	1	0	1	-	1	3	-	2	0	1	-	1	-
Other and unknown	2	1	0	2	0	0	0	2	1	0	2	1	0	1
Total	58	68	67	73	76	74	75	100	100	100	100	100	100	100

Note. From Hungarian Family Planning Surveys, 1958-1974.

[a] Dash indicates not yet in use.

[b] C-film, introduced and used 1968-1970, withdrawn because of ineffectiveness.

abortion because of the unavailability of effective and appropriate contraceptive methods, not because of carelessness or irresponsibility.

By 1977, pill use rose to 49 percent among the general population of married contracepting women aged under 35 (TCS 1974), while all other methods declined in popularity. Although coitus interruptus declined the most, it was still practiced by 23 percent of couples. Natural methods combined were favored by fewer contracepting couples (28 percent) than the pill (49 percent). Data from the 1975 reinterview of the 1966 marriage cohort reveal that, after nine years of marriage 47 percent of women under 35 practicing contraception were taking pills; half of the 1972 pill takers had used only natural methods or no contraception three years previously. However, the longitudinal data also showed that only 59 percent of the respondents taking pills in 1969 were still doing so three years later; 22 percent changed in the interval to a traditional method and 19 percent had stopped contraception, mostly in order to have a child.

When former pill users were asked in 1972 why they had dropped this method, 41 percent mentioned unpleasant side effects and 24 percent considered them harmful to health. (Eighteen percent were currently pregnant, breast feeding, or wanted to become pregnant.) The majority of respondents who had not yet tried oral contraception mentioned the same reasons for not using this method.

CHARACTERISTICS OF ABORTION SEEKING

Pilot Survey of Psychological Factors in Repeated Abortion Seeking, 1970

The first (March 1970) of the two studies on psychological factors associated with repeated abortion-seeking behavior was designed as a pilot study for a broader effect to identify groups of women at high risk for repeated abortions who might then be given special counseling to encourage more effective use of contraceptives. The survey was primarily of methodological importance and the data obtained can be considered only tentatively of statistical importance, particularly because there was no matched control sample of women who had shifted from abortion to more efficient contraception. To some extent, this survey and its companion of winter 1970-1971 served as predecessors of the 1974 survey of subsamples of women who had continuously used pills or had an abortion in 1972.

The survey covered 279 women of reproductive age (78 percent aged 20-34) who had just given birth (30 percent), had an abortion (29 percent), or received gynecological treatment (41 percent) in three university women's clinics and three Budapest general hospitals. Conducted by physicians (except for one midwife), the interviews of one to one-and-a-half hours covered 92 questions, of which 51 percent were on psychological factors and induced abortion. The women generally seemed willing to answer, in part perhaps because of their recognition of the confidentiality of the physician-patient relationship. However, even in these favorable circumstances, many women either did not reply to the psychological questions, particularly those regarding sexual life, or else gave responses tending to reflect their views of socially acceptable behavioral norms.

The prevalence of induced abortion in Hungary by 1970 is evident from the finding that virtually three-quarters of the respondents (74.6 percent) had had at least one abortion, with nearly one-quarter (23.7 percent) having had three or more. By the end of reproductive life, in the age group of 40-49 years, little more than one-tenth (13.3 percent) of the respondents had never had an induced abortion. The study, however, showed that this was due not to a preference for abortion but to the poor quality or inadequate use of contraceptive methods.

The women's attitude toward induced abortion was examined in three respects. First they were asked if they would be willing to undergo an induced abortion in the future. More than half of the total group (56.8 percent) responded positively, with the lowest proportions among those who had never had an abortion (46.2 percent), who were mostly younger women, and highest among the mostly older women who had had three or more (72.7 percent). These findings suggest that women become accustomed over time to the idea of pregnancy interruption.

To the question, "What would you do if the prevailing legal system were abolished?" the great majority (78.1 percent) replied that they would use a more effective contraceptive method than the one currently employed. This suggests that a completely permissive abortion system induces some contraceptive neglect and that stricter regulations might encourage more responsible attitudes. On the other hand, previous fertility research demonstrates that, over the long run, prohibition of abortion increases the number of illegal abortions, although this may hold less true at the present time with readier access to more convenient and effective modern contraceptives.

The respondents were also asked, "What would you do
if you were pregnant and interruption of pregnancy were no
longer permitted?" Slightly more than half (58.6 percent)
would continue their pregnancy, while 41.4 percent would try
to terminate pregnancy in some way, though mostly be seeking
private medical help rather than attempting self-induced abortion. The more abortions a respondent has had the less likely
she is to tolerate an unwanted pregnancy. However, the majority of respondents who had three or more abortions (54.4
percent) said they would bear the child if legal terminations
were difficult to obtain.

The number of induced abortions is correlated with attitudes towards sexual intercourse. The possibility that sexual intercourse can lead to undesired pregnancy and, thus, to
an abortion, never occurs to the majority of women with no
previous abortions (52.1 percent), but this fear increases
with numbers of abortions. Only 7.6 percent of women who have
experienced three or more abortions are not afraid of getting
pregnant. Two-thirds either always fear it or are disturbed
by this possibility during sexual intercourse.

After becoming pregnant, the relationship of respondents with their husbands becomes more intimate. This was the
case without exception among women with no prior abortions and
still characteristic of three-fifths of those who had had
three or more.

Husbands' reactions to pregnancy were also queried.
Husbands of women who have not had an abortion overwhelmingly
prefer continuing the pregnancy (92.5 percent) or leave it to
the wife to decide (6.5 percent). Generally, younger couples
belong to this category. However, husbands' desire for the
wife to carry the pregnancy to term decreases considerably after the first abortion and does not change significantly with
an increasing number of abortions. In the sample as a whole,
less than one-third of husbands (28.9 percent) urged their
wives to continue pregnancy. In over half the cases (56.4
percent), husbands agree with their wives' decision to terminate pregnancies and only 2.8 percent remain indifferent. With
an increasing number of abortions, the husband leaves the decision more and more to his wife. This is the case for only
6.5 percent after one abortion, but increases to 15 percent
after three or more. Just 1.4 percent of husbands deny their
responsibility in pregnancy.

Two-thirds of couples decide jointly on interruption
of pregnancy; wives decide alone in almost all other cases,
and only rarely (0.5 percent) do husbands decide without regard for the wife's feelings. An increase in numbers of

previous abortions is associated with an increase in wives'
responsibilities and rights in decision making and a decline
in common responsibility and joint decision making.

Findings from the 1974 TCS Subsurvey

As previously mentioned, the 1974 TCS national random
sample included 3,142 married women under age 35 with subsamples of 1,142 women who had used oral contraceptives continuously throughout 1972 and 1,117 women who had a recorded
induced abortion during that year.

Three socio-occupational groups are widely recognized
in Hungary: agricultural workers, nonagricultural manual
workers, and skilled workers. No differences were noted in
occupational groupings between women having one or two abortions and women having three or more terminations.

There have been some suggestions in the psychiatric
literature that being prone to spontaneous abortion may be indicative of rejection of the female role. No relationship was
noted between number of spontaneous abortions and number of induced abortions, although perhaps in some cases spontaneous
abortion may not occur if the induced abortion is performed at
an early stage.

Interpretation of the responses to attitudinal survey
questions is more difficult. In the basic sample of married
women, 41 percent disapproved of abortion for unmarried pregnant women. Among married women who had three or more abortions, 35 percent expressed similar disapproval. Since it
seems unlikely that married women have less empathy for pregnant unmarried women, it can only be surmised that the response
given was deemed more socially acceptable by the respondent.
In actual practice, unmarried pregnant women usually receive
routine authorization for elective abortion.

Elective abortion among married women was approved by
60 percent of the basic sample, 65 percent among women taking
pills, 63 percent among women having had one or two abortions,
and 73 percent among women with three or more terminations.
Ninety-four percent of the basic sample approved induced abortion in cases of physical risk for the pregnant woman; 90 percent approved if the conception resulted from rape. However,
in cases of "bad" socioeconomic circumstances, only 75 percent
of the basic sample approved compared to 80 percent of women
having had one or two abortions and 86 percent of women with
three or more terminations.

Comparison of Abortion Findings from the 1966 TCS
and 1966-1972 Longitudinal Survey

Comparison of findings from these two surveys, with
due controls for marital duration and woman's age, casts some
light on recent trends in attitudes toward abortion and birth
control practices. The most notable difference is in the degree of frankness in reporting abortions. The 1966 TCS attempted to measure the prevalence of abortion both by direct
questioning and by independent analysis of respondents' fertility history. Although abortion had by then been legal for
a decade, the numbers of abortions per live births for the
years 1960-1965 directly reported by respondents in this survey amounted to only 50-56 percent of the actual abortion/
birth ratios for these years available from the continuing
hospital statistics. In addition, only 28.6 percent of the
1966 TCS respondents directly reported having had an abortion.
In examining the data for evidence of induced abortion, respondents were classified as "induced abortion unknown" if
their fertility histories contained long intervals that could
not be explained on the basis of replies to other questions
(marital separation, sterility, contraception). Nearly 30
percent of respondents fell into this category. Thus, it was
estimated that 58 percent of this representative cross section
of married women aged 15-49 had had at least one abortion by
1966. Among respondents married six-to-seven years, it was
estimated that some 42 percent might have had an abortion, but
only 34 percent directly reported this. By contrast, in 1969,
after three years of marriage, 30.1 percent of respondents in
the 1966 longitudinal survey directly reported having had an
abortion (exceeding the 28.6 percent of direct admissions for
the total 1966 TCS sample). In 1972, after six years of marriage, this rose to 41.3 percent, and in 1975, after nine
years of marriage, to 47 percent. It is likely that under the
effect of repeated interviewing, the concealment of induced
abortions decreased considerably, particularly among younger
women.

Abortion-Contraceptive Practice by
Martial Duration and Age

Findings on birth control practices by marital duration
show similar patterns in the two surveys, although these can
be compared only for the first three years of marriage and, of
course, refer to differing periods before 1966 in the case of
the 1966 TCS and only to 1966-1969 for the longitudinal survey.
In the first year of marriage, just over one-third (40 percent)
of the 1966 TCS respondents had used contraception and less
than one-third (31.0 percent) of the 1966 marriage cohort.

Abortions were very rare in both groups. After three years of
marriage, 70.1 percent of the 1966 TCS respondents were then
using contraception--19.0 percent in combination with abortion.
At the same marital duration, 66.5 percent of the 1966 marriage
cohort were practicing contraception, 79.2 percent had contracepted at some time since marriage--25.9 percent in combination
with abortion. These data again indicate that almost all Hungarian married couples attempt conscientiously to control fertility first by contraception, but were forced, prior to 1969
at least, to resort to abortion because of deficiencies in
their contraceptive knowledge or the methods used.

        Data from the two surveys on birth control practices
by age show highest proportions of women practicing birth control among women aged approximately 23-32, with the majority
of women in these age groups using only contraception. In
both surveys, some three-quarters of the youngest married
women also practiced birth control, but apparently with less
success--in the 1969 survey, for example, over 30 percent of
women aged 17-22 either combined contraception with abortion
(26.2 percent) or used abortion only (4.1 percent). For older
married women, contraceptive use declines and induced abortion
increases. In the 1969 survey, use of contraception exclusively dropped from a high of 57.1 percent among women aged
23-27 to a low of 30.1 percent among women aged 38-42. Use of
abortion rose from a low of 2.8 percent to only 14.2 percent.

Abortion Differentials by Urban-Rural
Residence and Occupation

        As seen in Table 8-7, both the 1966 TCS and the 1972
and 1975 reinterviews with the 1966 marriage cohort indicate
that abortion experience and the average number of abortions
per woman reporting abortion are highest in the capital, Budapest; somewhat lower in provincial towns; and lowest in rural
villages. This differential is partially a reflection of differences in family size desires: in 1972, respondents living in Budapest desired an average total of 1.77 children;
women in provincial towns desired 1.90; rural women desired
2.08. However, because the percentage of respondents practicing contraception was not much higher in urban than in rural
areas, it is also an indication that urban women in Hungary
are much more determined to realize their smaller family plans
than rural women, even at the cost of undergoing an abortion.

        Data from the 1966-1972 longitudinal survey by woman's
occupation reflect a comparable pattern. Nonmanual workers
had the highest proportion of respondents using only contraception and lowest proportions of those relying only on abortion for birth control, but were very likely to resort to

Table 8-7

Abortion Levels among Married Women by Urban-Rural
Residence: Hungary, 1966, 1972

Residence	1966 TCS[a] (total sample of married women, aged 15-49)	1972 Reinterview with 1966 marriage Cohort (after six years of marriage)	1975 Reinterview with 1966 Marriage Cohort (after nine years of marriage)
Percent of women having had one or more abortions			
Budapest	65.0	56.8	60.5
Provincial towns	57.6	42.3	49.0
Rural villages	55.5	34.7	40.9
Average number of abortions per woman reporting abortions			
Budapest	2.07	1.88	1.98
Provincial towns	1.75	1.60	1.70
Rural villages	1.59	1.57	1.68

[a]Data corrected for underreporting

abortion when faced with an undesired pregnancy. Agricultural
workers, on the other hand, also had relatively high proportions
of contraceptors, but when contraception failed were more likely
to carry undesired pregnancies to term than either nonmanual
or nonagricultural manual workers.

Willingness To Have an Abortion
in the Future

    That Hungarian women increasingly tolerate induced abor-
tion only as a last resort is indicated by replies to the

following two questions, asked of the 1966 marriage cohort in their 1972 reinterview: (1) Will you undergo an induced abor‑ tion in the future, or what do you do to prevent it? and (2) If you got pregnant in the near future would you maintain this pregnancy? Only 18.2 percent of the respondents said ex‑ plicitly that they would undergo an abortion in the future (in contrast to the 56.8 percent of respondents in the 1970 pilot survey of repeated abortion seeking who said they would be "willing" to undergo abortion in the future). However, nearly half (48.6 percent) of the 1972 respondents declared that if they became pregnant they would not maintain the preg‑ nancy. In other words, although the great majority of these women, married for six years, do not approve of abortion as a birth control method, a large proportion are nevertheless un‑ willing to bear an unwanted child. It should be noted that nearly half of the 18.2 percent of respondents who indicated their intention to undergo an abortion in the future if neces‑ sary had not yet had an abortion and that four-fifths of these women also said in 1972 that they definitely wanted no more children.

Reasons For Having Abortions

Data from the 1972 follow-up of the 1966 marriage co‑ hort casts light on subjective motivations for having abortions. These motivations are subjective, however, only in the sense that respondents could choose for themselves among prestruc‑ tured replies concerning each abortion. The detailed findings are presented in Table 8-8.

When sorted into main groups, it can be seen that the largest proportion of reasons overall (34.2 percent) for not having borne a child at that time can be loosely categorized as "financial-economic." Among these, inadequate housing con‑ ditions was the largest single subcategory, with 21.9 percent. Next in overall importance are child spacing and fertility limitation motivations, with 24.9 and 23.7 percent, respec‑ tively, although, as might be expected, with each succeeding abortion child spacing becomes less of a motivation and fertil‑ ity limitation becomes increasingly important. Abortions prompted by the poor health of the woman or possibly of her unborn child, or by the respondent's or her husband's advanced age, represent only 8.5 percent of cases. Other miscellaneous reasons make up the remaining 8.6 percent.

Abortion Data from Surveys of Women Using Oral Contraceptives

Data from surveys of women using oral contraceptives at varying periods between August 1970 and December 1975 suggest

Table 8-8

Percentage Distribution of Main Reasons for Induced Abortion by Serial
Number of Abortion, 1972 Reinterview of 1966 Marriage Cohort

Why the Woman Did Not Bear That Child	Serial Number of Induced Abortion					Total
	1	2	3	4	5	
Fertility termination						
She did not want to have more children	21.0	23.6	38.8	43.3	38.4	24.9
Child spacing						
The last child was still small	25.8	12.5	4.6	3.3	7.7	20.1
Prolongation of interval between pregnancies	1.9	1.8	1.1	1.7	-	1.8
Wanted herself to determine date of birth	3.3	2.4	3.4	1.7	-	3.0
					Subtotal	24.9
Financial-economic						
Inappropriate housing conditions	20.4	25.6	22.3	23.3	23.1	21.9
Current financial difficulties	7.1	9.6	7.4	3.3	-	7.6
Maintenance of living standards	1.9	3.1	1.7	6.7	-	2.3
Taking of employment	0.8	1.6	1.1	1.7	-	1.1
Education	1.4	1.3	0.6	-	-	1.3
					Subtotal	34.2
Health-biological						
She or her husband was too old	0.8	1.6	2.3	6.7	23.1	1.4
Previous difficult pregnancy or labor	2.5	2.7	0.6	-	-	2.3
Health reasons	3.0	4.2	4.6	3.3	-	3.4
Anxiety about health of child to be born	1.3	1.5	1.7	1.7	-	1.4
					Subtotal	8.5
Miscellaneous						
Troubles connected with a child	1.0	2.0	2.3	-	-	1.3
Anxiety about the child's future	0.2	0.5	0.6	-	-	0.3
Influence of other persons	0.2	0.2	0.6	-	-	0.2
Other reasons	7.3	5.8	6.3	3.3	7.7	6.8
					Subtotal	8.6
Total	100.0	100.0	100.0	100.0	100.0	100.0

that women who adopt modern contraceptives are perhaps more highly motivated to control their fertility than the general population of Hungarian women of reproductive age (see Table 8-9). Prior to taking pills, 61.5 percent of these women had had an abortion, compared to the 58 percent estimated for the representative sample of married women aged 15-49 interviewed in the 1966 TCS. The rate of previous abortions for oral contraceptors also exceeded that of the 1966 TCS respondents overall--nearly 118 compared to 110 per 100 women. (The youngest group cannot be compared, since there were no 15- and 16-year-olds among the oral contraceptors.)

Among the 55,500 oral contraceptors covered in this survey, the majority had had one or two live births; just one or no induced abortions were reported. Women who already had had two live births and at least two induced abortions were much less likely to be taking oral contraceptives. Only 4.7 percent of the sample had never been pregnant.

Table 8-9

Rate of Previous Abortions among Oral Contraceptors and Married Women by Age of Woman at Interview: Hungary, 1966, 1970-1975

| | Average number of previous abortions per 100 women | |
Age Group	Women Taking Pills 1969-1969	Married Women Interviewed in 1966 TCS
17-19	37	-
20-24	64	54.2
25-29	110	118.4
30-39	162	174.4
40-49	180	154.1
Total	118	110.0

SUMMARY

Following legalization of abortion on request in 1956, abortion became a mass phenomenon in Hungary. Total numbers of legal abortions performed annually reached a peak of over 200,000 in 1969, some 50,000 more than both the number of live births in that year and the highest estimates of illegal

abortions calculated to have occurred annually before 1956.
With increasing use of effective modern contraception, abortion levels have dropped in recent years, most notably after
1974, following institution of official population policy measures deliberately designed to reduce reliance on abortion, encourage adoption of effective contraception, and raise average
family size.

Extensive research into the correlates of abortion
has been conducted since the late 1950s by the Hungarian Central Statistical Office and the Ministry of Health. Based on
continuing statistics supplied by health institutions since
1956, and on findings from special abortion and contraceptive
surveys and a series of national family planning surveys, this
research has dealt mainly with the demographic, socioeconomic,
and health aspects of abortion. The psychosocial aspects of
abortion have been specifically investigated thus far only in
two pilot surveys of 1970-1971 and in a subsection of the national TCS (KAP) survey of 1974. Inferences regarding psychological determinants of abortion can be gleaned from the various studies.

As a first step, we traced the remarkable recent convergence of the fertility behavior and desires of Hungarian
couples on the two-child family. Such a small family size implies a compelling need for effective birth control, by whatever means may be available. The survey findings indeed
indicate a rise in the percentage of married women of reproductive age currently practicing birth control, from 58 percent
in 1958 to about 90 percent in 1974. From the late 1960s, the
relative share of abortion in overall birth control began to
drop. This is due, first, to the growing practice of contraception, but more importantly in recent years to the shift
from traditional to more reliable modern contraceptive methods,
primarily pills, which have reduced the incidence of undesired
pregnancies and, hence, need for abortion. The survey findings clearly show that, prior to the introduction of oral contraceptives in 1967, Hungarian couples wishing to limit their
fertility were forced to resort to induced abortion because of
the unavailability of effective and appropriate contraceptive
methods and information, and not because of carelessness or
irresponsibility. By 1974, the proportion of contraceptors
using pills among married women aged under 35 had risen to 36
percent, while all other methods had declined in popularity.
However, coitus interruptus was still practiced by an almost
equal proportion of these contracepting couples--35 percent.
A 1972 follow-up of a 5 percent sample of the 1966 marriage cohort revealed that although here, too, 36 percent of contraceptors were taking pills after six years of marriage, many
had tried and dropped them and many more hesitated to begin
pills, mostly because of their actual or presumed side effects.

Detailed abortion findings indicate that the proportion of unmarried women among all abortion seekers has steadily
risen, amounting to 30 percent in 1975. Among married women,
resort to abortion increases with marital duration and woman's
age, and is highest among urban women and nonmanual workers.
Data on abortion by age were presented only from surveys of
1969 and 1972. The higher incidence of abortion noted among
the older respondents probably reflects in part the cumulative
effect of the unavailability of the most effective modern contraceptive methods during most of their reproductive lifespan.
With easier access to pills, it can be expected that abortion
levels at similar ages will be lower among the women now entering childbearing years. In 1974, 32 percent of all Hungarian
women aged 20-24 and 28 percent of those aged 25-29 were using
oral contraceptives; and 87 percent of all pill takers were
aged under 35.

Financial or economic difficulties, particularly housing inadequacies, were reported in 1972 as the most common
reasons for interrupting pregnancies, followed by the desire
to space or limit numbers of children. According to a 1970
pilot survey of repeated abortion seeking among 279 women,
two-thirds of abortions are decided upon jointly by couples.
When asked if they would willingly undergo an abortion in the
future, over half of these respondents indicated that they
would. Two years later, a similar question drew less than
one-fifth positive responses from women interviewed in a follow-
up of the 1966 marriage cohort, although nearly half of this
sample stated that they would not willingly carry any future
pregnancy to term. This suggests that Hungarian women increasingly disapprove of abortion as a birth control method but are
nevertheless unwilling to bear an unwanted child. Only 28
percent of a national cross section of married women, aged
15-49, interviewed in 1966, directly admitted to having had an
abortion (about half the actual percentage, as estimated from
national statistics and analysis of the respondents' fertility
histories), compared to 41 percent of respondents interviewed
in the 1972 longitudinal follow-up of the 1966 marriage cohort
six years after marriage. This difference is probably due to
the greater accuracy of data obtainable with prospective survey methods compared to the retrospective method used in the
earlier survey, but may also reflect a growing frankness in
admitting abortion.

There is little doubt that the population policy measures implemented in January 1974 have changed Hungarian fertility trends, contraceptive practices, and abortion patterns. By
1976 the number of induced abortions had declined to nearly
half the figure reported in 1973. At the same time, wanted
fertility increased: the number of live births grew by 20
percent. To prevent unwanted pregnancies, modern contraception

is practiced more widely and more effectively; for example, use of oral contraceptives per 100 females aged 17-49 years increased from 15 in 1974 to 20 in 1976. There is increasing reliance on modern fertility-regulating behavior, reducing dependence on induced abortion.

REFERENCES

Klinger, A. Fertility and family planning in Hungary. Studies in Family Planning, 1977, 8, 166-176.

Szabady, E., & Klinger, A. Report from Budapest: Pilot survey of repeated abortion seeking. In H. P. David & J. Bernheim (Eds.), Proceedings of the Conference on Psychosocial Factors in Transnational Family Planning Research, Geneva, April 1970. Washington: American Institutes for Research, 1970.

Selected Publications from the
Hungarian Central Statistical Office

● Data on family planning, birth control, and interruption of pregnancy. Budapest: Author, 1963.

● Sample survey of obstetrical events. Budapest: Author, 1964.

● Abortion data. Budapest: Author, 1970, 1973, 1974, 1975.

● Data on premature infants. Budapest: Author, 1970.

● Perinatal mortality. Budapest: Author, 1972.

● Population and policy in Hungary. Budapest: Demographic Research Institute, 1972.

● Use of modern contraceptives. Budapest: Author, 1973.

● The 1966-1972 years' family planning, fertility, and birth control attitude of couples married in 1966. Budapest: Author, 1975.

● Principal results of 1974 TCS survey of family planning, fertility, and birth control. Budapest: Author, 1975.

● Public opinion survey concerning population questions. Budapest: Author, 1976.

PART FOUR

ABORTION DENIED

9

Children Born
to Women Denied Abortion
in Czechoslovakia*

Zdeněk Dytrych, Zdeněk Matějček, Vratislav Schüller,
Henry P. David, and Herbert L. Friedman

*Editors' Note: It has rarely been possible to
follow the natural history of pregnancies in
women who sought but were denied abortion. The
overview presented in this chapter follows the
only known cohort of children, born in 1961-
1963, to women twice denied legal abortion for
the same pregnancy, and a similar number of
matched controls whose mothers had not applied
for abortion. Unwantedness was operationally
defined in terms of requesting or not requesting abortion. The children, now adolescents,
continue to be followed.*

INTRODUCTION

Although effective contraception and legal abortion
have helped reduce unintended fertility, even in countries
where both are legally available and readily accessible compulsory childbearing has by no means been eliminated entirely.
Problems inherent in contraceptive practice and effectiveness,
limitations imposed on legal abortion after the first trimester, moral or ethical constraints, and personal inability

─────────────────

*A joint research project of the Psychiatric Research
Institute (Prague) and the Transnational Family Research Institute, supported, in part, by the Czechoslovak State Research
Plan, the World Health Organization, the (US) National Institute of Child Health and Human Development (HD-05569), and the
Ford Foundation. Reprinted with permission from Family Planning Perspectives, 1975, 7, 165-177. The authors are pleased
to acknowledge the continuing methodological contributions of
Ludek Kubicka of the Psychiatric Research Institute. Additional reports are in preparation.

or unwillingness to practice contraception or to utilize abortion continue to result in unplanned conceptions that are carried to term.

Little is known about the personal and social development of children born under conditions akin to compulsory pregnancy. Do they remain unwanted as children, suffering neglect, psychological harm, and physical damage? Or are they as healthy, psychologically and physically, as their contemporaries of similar socioeconomic background whose mothers did not seek abortion? Is their social development normal, or is there evidence of impairment? The landmark Swedish study that found serious personal and social maladjustments among young adults who had been born to women denied abortion was suggestive, but it was flawed by the failure to match the study population with controls of similar background (Forssman & Thuwe, 1966). In an effort to examine the consequences to children born of unwanted conceptions, we studied 220 boys and girls born in 1961-1963 to women twice denied legal abortions for the same pregnancy and a similar number of matched controls whose mothers did not apply for abortion, across a wide spectrum of physical, intellectual, social, and psychological parameters, beginning with their births. These children were about nine years old at the time of assessment. As we shall demonstrate, we found no gross maladjustment or maladaptation, but there were signs that these children suffered significantly more illness, were less socially acceptable to their peers and teachers, and seemed less able to live up to their inherent intellectual capacities. The expectation that unwanted conceptions would lead inevitably to the children being unwanted proved not to be the case; nor did the mothers invariably grow to love and accept the children they had been compelled to bear. As will be noted the results of the extensive examinations are also suggestive of higher potential for future social madadaptation of the unwanted children. In this respect, the boys are probably more endangered than the girls.

In December 1957, the government of Czechoslovakia liberalized its abortion statutes, permitting district abortion commissions to grant requests to terminate unwanted pregnancies on medical and social grounds during the first three months of pregnancy. During the subsequent decade, 92 percent of abortion requests were granted on initial application and an additional 6 percent were approved after appeal from the initial refusal. The remaining 2 percent were refused for a variety of reasons, primarily reasons of health, or because the pregnancy was of more than twelve weeks' duration, or because the woman had had another abortion during the previous twelve months.

Access was granted to the records of the Appellate
Commission of Prague for the years 1961-1963. Of 24,989 applications for abortion, 638 were rejected on initial request
and on subsequent appeal. After excluding 83 women who were
not Prague residents or were citizens of another country,
there remained 555 women whose request for termination of an
unwanted pregnancy had been twice denied. By 1977, it had
been established that 316 (57 percent) of these 555 women had
carried their pregnancies to term while they were resident in
Prague. Of the remaining 239 women, 43 obtained legal abortions after requesting termination from another district abortion commission either in or outside the City of Prague; 80
were alleged to have aborted spontaneously; 6 were found not
to have been pregnant; 31 moved out of the city before giving
birth; 62 had no record of having given birth at any of the
Prague clinics for obstetrics and gynecology; 9 gave false
addresses on their abortion applications; and 8 were untrace-
able for other reasons. The percentage of "spontaneous abortions"--about one-third--was twice that normally expected.

The 316 traceable Prague women who carried their pregnancies to term gave birth to 317 live children; of these, six
died (five during the first year), 19 were offered for adoption, 39 moved out of the City of Prague, and 2 were placed
permanently in child care institutions. In four cases the
mothers denied that the children had been born. The remaining
247 children were located in Prague when the studied was initiated in 1971. Only 7 mothers explicitly refused to be
interviewed, and 6 were unable to participate for other reasons (e.g., 3 had died). Thus, of the 316 women who gave
birth, 233 and their children constituted the initial study
group.

To avoid some of the pitfalls of Forssman and Thuwe's
(1966) study of unwanted children in Sweden, efforts were made
to match children born of unwanted pregnancies with children
born to women who accepted their pregnancies.

The two groups were paired with respect to grade in
school, sex, birth order, number of siblings, mother's marital
status, and father's occupation. The object of this matching
was to achieve comparable socioeconomic background and family
situations for the study and control group children. Eventually, it was possible to match 220 children born to women
twice denied abortion for the same pregnancy, 110 boys and
110 girls, with 220 control children born to women who had not
requested abortion. The study also involved all the children's
mothers and, to a lesser extent, their fathers. The research
data were collected by staff who were not involved in the

matching procedure, and who did not know which child belonged
to which group.

It was hypothesized that the environment in which an
unwanted child grows up will be somewhat inferior because of
a less accepting family, and that the detrimental effects may
be evident in the child's physical development and medical
history, social integration, educational achievement, psychological condition, and family relations.

It was also believed that inadequate relationships between the mothers and fathers of such children would be more
common than usual, at least partially attributable to a negative attitude of the mothers toward males. That hypothesis,
together with the widely accepted fact that boys are more vulnerable to adverse environmental conditions, led to the prediction that male children would suffer relatively more than
female children.

It was understood that although the study group was
selected because the children were not wanted before birth,
many of them were likely to become accepted and, indeed, loved,
after they were born. This was thought to be especially true
because a sizable number of pregnant women who also had been
twice denied abortion managed not to give birth; therefore,
the study group mothers were not at the extreme end of the
scale in their desire not to bring their pregnancies to term.
Moreover, extreme cases of "unwantedness" after birth had also
been excluded, such as children offered for adoption or placed
in the permanent care of others. The children studied are
those living with their parents or at least with their mothers,
who represent those women most affected by legislative restrictions on abortions: they accepted the consequences. For
children of those mothers who continued to feel negative about
the child after it was born, it was hypothesized that manifestations both of rejection and overcompensation would appear
within the group. It was expected that group differences might
therefore be more apparent in the distributions of the variables than in the overall averages.

DATA COLLECTION AND ANALYSIS

The data collected in this study cover many aspects
of child development and parent-child relationships. Sources
of data about the children include delivery, pediatric clinic
and school health service records; the child's case history,
drawn from interviews with the mother by an experienced social worker and by a psychiatrist; a highly detailed physical
examination of the child at the time of the study conducted

by an experienced pediatrician; and a psychological examination of the child by a clinical psychologist.*

Information about the mothers also occupies a central place in this investigation, drawn from the original request of the study group women for an induced abortion; prenatal and delivery records; a case history interview with the mother based on a 56-item model, conducted by an experienced social worker; a structured interview with the mother conducted by an experienced psychiatrist, based on a specially designed questionnaire with scaled questions; and a series of standardized questionnaires and tests completed by the mother under supervision.[†] In addition, scales were developed by the social worker and the psychiatrist, independently, to assess the attitude of the mother during the interviews in regard to her family, her honesty of response, and her attitude toward the interviews themselves.

The data obtained included more than 400 different measures for each matched pair of children. A two-stage method of analysis was employed. Comparisons were made of study and control groups as a whole and of boys and girls separately. The significance of differences between samples was measured by means of t test, chi square, McNemar paired test, and, in

---

*The following measures were used: the Wechsler intelligence Scale for Children (WISC test); the Bene-Anthony Test of Family Relations; a measure of the relationship between aspiration and frustration; a projective test consisting of the child's drawing of his family; a story completion test; a structured interview focused on the child's relationship with his family; a sociogram done in the child's classroom to obtain a description of the child's social traits; a rating scale for traits familiar to those who know the child well, but which are difficult to assess in direct psychological investigation, completed independently by the child's mother and the child's schoolteacher; a rating scale used to assess the child's behavior during psychological testing; and a similar scale for the child's behavior during the physical examination.

[†]These included the Czech "Aims in Life" Questionnaire and a supplement called the "H2" Questionnaire; the Eysenck Personality Inventory of Neuroticism and Extraversion; the Bene-Anthony Test of Family Relations, modified for parents; the Gough Femininity Scale; a Risk Assessment Questionnaire developed by Weisz and Miller; and a Stress Reaction Questionnaire especially developed for the project.

some instances, correlation coefficients. Reported statistical
significances must be interpreted cautiously, and cumulative
evidence is required to substantiate eventual conclusions.

RESULTS

From the medical point of view, the pregnancies and
deliveries do not show any marked differences between the two
groups. Indeed, a few more complications during pregnancy
were found among the control group of mothers (35 percent) than
among those who were denied abortion (26 percent); the same is
true for puerperium complications (17 percent, compared to 9
percent). About the same proportion delivered at full term.
There were also no significant differences in the children's
weight and size at birth.   '

There was no significant difference between the two
groups of children in the incidence of congential malformations
(40 percent of the study group children and 38 percent of the
controls had some). Nor did thorough pediatric and neurologic
examinations reveal any important differences in the incidence
of minimal brain damage. (Seventy percent of the study group
children and 75 percent of the controls had none.) Health
care was not grossly neglected in either of the groups.

In general, it can be said that insofar as the biological start in life is concerned, both groups are on a par.
(There is indication of a slightly higher incidence of perinatal problems in the control group, but this group includes
children of women who wanted to have the child despite health
problems.)

The physical development and medical history of the
children in each group was also similar. As Table 9-1 shows,
such health-related events as long-term disease, accidents,
surgery, and hospitalization showed no significant differences
between the two groups. Acute illness was significantly more
common among the study children. There was a tendency (falling
short of statistical significance, however) for more of the
children of mothers denied abortion to suffer chronic diseases,
frequent hospitalization, minor accidents, and minor surgery.
(Serious accidents were more common among the control children.)
In each of these categories, the number of control children who
exhibited none of these problems was greater than among the
study children. From the point of view of somatic development
and state of health, no important differences were found in
any of the indicators that could be deduced from health service
documentation or from the thorough physical examination made
in the course of the study.

Table 9-1

Percent of Study and Control Children Experiencing a
Health-Related Event, by Specific Event

Event	Study	Control
Visual impairment		
none	80.9	81.4
some	19.1	18.6
Hearing impairment		
none	99.0	98.0
some	1.0	1.9
Acute illness[a]		
none or rare	24.1	30.3
average	55.9	58.0
frequent	20.0	11.7
Long-term disease		
none	71.7	76.5
some	28.3	23.5
Accidents		
none	82.2	83.6
minor	13.7	8.9
serious	4.1	7.5
Surgery		
none	68.0	70.1
minor	31.0	28.0
serious	0.9	1.9
Hospitalization		
none	33.2	41.6
1-2 times	48.9	44.8
more frequent	17.9	13.6

Note. [a]$p < .05$ MN paired chi square.

Data for evaluation of the children during the preschool period were collected from the study and control group
mothers during psychiatric examination. Although the women

denied abortion described their children as naughty, stubborn, and bad-tempered more often than did the control group mothers, only bad temper proved significant (see Table 9-2).

Table 9-2

Percent of Preschool Children in Study and Control Groups
Exhibiting Negative Behavior, According to Mother,
by Specific Behavior Characteristics

Behavior	Study	Control
Naughty		
above average	15.9	10.0
average	40.0	40.9
below average	44.1	49.1
Stubborn		
above average	35.5	33.2
average	32.7	34.1
below average	31.8	32.7
Bad-tempered[a]		
above average	30.0	19.5
average	28.6	32.7
below average	41.4	47.8

Note. [a]$p < .05$ MN paired chi square.

To determine whether there were significant differences among the children at school age on such characteristics as diligence, concentration, initiative, self-confidence, tidiness, and intelligence--considered important for school purposes--ratings were obtained from mothers, teachers, and the children's peers when they were nine years of age. Only in diligence were the study children rated significantly lower by the teachers (1.96, compared to 2.10, on a three-point scale); however, they also showed slightly, though not significantly, less concentration, initiative, and tidiness, but more self-confidence than the control group children (not shown).

Both mothers and teachers, independently, rated the children on 11 personal characteristics, as detailed in Table 9-3. Both rated the study children significantly more excitable

Table 9-3

Assessment by Mothers and Teachers of Personal
Characteristics of Study and Control Children,
on a 5-Point Scale (5 = Highest),
by Specific Characteristic

	By Mother		By Teacher	
	Study	Control	Study	Control
Ambitiousness	3.30	3.31	3.06	3.27
Conscientiousness	3.01[a]	3.22[a]	3.02[a]	3.29[a]
Obedience	2.74	2.89	3.26	3.50
Mobility	3.80	3.67	3.48	3.31
Dominance	3.13	3.07	3.01	2.93
Sociability	3.59	3.50	3.55	3.42
Sense of humor	3.60	3.53	3.31	3.21
Sensitivity	3.69	3.56	3.23	3.18
Excitability	3.04[a]	2.81[a]	2.92[b]	2.75[b]
Stubbornness	3.13	3.08	3.18	3.13
Demandingness	2.59	2.70	2.74	2.72

Note. [a]$p < .05$ MN paired chi square.

[b]$p < .01$ MN paired chi square.

and less conscientious. On all the other characteristics except "demandingness," the mean ratings of both teachers and
mothers were in the same direction. The study children were
considered less demanding than were the control children by
their respective mothers, while the teachers considered the
study children slightly more demanding (see Table 9-3).

SCHOOL CAREER

An important sphere of socialization for the child is
the school. On the basis of school documents, report cards

and questionnaires completed by teachers, comparisons were
made on a number of indicators. In all school subjects, as
measured by the most recent school grades, the results achieved
by children born to mothers denied abortion are somewhat poorer
than those of children from the control group (see Table 9-4).
The clearest differences are in marks for the Czech language,
where the influence of the child's social environment is strong-
est. With a scoring system in which five is highest and one is
lowest, the study and control children show respective mean
grades of 2.83 and 3.01 in Czech language. Not only is performance in language generally assumed to be an indicator of intelligence (in the absence of other measurement), but it is
also usually related to social development, particularly within
the family. As the social standing of the two family groups
was roughly equal, the children's poorer performance is language is attributable to their social environment. On the other
hand, marks in arithmetic, which under normal conditions have
the highest correlation with intelligence and are less vulnerable to environmental factors, demonstrate very small differences (3.20 and 3.29, respectively, for the study and control
children). The other subjects--physical training, drawing,
music, and arts and crafts--all show differences in the same
direction, but these are not statistically significant.

Table 9-4

Average School Grades of Study and Control
Children (Converted to 5-Point Scale,
5 = Highest)

Subject	Study	Control
Czech[a]	2.83	3.01
Arithmetic	3.20	3.29
Physical training	3.81	3.85
Drawing	3.33	3.43
Music	3.73	3.74
Arts and crafts	3.58	3.62

Note. [a]$p < .05$ t test.

Assessment of differences in school performance is valid only if the intellectual capabilities of the child for doing schoolwork are known. Both groups of children obtained similar scores on the Wechsler intelligence test--102.4 for the experimental group, compared to 103.3 for the controls. The number of children who are slightly mentally retarded is the same in both groups. The assessment by the teacher of the children's behavior and performance at school, their capacity for work, and their intelligence was less favorable for the study than the control group children, although in no case was the difference statistically significant.

The third sphere of socialization for the child is his peer group. An attempt was made to ascertain how their classmates characterized the experimental and control group children.

The children's classmates ascribed less desirable social characteristics to the study children than to the control children, as Table 9-5 shows. As a group, the study children were less often chosen as "best friend" than the control children, were more often described as "fights a lot," were thought to be more reclusive, more boastful, less intelligent and both more audacious and more cowardly. They were also considered by their classmates (and mothers and teachers) as having more of a "sense of humor." But, since this was synonymous with clowning and showing off, it was not considered a desirable trait. The only negative characteristic that reached significance was "refused as a friend." Overwhelmingly, although usually by only a small aggregate mean difference, three separate groups of observers ·-mothers, teachers, and classmates--tended to give the study child less favorable ratings on personal characteristics than they gave the control child. One may conclude that a real tendency toward poorer adjustment is manifest in these data.

On several other dimensions there appears to be a poorer adjustment on the part of the study children. Thus, the study mothers more commonly believed that their children did not accept the authority of the teacher when they began to attend school, although there was no difference in the view of both groups of mothers that their children had adapted well to school. The behavior of the study group children in the face of frustration was significantly less adaptive. This characteristic is usually correlated with intelligence, so a correlation of individual performance with scores on the intelligence test was performed separately for the two groups. The results suggested that the study group children were not taking full advantage of their intelligence (not shown in tables).

Table 9-5

Average Number of Votes Received from Classmates by Study
and Control Children, by Specific Social Characteristic

Characteristic	Study	Control
Best friend	2.74	2.90
Refused as friend[a]	3.15	2.69
Fights a lot	3.15	2.95
Has sense of humor[b]	2.65	2.15
Audacious	2.65	2.53
Cowardly	2.84	2.39
Intelligent	2.21	2.58
Reclusive	2.10	2.08
Brags a lot	2.56	2.43

Note. [a]$p < .05$ MN paired chi square.

[b]Synonymous with clowning, showing off.

BOY/GIRL DIFFERENCES

As noted earlier, the two groups of children show no significant differences with respect to their biological start in life. The differences emerge as they are growing up. It was hypothesized that male children in the study group would suffer more, proportionately, than female children as a result of being both more vulnerable and more likely to have been born to mothers prone to having a poorer relationship with men. Interaction analysis was performed. In general, the evidence points in this direction, for when differences attributed to gender are uncovered they almost invariably show greater problems for the boys of the study group than for the girls. When the differences are examined one by one, however, only a few reach the level of statistical significance.

With respect to physical development, the study group boys show a significantly greater incidence of chronic disease than the control group boys (33 percent, compared with 19 percent--p < .025), while there is no significant difference between the girls for this variable (24 percent compared with 28 percent). As for preschool behavior, mothers' ratings indicate that only "naughtiness" differentiates significantly when both sex and wantedness of the birth are considered (see Table 9-6).

Table 9-6

Preschool Behavior of Study and Control Children,
As Rated by Mother (3-Point Scale, 3 = Highest)

Behavior	Boys		Girls	
	Study	Control	Study	Control
Bad-tempered	.87	.85	.90	.59
Stubborn	.83	.86	1.25	1.15
Naughty[a]	.85	.61	.58	.61

Note. [a]p < .05 MN paired chi square, Interaction Analysis.

A considerable amount of data was collected on the personal characteristics of the child during the school years from teachers, mothers, and peers. As Table 9-7 shows, teachers rated boys born to mothers denied abortion lowest on diligence, concentration, initiative, self-confidence, and tidiness, as well as on intelligence (although there are no objective differences as measured by the intelligence test). In initiative and self-confidence, the girls born to mothers denied abortion scored highest and the interaction analysis confirms the significant difference by wantedness and sex.

With respect to personal characteristics, there is considerable agreement, as may be seen in Table 9-8, between the mothers and teachers in their ratings of the children. For both, the study group boys show the greatest degree of mobility, excitability, and sense of humor (clowning), while they are rated least conscientious, obedient, and ambitious. The study group girls are relatively dominant, demanding, stubborn, sensitive, ambitious, and obedient. The interaction analysis for mothers' ratings shows significant differences by wantedness and sex on two of the items, demandingness and obedience.

Table 9-7

Mean Differences between Study and Control Boys and Girls
in Teachers' Ratings of Selected Characteristics

	Boys	Girls
Characteristic	Study/Control	Study/Control
Diligence[b]	-.13	-.15
Concentration[b]	-.15	-.16
Initiative[ab]	-.19	+.09
Self-confidence[ab]	-.08	+.23
Tidiness[b]	-.15	-.12
Intelligence[c]	-.46	+.02

Note. [a]$p < .05$ interaction analysis for gender
       [b]Three-point scale.
       [c]Nine-point scale.

The sociograms taken from the children's classmates do
not show significant interaction differences; however, as
Table 9-9 shows, the trend is seen there as well. The idea of
having a study boy as a friend is most often rejected by classmates. The study boys also receive the highest average number
of votes for fighting, sense of humor (clowning), boldness,
and cowardliness.

They receive the lowest mean number of votes for intelligence. The study girls are not very different from the control girls, except for being chosen as best friend, on which
they score the lowest of all.

Neither the Aspiration/Frustration test, nor the Bene-
Anthony test of relations between the child and the mother and
the father, shows any interaction differences between the children born to mothers denied abortion and the control children;
but school grades for the study boys are consistently the poor-
est of all four subgroups, while the girls' school grades are
much closer (see Table 9-10).

Table 9-8

Combined Mean Ratings by Mothers and Teachers of Personal
Characteristics of Study and Control Children,
by Sex of Children

Characteristic	Boys		Girls	
	Study	Control	Study	Control
Ambitiousness	2.98	3.13	3.37	3.46
Conscientiousness	2.72	3.05	3.31	3.44
Mobility	3.71	3.63	1.85	3.35
Dominance	2.97	3.02	3.18	2.97
Obedience	2.67	3.03	3.33	3.37
Sociability	3.61	3.40	3.51	3.52
Sense of humor	3.60	3.44	3.31	3.29
Sensitivity	3.38	3.35	3.53	3.38
Demandingness	2.55	2.72	2.77	2.69
Excitability	3.19	2.99	2.77	2.57
Stubbornness	3.04	3.06	3.27	3.13
Intelligence[a]	1.35	1.55	1.73	1.67

Note. [a]Subtracted from five in order to equate to this scale
in which one is lowest and five is highest.

Overall, it does appear that whether because of greater
vulnerability to adverse familial conditions, or because the
conditions themselves are worse owing to greater frequency of
inharmonious relations with their mothers, the study boys do
tend to show greater adverse effects than the study girls, relative to their control groups, although aggregate differences
are generally small.

THE FAMILIES

Both teachers and social workers were asked to assess
the children's families, each of whom they had visited at least

Table 9-9

Interaction of Study and Control Group Children with Their
Classmates, by Average Number of Votes from Classmates
on Specific Characteristics, by Sex of Children[a]

| | Boys | | Girls | |
Characteristic	Study	Control	Study	Control
Best friend	2.86	2.81	2.62	3.00
Refused as a friend	4.83	4.10	1.41	1.28
Fights a lot	6.07	5.78	0.23	0.12
Sense of humor	3.76	2.97	1.53	1.33
Bold	4.11	3.97	1.19	1.10
Cowardly	3.52	2.94	2.16	1.85
Intelligent	1.65	2.29	2.77	2.87
Reclusive	2.73	2.70	1.46	1.45
Brags a lot	3.21	3.27	1.91	1.59

Note. [a]No significant differences by gender when tested for
interaction.

once. On all four variables--cultural level, internal family
life, care of child and cooperation with school--the teachers
rated the families of the study group children lower than the
control group families, albeit statistical significance was
reached only on the last two items (see Table 9-11). The social workers also found the study group families inferior, and
rated the mothers as significantly less informed about the
child and significantly more detached.

It was expected that the study children would perceive
their mothers' attitudes toward themselves, their relationships
with their mothers and their fathers, and their status within
the family all more negatively than the control children. The
Bene-Anthony Test of Family Relations was used to test this
hypothesis, but no significant differences or clear trends
were apparent from this measure.

Table 9-10

School Grades (Converted to 5-Point Scale, 5 = Highest)
of Study Boys and Study Girls Compared with Control
Boys and Control Girls, by Subject[a]

Subject	Boys		Girls	
	Study	Control	Study	Control
Czech	2.58	2.83	3.07	3.18
Arithmetic	3.13	3.24	3.26	3.34
Physical training	3.68	3.78	3.94	3.92
Drawing	3.11	3.26	3.53	3.60
Music	3.58	3.66	3.87	3.82
Arts and crafts	3.43	3.51	3.72	3.72

Note. [a]No significant differences by gender when tested for
interaction.

Table 9-11

Differences (5-Point Scale, 5 = Highest), between the
Families of the Study Children and the Families of
the Control Children

Family Characteristics	Study	Control
Teacher Assessment		
Cultural level of family	3.15	3.25
Internal family life	3.18	3.37
Care taken of child[a]	3.45	3.65
Cooperation with school[b]	2.77	2.92
Social Worker Assessment		
Mother informed about child	2.82	2.93
Mother's attitude to child[b]	2.91	3.03

Note. [a]$p < .05$ MN paired chi square.

[b]$p < .01$ MN paired chi square.

Although the major focus of this study was on the children, it was believed that their unwanted conception might relate in part to factors inherent in their parents. No unfavorable hereditary factors were found or inferred from the interviews with the mothers.

It was also hypothesized that in comparison to mothers in the control group, the study group mothers would more frequently report unhappy childhoods. No significant differences were noted in the interviews, although divorce may have been more common. The hypothesis that they would come from families with fewer children was confirmed. Compared to the control group mothers, more study group mothers were only children, and fewer had three or more siblings.

A number of measures* of the mother's personality, character traits, and values were taken to test the hypothesis that she might be suffering from more problems that initially led to the birth of a child unwanted at conception. In general, this hypothesis was not supported. Only on the Gough Femininity Questionnaire was a significant difference shown-- in a lower score for the study mothers--although the mean difference was quite small. It is possible that situational factors played a more important role in most unwanted pregnancies. If they interacted with some aspects of the women's own characteristics, they remained largely undetected by the measures used in this study.

One of the more striking differences in the families of the two groups of children was the greater instability of the study group families from the time of the abortion request until the time of the study, as Table 9-12 shows. Changes in family status, as represented by marriage, divorce, pregnancy, and widowhood, were significantly more common for the study group. Both study group mothers and fathers were significantly more often married to someone else and were more often divorced. The study children significantly more often lived with a stepfather.

It was predicted that there would be less harmony in the marital relations of the study group. Both social workers

---

*The measures, including those of optimism, social integration, the Eysenck EPI of Extraversion, Neuroticism (as well as the Lie score), and risk-taking behavior, as well as some 15 measures of "Life's Aims," all show no significant differences between the two groups of mothers.

UNWANTED PREGNANCIES IN CZECHOSLOVAKIA

Table 9-12

Percent Distribution of Changes in Parental Status of the
Study and Control Children at the Time of Study

Changes in Parental Status[a]	Study	Control
All changes		
None	75.0	84.5
One or more	25.0	15.5
Status of mother[b]		
Unmarried	1.8	0.0
Married to child's father	73.2	86.4
Married to another man	10.0	3.6
Divorced	13.2	8.2
Widowed	1.8	1.8
Status of father[c]		
Unmarried	0.5	0.5
Married to child's mother	75.2	86.7
Married to another woman	11.7	3.2
Divorced	10.3	7.8
Widowed	0.0	0.0
Died	2.3	1.8

Note. [a] $p < .025$ chi square.

[b] $p < .005$ chi square.

[c] $p < .025$ chi square.

and psychiatrists found that, compared to the control group mothers, the study group mothers significantly more often had a negative attitude toward their husbands (12.2 percent compared to 4.5 percent and 14.7 percent compared to 8.3 percent, respectively); and there was a significantly greater number of study group mothers who considered their marriages as definitely unhappy (14.4 percent compared to 7.0 percent).

Although the birth of the child, not surprisingly, was significantly less often received with pleasure by the study group mothers, the differences tended to lessen by the time of the investigation. Although the differences were not

significant, somewhat fewer study group mothers found them-
sèlves satisfied, and more were actively dissatisfied, with
their children.

The study children were significantly more often
reared by persons other than their natural parents; and 47 percent of study children were educated elsewhere than at home,
compared to 29 percent of control children. Although it was
expected that mothers of study girls would have relatively
more positive attitudes toward their children than mothers of
study boys, the data show that maternal attitudes were equally
poor for both sexes relative to control mothers' attitudes toward their children.*

It was hypothesized that study group mothers were more
likely to have had induced abortions, both before and after
the delivery of the unwanted child. Although the total number
of abortions showed no significant difference for the two
groups (bearing in mind that there was some evidence that study
group mothers were somewhat less accurate in their self-
histories), there were some striking differences, nonetheless.
A history of three or more abortions was four times greater
among the women denied abortion than among the control group
women (8 percent compared to 2 percent). The number of abortions in the nine-year period since the birth of the child was
also significantly ($p < .01$) greater for study group women.
There is thus evidence of a repeated abortion syndrome. It is
also of interest to note contraceptive practices. Although
coitus interruptus was the most commonly used method for both
groups, if the use of this method is compared with "female"
methods, including the pill and the IUD, significantly more
study group mothers used female methods, albeit unsuccessfully.
This may be a reflection of lack of clear consensus on the part

---

*However, psychiatric interviews with the mothers re-
flect their belief that fathers of study boys are significantly
different ($p < .001$) in the degree to which they accepted the
births of their sons, but both groups of fathers show no difference with respect to their daughters' births. Another difference shows that, currently, the control fathers devote more
time to their sons than to their daughters, whereas the reverse is noted of study fathers. The interaction analysis is
significant for gender at the .05 level. Overall, a number of
indicators suggest that one of the consequences of unwantedness is paternal rather than maternal deprivation, unless it
is simply a consequence of the mothers' projection onto the
fathers of their own views.

of the couple about prevention of the birth in question, or uncertainty of the mother about the father's willingness to prevent the birth in question.

One of the more unusual findings was that at the end of the psychiatric interview, 38 percent of the study group women placed themselves in a category of not having asked for an induced abortion at the time they were carrying the study child. It was noted, however, that they were significantly more likely to give this response to a female rather than a male psychiatrist.

Finally, it was hypothesized that an initially rejecting attitude on the part of the study group mothers would change to a more positive one, but that the change would be associated with the mother's personality, the quality of her marital life, and the sex of her child. By and large, the study group mothers did move from initial rejection to ultimate acceptance at the time of the study. However, some mothers continued to be dissatisfied with their children. Positive acceptance seems to be most strongly related to two factors, the age of the parents and the relationship that causes them to live together or apart. The continuing negative attitude of the mother to the child appears to be a function of her relationship with the father of the child and of her own psychosexual development.

CONCLUSIONS

Compulsory childbearing has varied and sometimes unfavorable consequences for the subsequent life of the child. Although the aggregate differences between the children born following unwanted conception and the control children are not dramatic at nine years of age, the observations tend to support many of the major hypotheses. The higher incidence of illness and hospitalization despite the same biological start in life, slightly poorer school marks and performance despite the same level of intelligence, somewhat worse integration in the peer group--all these point to a higher-risk situation for the child and the family, as well as for society.

These higher risks concern, above all, the emotional and social development of the children, indicated, for example, by the differences between boys and girls. The gross data available so far reveal that boys born from unwanted pregnancies are more endangered in the development of their personalities than girls, although there are no marked differences between the sexes on indicators concerning the biological foundation, the intactness of the central nervous system, and the development of intelligence. This is in accord with day-to-day experience, where boys under less positive conditions of family interaction have more pronounced reactions and exhibit less adaptive behavior. They thus find themselves in a vicious circle of interaction, where the expectations of parents are repeatedly frustrated. This, in turn, leads to reactions on the part of the child, which then increase the chances for maladaptive behavior in the future.

If we sum up all the differences between children born from unwanted pregnancies and their controls, concerning performance, attitudes, and behavior, one common denominator emerges from the objective data and from the perceptions of mothers, teachers, and classmates. In our opinion, this common denominator is an increased defensive position against stress and frustration among the study children. The early and frequent need of such children, especially boys, to achieve satisfaction and to assert themselves is a strong source of stimulation leading to a certain behavior pattern which, in a given situation, is systematically enhanced and may become a more or less permanent trait. At present, this trait is well within the bounds of social viability; there have been no excessive cases of breakdowns or conflicts that have come to the attention of psychological dispensaries or child psychiatric clinics. Nevertheless, there may be a question concerning the future development of these children. What will they be like in puberty and adolescence?

Our findings suggest that the commonly held belief among professionals, that a child unwanted during pregnancy remains unwanted, is not necessarily true. However, the opposite notion, more common among the lay public, that the birth of a child causes a complete change in attitude and that every woman who becomes a mother will love her child, is also untrue. The child of a mother denied abortion is born into a potentially handicapping situation. At the same time, it seems evident that in the common life of mother and child there are some factors that tend to have a positive impact. To identify these variables and their relative weights will be the subject of further analysis and statistical evaluation.

It should also be borne in mind that the study children were born to women who, after all, accepted the commission's ruling and bore the child, and thus were not the most extremely negative prospective mothers in the original group (who found a way to avoid childbirth or to place the child). It should also be remembered that this report deals with group mean data. There is some indication that the recurrent differences between the groups are attributable to a small subgroup who bear closer attention, and for whom a secondary data analysis may be merited. This might help to predict and avert births that could be irretrievably damaging.

Prospective studies are needed to learn more about the positive and negative mechanisms that affect child development so as to provide opportunities for support when unwantedness threatens healthy child development.

POSTSCRIPT

A subsequent report (David et al., 1977) described the development of the Maladaption Score as a global indicator of the child's social adjustment within the family and society. Sixty items were selected from the case history, question-naires, rating scales, and other psychological assessment measures, which could be interpreted as providing evidence of the child's maladaption. A score was calculated for each study and control child by summing the "unfavorable" or "mal-adaptive" items, thus forming the Maladaption Score (Matějček et al., 1976, 1978).

It was noted that the children born from unwanted preg-nancies had a significantly higher Maladaption Score than the control children. Differences between the study and control children, which were not so definitive when viewed in terms of individual indicators, came into sharper focus when the cumu-lative effects of negative factors were noted. The study boys manifested the highest maladaption scores and were generally assessed more negatively than the control boys. The same find-ing was observed among the girls. Interaction analysis re-veals that the significantly higher maladaption score is a de-velopmental trait of both unwanted boys and girls, and not of unwanted boys specifically. Children born from unwanted preg-nancies appear generally less adaptive, less socially mature, and less well-accepted by their classmates. They find them-selves more often in an unfavorable social situation and seem to be at greater risk (Matějček et al., 1978).

In another substudy a regression analysis was per-formed with the Maladaption Score as a dependent variable. Signs of minimal brain dysfunction (MBD), assessed by medical examination, were found to be second only to the sex of the child in having the greatest relationship to the Maladaption Score. Although the number of children diagnosed as MBD was just about the same in both groups, differences between MBD study and control children on the Maladaption Score was sta-tistically very significant ($p < .001$). This finding suggests that in the unfavorable context of emotional and social fac-tors associated with the original "unwantedness" of the child the MBD syndrome becomes more marked and socially disturbing.

Highest maladaption scores were obtained by "only children" in the study group, and lowest scores were noted among "only children" in the control group. This may reflect a rejection of the maternal role among women compelled to carry to term the only pregnancy they have been unable to control. The sociopsychological effects of this situation appear to deserve particular consideration.

With the passage of time additional information has accumulated. By 14 years of age, 43 study children (31 boys and 12 girls) and 30 control children (18 boys and 12 girls) had been examined in child psychiatric and/or school counseling centers in Prague for reasons entirely independent of this research and without any awareness of their identity among the professional staff. Although differences in number of referrals is slight, the study children were seen significantly more often because of serious behavior disorders requiring therapeutic, educational, and social attention and/or treatment. The control children came to attention because of comparatively less serious developmental deficits or irregularities which required primarily administrative and organizational actions, e.g., special schools, delay of school entrance, remedial treatment, etc. These highly significant differences in the needs of study and control children for professional services are very much along the lines previously anticipated.

REFERENCES

David, H. P., Matějček, Z., Dytrych, Z., Schüller, V., & Friedman, H. L. Developmental consequences of unwanted pregnancies: Studies from Sweden and Czechoslovakia. In Y. H. Poortinga (Ed.), Basic problems in cross-cultural psychology. Amsterdam: Swets and Zeitlinger, 1977.

Forssman, H., & Thuwe, I. One hundred and twenty children born after application for therapeutic abortion refused. Acta Psychiatrica Scandinavia, 1966, 42, 71-78.

Matějček, Z., Dytrych, Z., & Schüller, V. Prague study on children born from unwanted pregnancies. III. Maladaption Score. (In Czech) Psychologia a Patopsychologia Dietata, 1976, 2, 99-112.

Matějček, Z., Dytrych, Z., & Schüller, V. Children from unwanted pregnancies. Acta Psychiatrica Scandinavia, 1978, 57, 67-90.

10

The Preferred Risk
of Illegal Abortion
in the Dominican Republic*

Cándida E. Ramírez E., Antoinette Russin,
and Raymond L. Johnson with Antonía Ramírez M.,
Ezequiel Garcia, and Alberto E. Noboa Mejia

Editors' Note: Following an earlier coopera-
tive study of family planning attitudes of a
sample of male heads of households in selected
regions of the Dominican Republic, a coopera-
tive study evolved on the public health and
socioeconomic costs of illegal abortion. Im-
pediments to effective family planning are
noted and recommendations made. A more exten-
sive Spanish-language report has been dissemi-
nated in the Dominican Republic.

INTRODUCTION

The Dominican Republic, with estimated rates of 48.5 births and 14.7 deaths per 1,000 population (United Nations, 1971), has one of the highest fertility growth rates in Latin America. The dangers to the country of the continuing

---

*A joint project of the Research Center of the Universidad Nacional Pedro Henriquez Ureña (UNPHU) and the Instituto Nacional de Educacion Sexual (INES) in cooperation with the Transnational Family Research Institute. The authors are pleased to acknowledge the generous cooperation received from Drs. Vinicio Calventi (Maternidad Nuestra Señora de la Altagracia), Pedro Pichardo (Hospital José María Cabral y Báez), and Humberto Sangiovanni (UNPHU School of Medicine). A more extensive Spanish-language report, entitled Estudio del Aborto en 200 Mujeres en la Republica Dominicana, is available from the Centro de Investigaciones, Universidad Nacional Pedro Henriquez Ureña, Santo Domingo, Dominican Republic.

population explosion are such that the President of the Republic, in spite of considerable opposition, has been one of the
few Latin American heads of state to openly proclaim the need
for a change in fertility patterns. Since it is rare, anywhere, for individuals or families to consider abstract societal needs in their daily activities, and most especially in
behavior not open to public scrutiny, such as sexual behavior,
it is not surprising that in many countries family planning
campaigns have had only limited success in inducing major
changes in individual behavior. Even where the motivation to
avoid unwanted children is apparently present, adoption of
modern contraception has not always occurred.

The objective of this study was to contribute to solv-
ing the puzzle of why women apparently highly motivated to
avoid unwanted births are not motivated to practice effective
contraception. It deals with a segment of the Dominican public that is often beyond the reach of family planning recruit-
ment efforts. These are the younger women with a number of
fertile years remaining who are typical of the uneducated,
marginally employed urban poor crowding the shanty slums and
the cinturones de miseria surrounding most cities of Latin
America (Gonzáles-Cortes & Errázuriz, 1973). The women in
this study also occupied the most dense region of hard-core
resistance to modern contraceptive use (Rogers, 1973a). Yet,
despite their apparent lack of enthusiasm for family planning,
they did act purposefully to limit family size by seeking and
obtaining abortions.

THE SAMPLE

Two hundred women were interviewed in two hospitals
following treatment for incomplete abortions or for complications stemming from abortions (which in every case were
strongly suspected by the hospital staffs to have been induced)
Of these, 150 women were interviewed at the Maternidad Hospital Nuestra Senora de la Altagracia in Santo Domingo, the
largest maternity hospital in the country (about 1,500 deliveries per month). An additional 50 women were interviewed at
the Hospital José María Cabral y Báez in Santiago de los
Caballeros. This is a general hospital serving the second
largest city of the country and its surrounding rural area; it
averages 580 deliveries each month. Both are public hospitals
providing free medical care to poor families. La Maternidad
averages approximately 260-280 induced and spontaneous abortion cases per month. Cabral Hospital treats about 80 abortion cases monthly.

The sample represents 200 consecutive cases of suspected induced abortion treated in the two hospitals over a

period of one-and-a-half months in the summer of 1973. The
interviewing was conducted by two male medical students and a
young male psychologist. (The three had earlier participated
in a pretest of the interview questions and procedures with
15 women patients.)

The mean age of women in the sample was 26 years, and
three out of four were living in some type of permanent union
(18 percent were married, 57 percent were in consensual union).
For half the women, the present union was their first; 34 percent had had one previous union. For half the couples, the
union was four years or less in duration; 20 percent of the
unions had been established less than a year previously. Fourteen of the women (7 percent) were single.

The average number of live births was 3.2, but 76 (38
percent) of the women had more than five children.

The group was predominantly Roman Catholic (68 percent), but overall could not be characterized as devout. Nearly
half (48 percent) of the professed Catholics attended church
very infrequently--no more than a few times a year--contrasted
to the 34 percent who attended at least once a week. There
was a significant number (55 women, or 28 percent of the total
sample) who claimed no religious affiliation whatever. Prot-
estant representation was negligible (about 4 percent).

The large majority (86 percent) of the women had completed less than six years of primary education; a quarter
were illiterate. More than two-thirds (68 percent) did not
work outside the home at all, a quarter held regular jobs, and
the remainder worked only occasionally. Of those who worked,
57 percent were domestics and 79 percent earned 40 pesos or
less per month. Among the women who did not work, nearly all
(92 percent) depended on the husband or male partner for support; 71 percent of the men held permanent jobs. For 53 percent of the families, monthly family income was less than 100
pesos, which falls between the marginal and low levels in the
income classification scheme of the National Planning Office
(Dominican Republic, 1970).

Three-quarters of the sample lived in either Santo
Domingo (62 percent) or Santiago (13 percent). Less than one-
quarter (22 percent) lived in rural areas or small towns. Thus,
the group was predominantly urban, both with respect to current residence and birthplace (60 percent were born in large
cities).

FINDINGS

Following the Napoleonic Code, abortion in the Dominican Republic is illegal, without exception (Law No. 1690 of
April 19, 1948). Although penalties are severe both for the
practitioner and the woman, there appear to have been very
few if any prosecutions in recent years. Although the law is
not rigorously enforced, the social stigma persists (Montás.
1973); women seek abortions stealthily and are secretive about
them afterwards. As a consequence, the interviewers encountered a nearly unbreachable wall of silence in attempting to
discuss with the women the abortions that led to their hospitalization. Only 14 acknowledged having had an abortion and
16 even denied having been pregnant. Nevertheless, the women
were quite willing to answer questions not dealing with the
immediate past abortion itself, but with experiences and attitudes that were not incriminating. Their responses are summarized below.

Most Women Were Familiar with the Family
Planning Concept, but Many Were Doubtful
about the Safety of Contraceptives

Condoms, oral contraceptives, foams, and jellies are
readily available in the Dominican Republic and awareness of
family planning was widespread in the sample. But, although
155 (78 percent) of the women said that they had heard about
birth control, a scant 47 (30 percent) of those who knew about
contraception had ever used any method. Of these, 20 (43 percent) had taken the pill, almost always obtained from family
planning clinics. Only 3 women reported using coitus interruptus and 2 the rhythm method.

Among the several reasons women gave for not practicing
contraception, one stood out most prominently. More than a
quarter of the women (28 percent) objected to the use of birth
control methods on the grounds that these could be hazardous
to health. The second most common reason (offered by 22 percent of the women) was that the husbands or male partners objected to contraception. The main reason for this male opposition? More than half the women (51 percent) said that their
men considered contraceptives a risk to health.

Table 10-1 lists the variety of reasons for resisting
modern contraception among the 108 women who knew about family
planning but did not use any method.

Table 10-1

Reasons for Not Using Contraception among Women Who
Knew about Family Planning

Reasons	Number	Percent
Birth control is bad for health	30	28
Husband is opposed	24	22
Neglected to obtain supply	14	13
Not interested in using contraceptives	11	10
Want to have another child	10	9
Don't know how to use methods	7	6
Difficult to obtain supply	4	4
Fatalistic, accepts God's will	4	4
Didn't think she could become pregnant	3	3
No answer	1	1
	108	100

Most Women Did Not Want Any More Children and Said They Were Considering Contraception in the Future

A significant majority of the women (140, or 70 percent) did not want to become pregnant again; only 42 (21 percent) said they desired another child. Among those wishing to avoid another pregnancy, 116 (83 percent) said they had been thinking about using a contraceptive once they left the hospital. However, half this number (58) were unable to say which specific method they would choose. Of those who expressed a preference, 13 (22 percent) favored oral contraceptives and 9 (16 percent) mentioned female sterilization. When there was a preference for a method, it was typically based upon the recommendations of "girl friends" and other women acquaintances.

The Women Tended to Accept Abortion as a Familiar, Reliable Method of Preventing the Births of Unwanted Children

One indication of the Dominican women's matter-of-fact view of abortion, despite the legal and social sanctions against it, was the fact that abortion seeking was not dangerously postponed. Nearly 30 percent (59) of the women confirmed their pregnancies by going to a doctor or to a hospital for a pregnancy test. According to estimates of hospital personnel, 169 (84 percent) of the abortions occurred prior to the twelfth week. The dispatch with which pregnancies were confirmed and abortions performed is reflected in the relatively low incidence of serious complications leading to prolonged confinement. In our sample, two women died while in the hospital and 14 others were seriously ill. But 150 (75 percent) of the women were hospitalized for no more than 48 hours and 80 (40 percent) for no more than a single day.

The short average stay in the hospital was also the result of the promptness with which the women sought medical care when complications did occur, and further indicates that Dominican women profited from a considerable body of shared experience about abortion. Although the women we interviewed were extremely reticent about discussing the reasons for their present hospitalization, 76 (38 percent) admitted that they knew how to induce an abortion and 68 (34 percent) could describe at least three methods, usually of the folk variety. Of those admitting to such knowledge, about half (30) said that they had been told by "friends" and that the methods were reputed to be effective.

Many of the women in our study had had prior personal experience with abortion. Of an approximately 1,000 total pregnancies, 33 percent had ended in spontaneous or induced abortions. Three-fourths of the 177 women with previous pregnancies had terminated at least once by means of an abortion and 62 (35 percent) reported two or more consecutive abortions; 56 (32 percent) of the pregnancies immediately preceding the most recent one had been terminated. When the women were asked if they would consider seeking an abortion in the event of a future pregnancy, 132 (66 percent) said no, but 58 (29 percent) replied yes or perhaps. Overall, there were insistent clues that at least some of the women had been relying on induced abortion as a means of regulating fertility.

The tentative acceptance of abortion among those interviewed was further demonstrated in response to a question about whether they believed Dominican women should be able to obtain safe, legal abortions "when needed." Approval was expressed by 122 (61 percent), 64 (32 percent) said no, and 14 (7 percent) declined to state an opinion.

These findings, which suggest a widespread reliance on abortion, are consistent with those of a previous Dominican survey of 880 male heads of households conducted in 1970-1971

(Friedman, Ramírez, & García, 1975). Although over 80 percent of the men totally disapproved of abortions, 11-12 percent admitted that their female partners had obtained them in the past. This incidence was very likely underreported, but even so indicated that abortion was probably the single most practiced method of fertility regulation in the Dominical Republic.

The Abortion Experience Was Economically Costly

Even though the expenses of hospitalization were not borne by the patients, other substantial costs associated with the abortion were incurred by the woman and her family. Prior to hospitalization, an average of $9.68 was spent on related expenses (which may have included the cost of the abortion itself). This amount represented 10-11 percent of the average monthly income of families in the study. An additional 3 percent of one month's average pay was spent in making arrangements to enter the hospital (travel, the purchases of personal items of clothing, etc.), bringing the total family cost of an abortion to about $13, excluding the loss of the woman's wages if she worked. For families struggling at a near subsistence level, this was a burdensome expense.

The hospitals bore an even heavier economic burden. It was estimated, from hospital records, that the total average cost of treating a woman whose abortion was without serious complications was $62.50 (including staff time, drugs, patient feeding, and other items). But when complications prolonged a woman's stay in the hospital, the average cost escalated to $175.65. In comparison, the cost to the hospital of a normal delivery was $14.55. The estimated total cost of caring for the 150 women interviewed at La Maternidad was $8,752.50.

The Male Partner's View on Fertility Regulation Was Often Influential, If Not Decisive

Slightly less than half (90) of the women had at some time in the past discussed family planning with their husbands or partners. There was a slightly greater inclination to discuss the matter with the men sometime in the future; 102 (51 percent) said that they definitely intended to do so, an additional 30 (15 percent) said they might, while 52 (26 percent) indicated they would not. As already reported, the most common basis for male opposition, according to the women, was the belief that contraceptives were unsafe, a view with which many of the women themselves agreed.

When the most recent pregnancy was discovered, 156 (78 percent) of the women told someone about it almost

immediately. Usually it was the man who was first informed
(in 112 of the incidents), but only 11 of the women said they
asked the man, or anyone else, for advice on how to handle the
situation. The response to news of the pregnancy was mixed.
About 60 percent of those first told reacted favorably and the
other 40 percent were described as having been negative or at
least noncommittal.

The husbands and male partners were usually said to
have been aware of the hospitalization (166, or 83 percent),
and those who knew were more often than not characterized by
the women as being worried and concerned (57 percent). There
were relatively few reports of anger or rejection on the part
of the men (9 percent). It is not known, of course, how many
of the men were aware of the actual reason for the hospitalization.

CONCLUSIONS AND RECOMMENDATIONS

The women in this study represent a promising but para-
doxical group for the advocates of family planning. Despite
the fact that these women were highly motivated to prevent
births of unwanted children and were generally aware of the
availability of modern contraceptive methods, there was very
little indication of adoption. In the national survey of male
heads of households cited earlier, a similar observation was
made. Of the more than 40 percent who approved of contraception, more than half did not use any of the available methods.
These are indications of the KAP-Gap which has been reported
throughout the developing world: making people aware of family planning and the advantages of small families does not
automatically result in a general acceptance of modern
contraception.

In an attempt to explain the continuing reluctance of
women throughout the world to practice effective contraception,
Bogue (1974) reviewed 10 factors which have been thought to
impede family planning in the past, and in each case discounted
their current importance. These factors are listed in Table
10-2, with summary findings from our own study to indicate the
state of affairs in the Dominican Republic.

None of the 10 factors would appear to be serious obstacles to the success of family planning in the group studied
in the Dominican Republic, and Bogue contended that they are
of diminishing significance throughout the developing world.
But in searching for alternative explanations for the KAP-Gap,
Bogue overlooked a barrier which, at least in the Dominican
Republic, appears to be of major importance: abortion competes

Table 10-2

Ten Impediments to Family Planning and their
Relevance in the Dominican Republic

Impediments to Family Planning	Situation in Dominican Republic
1. Unawareness that family planning is possible	Most women in study had heard about contraceptive methods
2. Lack of knowledge about reliable modern methods	Most women knew about specific methods, where to obtain them, and some had tried using them
3. Social disapproval of family planning on moral or religious grounds	No indication of strong moral and religious objections; only minority of women were devout
4. Prevalence of large family values; desire for large families	Average family size not large; nevertheless, most women did not want another child
5. Weak or ambivalent motivation	Having abortions despite risks was prima facie evidence that motivation was high
6. Shame and shyness in discussing sex and contraception with spouse, peers	Many women said they had discussed family planning with husbands, or intended to do so in the future
7. Fatalism	Few women gave fatalistic reasons for resisting family planning
8. Traditionalism: reticence to accept innovations or change	No direct evidence, but majority of women believed safe, legal abortions should be more easily available than at present
9. Social pressures for childbearing, especially early in union	Again, no direct evidence; but abortion terminated first pregnancy for 12 percent of women, first through third pregnancies for 41 percent
10. Lack of ego involvement in family planning	Some indication of repeated abortion seeking; number of women said they would have abortion in the event of future pregnancy

with contraception as an accepted means of regulating fertility. Illogical as it seems, women who have been hospitalized because of abortions are nevertheless fearful of the health hazards resulting from the use of contraceptives.

The opinion that abortion involves less risk than contraception would appear more logical if seen to be a plausible inference drawn from popular understandings of the causes of health, illness, and healing. Family planning workers know from experience that resistance to the adoption of contraceptives is often reinforced by the tenets of folk medicine. A Hindu woman, for example, is said to believe that blood is allotted to one at the time of birth and is naturally concerned that spotting caused by the pill will deplete her lifetime supply. Elsewhere, women have been reported to fear that the pill poisons the fetus, leaving it to decay within the woman's body. An abortion, in contrast, "cleanly" removes the fetus. A preference for abortion may also reflect the prestige of surgery, identified with modern scientific medicine, while the pill is viewed as not very different from traditional herbal medicine.

Anecdotes and surmises such as these may offer some insight, but are too fragmentary to be useful in constructing a complete account of a belief system. As a more comprehensive approach, D'Andrade (1976) describes a research method designed to uncover implicit beliefs about the causes and cures of illness. A model of a belief system is constructed from data obtained when informants supply the missing terms in sentences such as "you can have _____ and not know it," or "_____ runs in the family." The model specifies the logical relationships among diseases and also is a mechanism that simulates the way people may test the plausibility of statements they may encounter for the first time (e.g., "Poison ivy affects the heart.") Previously used in anthropological field studies in rural Mexico, this method could be adapted to investigate Dominican folk beliefs about contraception and abortion within the broader medical context of pregnancy and childbirth. Findings would provide guidance in understanding the fears aroused by contraceptives and in predicting the public response to reassuring "official" or "expert" statements about the safety of contraceptives.

However, research into belief systems should not postpone more immediate efforts to encourage Dominican women and their male partners to reevaluate the comparative risks of abortion and contraception. We recommend two communications tactics.

Attempt to Reassure the Population about the Safety of Modern Contraceptives by Meeting Head-on the Problem of Side Effects

Bogue (1974) observed that the belief that "family planning makes you sick" is nearly universal and has been sustained by the widespread experience of at least temporary discomfort. He concludes that

> the "product" is imperfect in this respect. Yet much too little effort is being devoted to acknowledging and dealing with this phenomenon. Instead, it is swept under the rug. Field workers pretend that it does not exist. In their desire to get their quota of adoptors they do not dare mention it, or denigrate its importance if it is mentioned. As a result, a huge credibility gap has developed between the public at large and the family planning establishment.

There is, of course, a common sense justification for neglecting to fully inform women about possible side effects: forewarnings may actually induce problems, especially among suggestible women. Common sense in this case, however, is not a reliable guide. It has been well demonstrated that negative experiences will usually have a less adverse impact if they already have been anticipated by a person. Advance warnings can have an emotionally dampening effect, but a person given little information about what to expect tends to overreact to negative experiences when these occur. Based on their reading of the research literature, Janis and Mann (1977) advocate "emotional inoculation" as a counseling technique and cite evidence that giving a patient full and accurate information about what to expect has been successful in reducing post-surgical discomfort and the pain associated with certain medical procedures. The technique is simple enough to be incorporated into routine contraceptive counseling and might prove useful both in emotionally inoculating women against stressful experiences with side effects, and also in stemming unfavorable word-of-mouth communication about these side effects.

Disseminate Information Which Factually Contrasts the Risks and Costs of Abortion (Especially when It Is Illegal) with the Problems Associated with Contraceptive Use

An important task of communication must be to convince members of the target audience that contraception offers significant advantages. Care should be taken, however, to refrain from scare tactics and exaggeration. Many Dominican women are knowledgeable enough about abortion to detect blatant distortion and false claims.

The use of the mass media to promote family planning is well established in the Dominican Republic (e.g., Marino, 1973; Ortega & Fernández de Cueto, 1973). Yet such media campaigns, anxious to avoid political and religious controversy, have tacitly imposed an information blackout on the topic of abortion. As a result, women and their male partners are deprived of information necessary to make a rational choice.

The taboo nature of the abortion topic also impedes the transmission of accurate information by word of mouth. Social taboos have characteristic patterns of interpersonal information exchange. There are strong social norms governing who may properly talk with whom about what, and under which circumstances. Even the most sensitive taboo topics, such as abortion, can be discussed with someone, somewhere, at some time (Marshall, 1971). But persons who may share information about abortions tend to be very similar in social background and experience; that is, taboo communications occur between very highly homophilous individuals (Rogers & Bhowmik, 1971; Rogers, 1973b).

The high degree of homophily among individuals who engage in abortion-related communications has the probable effect of impeding rapid and widespread diffusion of information. The same information (or, more likely, misinformation) keeps recirculating among members of a closed group--hence perpetuating the taboo status of the topic.

Schramm (1971) in reviewing research on communications in family planning concluded that both sides of an issue might as well be openly presented, because the audience is going to learn about the pros and cons anyway. Even though the subject of abortion is veiled in official silence, dissemination through informal word-of-mouth channels will continue to occur. And misinformation will be circulated along with the truth. The "grapevine" will always exist, and it is the responsibility of the communications strategists in family planning to prune and cultivate it.

REFERENCES

Bogue, D. J. Old and dying and new and virulent psychological threats to family planning. Unpublished paper, 1974. See also "Policy implications of theory and research on motivation and induced behavior change for fertility and family planning," a paper presented at the ECAFE Expert Group Meeting on Social and Psychological Aspects of Fertility Behavior, Bangkok, June 1974.

D'Andrade, R. G. A propositional analysis of U.S. American beliefs about illness. In K. H. Basso & H. A. Selby (Eds.), Meaning in anthropology. Albuquerque: University of New Mexico Press, 1976.

Dominican Republic, Government of. Primer plan de desarrollo económico y social - 15. Oficina Nacional de Planificación. Secretariado Técnico de la Presidencia. Santo Domingo, 1970.

Friedman, H. L., Ramírez, A., & García, E. F. Attitudes of a sample of male heads of households in the Dominican Republic. In Pan American Health Organization (Eds.), Epidemiology of abortion and practices of fertility regulation in Latin America: Selected reports. Washington: Pan American Health Organization, Scientific Publication No. 306, 1975.

González-Cortes, G., & Errázuriz, M. M. The marginal family: Social changes and women's contraceptive behavior. Paper presented at IXth International Congress of Anthropological and Ethnological Sciences, Chicago, 1973.

Janis, I. L., & Mann, L. Decision making: A psychological analysis of conflict, choice, and commitment. New York: The Free Press, 1977.

Marino, A. Radio and family planning in the Dominican Republic. In J. M. Stycos (Ed.), Clinics, contraception, and communication: Evaluation studies of family planning programs in four Latin American countries. New York: Appleton-Century-Crofts, 1973.

Marshall, J. F. Topics and networks in intra-village communication. In S. Polgar (Ed.), Culture and population. Cambridge, Mass.: Schenkman, 1971.

Montás, H. Dominican Republic. Country Profiles, January 1973.

Ortega, M. M., & Fernández de Cueto, J. M. Informe final del estudio comparativo de la escuela radiofonica de educacion familiar de la Asociacion Dominicana pro Bienestar de la Familia, Inc. Santo Domingo: Universidad Nacional Pedro Henriquez Ureña, Centro de Investigaciones, 1973.

Rogers, E. M.   Communication strategies for family planning in
    developing countries.   Paper presented at the Population
    Association of America Meeting, New Orleans, April 1973.   (a

Rogers, E. M.   Mass media and interpersonal communication.   In
    I. de sola Pool et al. (Eds.), Handbook of communication.
    Chicago: Rand McNally, 1973.   (b)

Rogers, E. M., & Bhowmik, D. K.   Homophily-heterophily: Rela-
    tional concepts for communications research.   Public
    Opinion Quarterly, 1971, 34, 523-538.

Schramm, W.   Communication in family planning.   Reports on
    Population/Family Planning, April 1971, No. 7.

United Nations, Department of Economic and Social Affairs.
    Demographic yearbook, 1970:   Special topic--population
    trends.   New York: Author, 1971.

PART FIVE

SERVICE PROVIDERS

11

Physician, Nurse, and Midwife Opinion in Jamaica*

Karl A. Smith and Raymond L. Johnson

Editors' Note: One of the first instances of the use of the Delphi method in population research, the national survey conducted in Jamaica questioned participants separately and anonymously, and subsequently provided respondents with a summary of results, offering opportunities to revise judgments or repeat them. The findings have been of national significance, well circulated among government decision makers.

INTRODUCTION

For a number of years, political leaders in Jamaica have recognized the need for a deceleration of population growth, and within the past seven years or so there have been national efforts at family planning. Just as previous governments tended to avoid the controversial issue of a national family planning program, the present government is reluctant to make decisions affecting the use of abortion for fertility control. At the same time, it is widely recognized not only that abortion has been practiced for a long period of time in Jamaica but also that abortions are being performed increasingly

*A joint project of the Family Planning/Epidemiology Unit, Department of Social and Preventive Medicine, University of the West Indies and the Transnational Family Research Institute. The authors appreciate the endorsement and cooperation of the Medical Association of Jamaica and the contributions of Pamela Grant, Sybil McCaw, and Jeanne P. Ebanks of the University of the West Indies. Reprinted with the permission of the Population Council from Studies in Family Planning, 1976, 7, 334-339.

241

242   *ABORTION IN PSYCHOSOCIAL PERSPECTIVE*

frequently--many of them under clandestine and medically unsafe circumstances.

     Jamaica is currently in the throes of controversy
over efforts to liberalize or repeal its present abortion law.
Based on old British law, the existing statute declares the
act of abortion to be a felony, punishable by life imprisonment (Jamaica, Government of, 1953). A pregnant woman who
seeks an abortion and anyone helping her to obtain one are
subject to prosecution. The Bourne decision in England in
1938 set the precedent for a physician, when brought to trial
for performing an abortion, to be defended on the grounds
that continuation of the pregnancy endangered the life of the
mother or threatened to make her a "physical or mental wreck."
Since the Bourne decision only represents a precedent but does
not offer real protection from prosecution, many doctors are
unwilling to risk the possibility of legal confrontation, although the law is, in fact, rarely if ever enforced. According to Robert Rosen (1973), even nonmedical abortionists go
unprosecuted in Jamaica, "performing their work with the knowledge and acquiescence of local police." This is, perhaps, an
exaggerated description of the situation. Nevertheless, this
de facto tolerance, it has been suggested by some, grants physicians a measure of protection as a matter of common law.

     Many in the medical community are dissatisfied with
this legally ambiguous situation, and so they continue to
press for a modification of the law. In June 1971, the Grabham Society, a professional organization of obstetricians and
gynecologists, issued a resolution that called for revision
of the law and offered several specific recommendations. The
Society urged that the termination of a pregnancy be considered
lawful whenever "a registered medical practitioner in good
faith considers that the pregnancy threatens the life or health
(mental or physical) of the mother bearing in mind all relevant,
present, and future foreseeable circumstances." The resolution
further recommended that a doctor not be obligated to perform
an abortion if this would offend his conscience; that facilities where abortions are to be performed be approved by the
Ministry of Health; that a client be a resident of Jamaica,
except in cases of emergency; and that each abortion be reported to the Ministry of Health, but in a manner that assures
the client's anonymity.

                        SURVEY OBJECTIVES

     It was against this background of debate and uncer-
tainty that we conducted a national survey of medical and related professional opinion in cooperation with the Medical
Association of Jamaica. Our study had three purposes:

1. To provide policymakers with an overview of attitudes and opinions of those who, in the long run, must implement policy on abortion if it is to have the intended consequences;

2. To identify a consensus of informed opinion among
medical personnel concerning their evaluation of proposed
changes in law or policy on abortion, their own recommendations for change, and their predictions of the likely impact
of these changes on existing health services; and

3. To elicit judgments of the comparative magnitude
of illegal abortion as a public health problem.

Any rewriting of the law or expansion of health services must, in the end, be accepted and carried out by the
"gatekeepers"--the physicians, nurses, and other medical personnel who hold key positions. Karl Deutsch (1963) refers to
this group as the strategic "middle level of communications
and control," without whose cooperation or consent very little
can be done and, particularly, very little can be changed.
These individuals may greatly help or hinder the day-to-day
implementation of any new policy or program, yet their views
are too often disregarded during the formative discussions and
deliberations. It was the purpose of our survey to gather, in-
tegrate, and refine the expert opinion of such personnel--to
determine how they perceived the abortion problem in Jamaica,
what they themselves would recommend, and how they reacted to
the proposed changes. In this way, it was hoped to make
policymaking less of a closed-chamber affair isolated from the
informed judgment of those who will, in large part, determine
the eventual fate of top-level decisions.

METHOD

To the best of our knowledge, this study represents
one of the first instances of the use of the Delphi method in
population research. The name derives from the Grecian oracle
at Delphi where priestesses with foaming lips were believed to
have predicted events, and where leaders of the Greek city-
states sought clues about the future. The Delphi method,
first developed at the RAND Corporation more than a decade ago,
is a technique for soliciting and refining "informed" opinions
on topics vexed by uncertainty, speculation, and a lack of
trustworthy information (Chambers, Mullick, & Smith, 1971).
For social and technological forecasting, it is most often applied in achieving consensus on major forthcoming events and
on their timing.

The Delphi method has many variations, but a common feature is the repeated interrogation of respondents on their expectations and understandings regarding a particular issue. They are questioned separately and anonymously to avoid band-wagon effects or conformity in the face of authority. A summary of results is then fed back to the respondents, who may revise their judgments or repeat them. In some cases justification is sought for deviant opinions, and these are also fed back to the respondents as further stimuli for reexamining their original judgments. Eventually, individual views tend to converge and a group consensus is achieved. The method combines group discussion and opinion polling techniques, but, in the domain of conjecture and uncertainty, it is considered superior to both. Repeated questioning with controlled feedback has been demonstrated to yield a more accurate consensus than does simply averaging the responses obtained from a single survey. Furthermore, closely guarding the anonymity of the participants reduces the influence of group pressure to conform and neutralizes the overwhelming dominance of prestigious figures (Dalkey et al., 1972).

In adapting the Delphi design for our study, we planned that each participant would be questioned in two successive rounds of data gathering. During round 1, 120 informants--doctors, public health nurses, and district midwives--were individually interviewed at length about their perceptions of the present situation with respect to abortion, the courses of action they themselves would recommend, their views on the proposed changes in the law, and their predictions on the consequences of those changes. Round 1 was conducted in July 1973. Following a preliminary analysis of round 1 data, a very short questionnaire, which supplied feedback to the participants in the form of frequency distributions for selected questions, was prepared for round 2. Participants then had the opportunity to reconsider their previous answers in the light of the views of their anonymous colleagues and co-workers. Answers to other open-ended probe questions in round 1 were converted to provide response categories for close-ended questions in round 2. The second round, which was carried out in September 1973, also allowed ambiguous responses to be clarified and permitted the follow-up of intriguing leads produced by the first round.

SAMPLING

The national sample for round 1 of the study consisted of 70 physicians, 16 public health nurses, and 34 licensed district midwives selected by a stratified random sampling procedure. In each case, stratification was by parish of residence, and the proportion was determined according to the distribution of the personnel throughout the country. The physicians were selected from the membership of the Medical Association of Jamaica, to which the overwhelming majority of physicians engaged in private practice belongs. These 70 physicians represented about 20 percent of the total membership of the Association and included 27 general practitioners and 8 specialists in obstetrics and gynecology. Eighty percent were men, and more than 50 percent practiced in the Kingston area--a reflection of the high concentration of physicians there compared with the other parishes. The public health nurses and midwives were selected from the personnel records of the Ministry of Health. All were women and, unlike the physicians, were likely to work in the small towns and rural areas.

The sample for round 2 consisted of 65 physicians and 37 nurses and midwives, most of whom had participated in round 1. We also sought the views of 20 physicians not included in the original random sample who were judged to be well informed or who had been outspoken on the abortion issue, either pro or con. Thirty-one of the physicians and 10 of the nurses and midwives whom we considered especially knowledgeable informants were interviewed in person in round 2. The remainder--34 physicians and 27 nurses and midwives--responded to the questionnaire by mail.

There was a 100 percent response in round 1, with few instances in which it was necessary to go into a reserve sample. The overall return rate for the mailed questionnaire was 60 percent (i.e., of the 101 mailed, 61 were completed and returned). Most responsive were the nurses (71 percent returned), followed by physicians (60 percent), and midwives (50 percent). Some attrition in the sample was due to the absence of some respondents from Jamaica during round 2.

RESULTS

In reviewing the findings of the survey, we will attempt to answer four main questions:

1. Do doctors and other health professionals favor a liberalized abortion law?

2. How do members of the medical profession perceive the seriousness of illegal abortion as compared with the seriousness of other health problems?

3. What is the expected impact of abortion law liberalization?

4. What innovations in health care delivery would be
advisable if the legal restrictions against abortion were
relaxed?

Does the Medical Profession Favor
a Liberalized Abortion Law?

Awareness of the Grabham Society resolution mentioned
earlier was not widespread, in spite of the fact that the
resolution was nearly two years old and had been fully reported in Jamaica's major newspaper. More than one-third of
the physicians had not heard about it prior to the survey, nor
had two-thirds of the nurses and midwives. Nevertheless, once
the respondents were informed of the position taken in the
resolution, 84 percent of the physicians and 88 percent of the
nurses and midwives expressed themselves to be in general
agreement with it.

An interesting difference was noted in comparing the
respondents' own opinions with their answers when asked to
guess the reaction of their colleagues toward the resolution.
Respondents tended to anticipate a less favorable evaluation
of the resolution by their peers than was actually the case.
Physicians and nurses underestimated the extent of support
only slightly--by less than 10 percent. But midwives very
much missed the mark. While 88 percent of the midwives questioned favored the resolution, only 65 percent thought that
most other midwives supported it. A somewhat more detailed
breakdown of medical opinion concerning the Grabham Society
resolution is shown in Table 11-1.

Even though the Grabham Society resolution found widespread acceptance among medical practitioners, there were important differences of opinion about specific provisions that
any revised law should include (see Table 11-2). Seventy-
four percent of the doctors wanted legal protection to include
coverage for abortions performed on minors; however, such extension of protection to cover minors was opposed by 65 percent of the nurses and midwives. A large majority of physicians (80 percent) would prohibit abortions after the twelfth
week of pregnancy. By contrast, approximately 84 percent of
the nurses and midwives objected to such a prohibition. Nurses
and midwives, however, were more inclined than physicians to
limit the number of abortions a woman could obtain.

There was substantial support among all respondents
for the use of abortion in cases of contraceptive failure.
Nearly 70 percent of the physicians favored abortion as a
backup method for regulating fertility, as did 54 percent of
the nurses and midwives. Most expressed the view that abortion should be offered under the auspices of the government.

Table 11-1

Medical Opinion Concerning the Grabham Society
Resolution on Abortion: Jamaica, 1973
(in percents)

Item	Physicians (N = 70)	Nurses and Midwives (N=50)
Awareness of resolution		
Had heard about it	60	32
Had not heard about it	39	68
Not sure	1	
Attitude toward resolution once informed about it		
Favorable	84	88
Unfavorable	10	4
Mixed	6	6
Undecided		2
Beliefs about colleagues' views on resolution		
Most support it	81	70[a]
Most oppose it	3	8
Don't know	16	22

Note. [a]Among the midwives, 88 percent said that they themselves favored it; 65 percent thought that other midwives
would support the resolution.

sponsored National Family Planning Board--particularly in
cases of contraceptive failure (not shown in table).

Abortions also should be available without cost to
women unable to afford them, according to 85 percent of the
doctors and 57 percent of the nurses and midwives. We sus-
pect, on the basis of our data, that one reason for the widespread advocacy of free abortion is that women often delay
seeking abortions until they have the money to pay the abortionist, and this delay increases the risk of complications.

Table 11-2

Medical Opinion on Abortion-Related Questions
Jamaica, 1973

Question	Percent Answering "Yes"	
	Physicians (N=65)	Nurses and Midwives (N=37)
Should a woman alone make abortion decision?	14	9
Should women and doctor together make decision?	68	62
Should prior approval of two doctors be required?	20	16
Should doctors be given legal protection for performing abortions on minors?	74	35
Should abortion be urged if child probably will be deformed or retarded?	57	57
Should abortions after 12 weeks be forbidden?	80	16
Should the number of abortions a woman can have be limited?	37	49
If a woman has had several abortions, should sterilization be required?	45	35
Should abortions be free for women who cannot afford to pay?	85	57
Should abortions be provided in cases of contraceptive failure?	68	54

Should we forget about changing the law and, instead, enforce the present one?	6	19
Should be forget about changing the law and concentrate on improving the national family planning program?	14[a]	30
Should the following be dropped from the Grabham Society Resolution?		
All abortions must be reported to the Ministry of Health	31	8
Only residents can obtain abortions	23	11
The Ministry of Health must approve places where abortions are performed	15	14

Note. The data in this table are from round 2. These issues were raised by the respondents themselves during round 1.

[a]The percentage of physicians opposed to the continuation of the existing law (86 percent) closely corresponds to the percentage favoring the Grabham Society Resolution (84 percent). The two questions were asked in different rounds, and the groups of respondents were not identical. Hence, we can have some confidence in the reliability of our data concerning physicians' opinions on this issue.

How Serious a Problem Is Illegal Abortion
as Compared with Other Health Problems?

        One aim of the survey was to obtain from medical and
related professionals their perception of the comparative magnitude of induced abortion as a public health problem. We
thought it worthwhile to question doctors, nurses, and midwives because, as a group, they constitute one of the most accessible "informed" sources of information about the extent
of illegal abortion. Through their day-to-day practice, they
are aware of women who become pregnant but do not give birth.
They see cases of women who have suffered complications or incomplete abortions at the hands of the medically unqualified
or who have attempted self-induced abortions. They are asked
for advice about how to obtain abortions, and some may perform
abortions themselves.

        We sought opinions about comparative occurrence be-
cause judgments of comparative frequency are closer to clinical experience and, hence, are likely to be more trustworthy
than are more quantitative guesses about incidence. The procedure we employed was simply to provide respondents in round
1 with a list of 18 diseases and medical conditions common in
Jamaica. The respondent's task was to judge whether the occurrence of illegal abortion was more or less common than the
diagnosis and treatment of each of the diseases on the list.
In round 2, this list was shortened by eliminating diagnostic
and treatment categories that a large majority of our respondents agreed were more common or less common than abortion, and
by retaining those for which opinion was more evenly divided.

        The results from round 2 indicate that physicians,
nurses, and midwives were in substantial agreement in the
judgment that appendicitis occurred less frequently than did
abortion; 64 percent of the physicians and 70 percent of the
nurses and midwives thought so. In contrast, the comparative
frequency of miscarriage relative to abortion evoked some disagreement among physicians, but not among nurses and midwives.
Slightly less than half the physicians (49 percent) believed
miscarriage was more common than abortion, while 42 percent
thought miscarriage less common. Nine percent could not say,
even on the second round. Among the nurses and midwives, however, 83 percent thought that miscarriage was less common than
illegal abortion, with only one percent unable to express an
opinion.

        A very common view among our respondents was that re-
peat abortion is not very common in Jamaica. It is thought
that few women have more than one. However, this question

also elicited a relatively large number of "don't know" re-
sponses--about 25 percent.

     To a considerable extent, the perceived magnitude of
illegal abortion as a public health problem is influenced by
who is thought to perform the operation. Our survey found
nearly unanimous agreement that pharmacists and licensed physicians are the most active in performing illegal abortions.
The only substantial disagreement emerged over the role of
nurses and midwives. The physicians in our sample suspected
a greater involvement of nurses and midwives in performing illegal abortions than did the nurses and midwives themselves.
Since pharmacists were not included in our sample, we do not
know how they would assess the extent of their colleagues'
involvement.

     The rate of complications from illegal abortions was,
not surprisingly, seen to be linked to who performed them.
For abortions performed by pharmacists, the risk of complication was believed to be at least 50/50 by most physicians (67
percent) and nurses and midwives (63 percent). But, for abortions performed by licensed physicians, the risk was believed
to be much lower--less than 25 percent of cases. This degree
of confidence in the skill of physicians was held by 77 percent of the nurses and midwives and 88 percent of the
physicians.*

What Will Be the Effect of Liberalization of the Abortion Law?

     Many physicians discounted the likelihood that re-
moval of legal restrictions on abortion would seriously undermine the acceptance and use of other fertility-regulating
methods. Quite the opposite effect was often expected, that
is, that the opportunity to choose between contraception and
abortion would stimulate interest in and increase awareness of
all birth control methods. The physicians did foresee an

----

     *In Husting's (1972) study of Jamaican women hospital-
ized with complications from abortion, it was reported that 30
out of 69 abortions (about 40 percent) were performed by doctors, and 14 (or 20 percent) were performed by pharmacists.
The incidence of complications serious enough to require hospitalization was roughly estimated to be one-fifth to one-
third of all induced abortions (which, by some admittedly pre-
carious extrapolation, was put at 15,000 to 25,000 per year in
Jamaica).

increase in the number of abortions, of course; and 87 percent
of those surveyed thought that a rise in demand would be experienced by health services within six months of any legislative
change.

Nurses and midwives held a different view. More than
half (57 percent) thought that women now using contraceptives
might become careless or irregular in their use because abortion would be available in the event of pregnancy. A majority
(51 percent) also expected many women to rely on abortion as
the preferred means of regulating fertility, with some dis-
continuing contraceptive use.

Does the Medical Profession Favor
New Abortion Procedures to Meet
an Increased Demand?

Most of our respondents expected that proposed legislation would lead to an increased number of abortions and that
the health services would have to undergo some changes in order to accommodate the demand. They were also queried about
their attitudes toward two specific innovations in service:
(1) the use of menstrual extraction for an early abortion* and
(2) the wider employment of medical professionals other than
doctors.

Although virtually all physicians (97 percent) said
that dilatation and curettage was still the most common abortion method used by Jamaican physicians during the first trimester, 63 percent had, prior to the interview, heard about
menstrual extraction.

However, among those already familiar with menstrual
extraction, most (78 percent) did not know whether it was being used in Jamaica. For the most part, knowledge of the
method came from reading published accounts. Given a brief
description of the procedure at the time of the interview, 76

---

*Menstrual extraction is a form of suction curettage
that is intended for use as early as six days after a missed
menses, and up to 40 days of amenorrhea. The technique causes
uterine bleeding as a result of suction being applied through
a 4 mm to 6 mm cannula attached to a syringe or small pump.
The entire procedure takes 5-10 minutes, requires neither
anesthesia nor dilation of the cervix, and causes only minimal
discomfort. A prior pregnancy test is not necessary (Brenner
et al., 1973).

percent of the physicians expressed a favorable attitude toward it, but more than half (53 percent) believed the method
should be subject to the same controls and safeguards as regular abortion. Thirty-eight percent of the physicians categorized themselves as likely to be either innovators or early
adoptors in their acceptance of menstrual extraction, in contrast to 28 percent who saw themselves as probably being late
adoptors or "laggards." When these data on the likely acceptance of this new method of fertility regulation are matched
with the theoretical and normal distribution of innovativeness
proposed by Rogers and Shoemaker (1971), it becomes apparent
that, as a group, Jamaican physicians may be skewed in the
direction of self-proclaimed "venturesomeness."

Physicians and nurses agreed that the main advantage
of menstrual extraction is the lower risk of complications
compared with the risk associated with abortions later in pregnancy. Another advantage, cited by many of the nurses and midwives, is that menstrual extraction may allay a woman's anxiety
about an overdue period since menses can be so simply induced.
Among the disadvantages mentioned was concern that women might
come to rely excessively upon menstrual extraction at the expense of effective contraception, and the possibility of complications or injury from repeated or improper use of the
procedure.

The successful introduction of menstrual extraction as
a new method of fertility regulation depends in part on the
ability of women readily to realize when their periods are
overdue. A large majority of our respondents believed that at
least one-half of their female patients know when their periods are seven or ten days overdue, well within the recommended
time limit for the safe use of menstrual extraction.

Because menstrual extraction is a simple procedure,
advocates in the United States and elsewhere have suggested
that the method can be safely and efficiently performed by
nonphysicians, thereby increasing its availability to women
and lowering its cost. Our survey found qualified support for
extending the role of Jamaican nurses and paramedical personnel. Over 60 percent said that nurses, midwives, and others
should be allowed to perform menstrual extraction, but there
were differences of opinion about the extent of control that
physicians should exercise. A sizable number of nurses (47
percent) and doctors (32 percent) believed that close supervision was not necessary. Some of the caution voiced by
others was based on the fear that, without adequate supervision,
nonphysicians might sometimes attempt to use the menstrual extraction technique when pregnancies were too far advanced, thus
risking serious complications.

DIFFERENCES IN ATTITUDES AMONG MEDICAL PROFESSIONALS

Although physicians, nurses, and midwives believed that many, perhaps most, of their colleagues would support abortion law liberalization, there was a tendency to underestimate the level of actual support. This is a tendency that has been observed elsewhere. V. D. Thompson and her collaborators discovered that among "elites" surveyed in urban North Carolina the extent of support for less restrictive population policies was underestimated and the degree of opposition overestimated (Thompson, Appelbaum, & Allen, 1974). An important implication of this finding was noted:

> Those who are most likely to be or to become policy implementers. . .are the most inaccurate in their perceptions. While they themselves have relatively high acceptance levels, particularly for nonrestrictive [policies], they do not accurately perceive others' relatively high acceptance of the same policies. . . . The consequence is no doubt one of inaction. (Thompson, Applebaum, & Allen, 1974, pp. 68-69)

In Jamaica, the discrepancy between actual and perceived levels of support was most marked among nurses and midwives. They were also somewhat less consistent than physicians in favoring a nonrestrictive abortion policy, and their ambivalence may well reflect role tension.

Physicians' judgments are heavily influenced by their identification with the special norms and values of their professional group. Once a question is defined as being primarily medical in nature, they tend to resist the intrusion of nonmedical points of view as irrelevant or incompetent. Hence, the abortion issue is perceived more as a medical problem to be dealt with by the physician than as a social problem to be solved by government action. The repeal of the restrictive abortion law finds strong support among physicians because it would remove "outside" interference with medical decision-making (Veatch & Draper, n.d.).

Nurses and midwives, on the other hand, are less influenced by the forces of professionalism that shape the views and conduct of physicians. The ambivalence reflected in the evaluation of their colleagues' opinions and in their attitudes toward abortion policies may be due to the lack of a complete role identification with the medical community. The nurses and midwives are women while most Jamaican physicians

are men, and nurses and midwives more often live and work in
the rural parishes than do physicians. Thus, nurses and midwives tend to hold attitudes and values more in common with
the nonmedical community. The fact that they nevertheless extensively support a relaxation of legal curbs against abortion
indicates that their motivation is not one of narrow professional control; that is, to fend off nonmedical interference
with the medical right-to-act. Rather, their concerns are
more broadly based and reflect the prevailing views of the
community at large.

The survey results show that, despite misgivings and
reservations, there is very solid support in these three segments of the medical community for a liberalization of the
current abortion law and for modifications in the organization and delivery of health services to accommodate an increased demand for abortion. It is significant that not one
of the 70 physicians interviewed said that he or she would
never perform an abortion, although 25 percent indicated that
they might be inclined to refer a case to another physician.
Large numbers of our respondents said that they had changed
their minds about abortion within the past three or four
years: about two-thirds of the medical personnel surveyed. In
the majority of instances, the shift was in the direction of
a more favorable attitude (see Table 11-3).

Table 11-3

Change of Attitude Toward Abortion among Medical Personnel:
Jamaica, 1973 (in percents)

Change of Attitude	Physicians (N=70)	Nurses and Midwives (N=50)
Has attitude changed during past 3-4 years?		
Yes	64	68
No	36	32
If attitude has changed, is it now more favorable or less favorable than before?		
More favorable	89	97
Less favorable	11	3

The trend toward the acceptance of abortion as a means of regulating fertility reflects the deep concern shown by the medical community for the population growth rate in Jamaica. It has been projected (Walsh, 1971) that if the present growth rate persists the population of Jamaica--which now numbers about 2 million--will rise to 6 million by the year 2000 and to over 12 million by the year 2020. Such growth would cause a severe drain on already inadequate resources and could undermine the present political and economic system. The evidence from our study indicates that this danger clearly is perceived by members of the medical and paramedical professions. Table 11-4 shows that among all respondents the control of a rapidly expanding population was ranked among the top three social problems confronting the nation.

Table 11-4

Ranking of Major Social Problems by Medical Personnel: Jamaica, 1973 (average ranks)

	Average Rank	
Social Problems	Physicians (N=70)	Nurses and Midwives (N=50)
1. Unemployment	2.8	3.0
2. Overpopulation	2.9	3.0
3. Lack of adequate housing	4.3	2.4
4. Malnutrition	4.0	4.1
5. Low level of educational attainment	3.4	4.8
6. Ignorance of health care	4.9	5.9
7. Inadequate water supply, sanitation	5.9	6.1
8. Poor roads, communication	7.0	6.7

CONCLUSION

The findings of this study indicate that, from the standpoint of the medical community, governmental action to relax legal curbs on abortion would be an evolutionary, not a revolutionary step. Those engaged in administration and policymaking in government work within existing systems. They prefer courses of action that improve efficiency and performance without the risks and disruptions involved in radical innovation (Fawcett, 1974). Lord Salisbury's analogy that foreign policy is like drifting downstream could apply as well to population policy. The thing to do, Salisbury advised, is to stick out a pole occasionally to keep the boat from colliding with the bank. The liberalization of the current abortion law would be no more than a slight correction in course, according to the views of Jamaican physicians, nurses, and midwives we surveyed.

A smooth and uneventful transition could be expected, following a removal of restrictions on the availability of abortion, for three major reasons:

1. The practice of abortion among Jamaican women is believed to be already widespread, and a number of physicians appear to be very much involved in providing abortion services, even under existing circumstances of legal risk.

2. The medical and related professions stand ready to adopt the changes in the health care delivery system required to adequately meet the expected increase in demand for abortions following modification of the law.

3. A nonrestrictive abortion law finds general support within the medical community.

REFERENCES

Brenner, W. E., et al. Suction curettage for "menstrual regulation." Paper presented at meeting of the American Association of Planned Parenthood Physicians, Houston, Texas, 1973.

Chambers, J. C., Mullick, S. K., & Smith, D. D. How to choose the right forecasting technique. *Harvard Business Review*, 1971, 49, 45-74.

Dalkey, N. C., et al. *Studies in the quality of life: Delphi and decision-making.* Lexington, Mass.: Lexington Books, 1972.

Deutsch, K. W. *The nerves of government.* New York: Free Press, 1963.

Fawcett, J. T. Social and psychological aspects of fertility issues and priorities. Paper presented at ECAFE Expert Group Meeting on Social and Psychological Aspects of Fertility Behavior, Bangkok, June 1974.

Husting, E. L. Preliminary report on interviews with post-
    abortal patients at Victoria Jubilee Hospital. Unpublished
    paper, University of Pittsburgh Graduate School of Public
    Health, 1972.

Jamaica, Government of. Offenses Against the Person Act,
    1861, Articles 65-66. In The laws of Jamaica, Vol. 6
    (revised edition). Kingston: Government Printer, 1953.

Rogers, E. M., & Shoemaker, F. F. Communication of innova-
    tions: A crosscultural approach. New York: The Free
    Press, 1971.

Rosen, R. C. Law and population growth in Jamaica. Medford,
    Mass.: The Fletcher School of Law and Diplomacy, Law and
    Population Program, 1973.

Thompson, V. D., Appelbaum, M. I., & Allen, J. E. Population
    policy acceptance: Psychological determinants. Chapel
    Hill, N.C.: Carolina Population Center, 1974.

Veatch, R. M., & Draper, T. F. Population policy and the
    values of physicians. Hastings-on-Hudson, N.Y.: Institute
    of Society, Ethics, and the Life Sciences (The Hastings
    Center), no date.

Walsh, B. T. Economic development and population control: A
    fifty year projection for Jamaica. New York: Praeger,
    1971.

12

Medical and Paramedical Opinion in Nigeria*

Christopher G. M. Bakare

Editors' Note: Building on the previously reported experience with the Delphi method in Jamaica, it was possible to demonstrate that illegal abortion constitutes a major public health and societal problem in Nigeria. The findings and recommendations have been widely disseminated and endorsed but continue to await governmental implementation.

INTRODUCTION

In spite of the very restrictive nature of the current abortion law in Nigeria, the phenomenon of abortion is known to be very widespread in the country. Although imprisonment of up to 14 years is prescribed under the Nigerian Criminal Code for any person convicted of inducing an abortion, it is nevertheless recognized that illegal abortion now constitutes one of the leading causes of maternal mortality and morbidity in the large urban areas of the country.

Dada (1974), for instance, estimated that there are at least 5,000 abortions performed in the Lagos area every year; Akinla and Adadevoh (1969) indicated that terminating unwanted pregnancies is common not only among young single girls but among married women as well. Likewise, Onifade (forthcoming) found that in a sample which he studied, 19.9 percent of the office workers and 34.7 percent of the factory

*A joint project of the Behavioural Sciences Research Unit, University of Ibadan, and the Transnational Family Research Institute. I am pleased to acknowledge the contributions of Sisters T. B. Craig, R. O. Francis, and J. U. Aredele; Mrs. C. R. O. Barlow; and Mr. A. O. Oyeneye, who collected and analyzed the data on behalf of the Behavioural Sciences Research Unit.

workers admitted to one or more abortions, and that 25 percent
of these were induced for nonmedical indications. In the same
vein, Akingba (1971), in a well-documented work, testifies to
the widespread incidence of abortion among Nigerian single and
married women and highlights some of the common complications
when such abortion is procured from quack doctors. On this
and other grounds he made a reasoned plea for the liberalization of the existing abortion laws in the country.

      The very high incidence of illegal abortion and its
dreadful complications is common knowledge in Nigeria. It has
been said that public concern over this rising incidence provided the major impetus for the promotion of modern family
planning in the country. It is perhaps such public concern
as well that has made abortion one of the most controversial
medical topics in and outside of medical circles in Nigeria
today.

      Informed public discussion on the abortion issue can-
not proceed in the absence of reliable data. Unfortunately,
collecting data on the phenomenon of abortion is beset by several difficulties. First, in countries like Nigeria where
abortion is still illegal, clandestine abortionists keep no
records and volunteer little or no information on their practice and their clients. Second, the women who have abortions
are careful to maintain their anonymity and are extremely reluctant to discuss an incident that they often consider to be
tinged with some degree of stigma. Thus, the two most reliable sources of data on abortion are closed or almost closed
to the research worker. Yet, there is an urgent need to provide trustworthy epidemiological and other data on the phenomenon of abortion; for, without such data, there can be no
sound basis for public policy on this important issue,

      In this situation, the one group in society from whom
the nearest simulation of reliable data on abortion could be
obtained would be members of the medical profession who primarily deal with women. In their everyday practice they are
aware of women who become pregnant but do not give birth, having terminated the pregnancy before term. They have to treat
women who suffer the complications of self-induced abortions
or of those performed by the medically unqualified. They are
asked for advice about how to obtain an abortion and some perform abortions themselves. Hence, the medical profession constitutes a repository of knowledge on the abortion phenomenon.
But the importance of this group does not stop there. Because
of their key position, their opinions carry far-reaching implications for policy, especially in regard to the liberalization of the existing abortion laws. And furthermore, the
stand of the medical profession on abortion will affect the

implementation of any new abortion policy because members of
the profession will be directly involved in its implementation.
These are some of the major considerations that motivated the
present study.

OBJECTIVES

The major objectives of the present study were:

1. to obtain from medical personnel an indication of
the relative magnitude of illegal abortion as a public health
problem in Nigeria;

2. to obtain background data on the abortion problem
by identifying the perceptions of medical personnel on various
aspects of the abortion phenomenon (e.g., characteristics of
women seeking abortion; attendant problems from the woman's
and the doctor's viewpoint; the type of people performing
abortion, the fees charged, the methods used, and the complications resulting, if any); and

3. to provide policy makers with an overview of the
attitudes and opinions of the medical personnel towards the
liberalization of the current abortion laws in Nigeria and of
the probable impact of such a move on the existing family
planning and health delivery systems.

METHOD

This study employed the "Gatekeeper" design (Johnson
et al., 1973), which was developed for the purpose of increasing the validity of information drawn from professionals and
paraprofessionals on sensitive and difficult topics, such as
abortion, by achieving an informed consensus. It employs a
modified version of the Delphi technique first developed by
the RAND Corporation. The technique is characterized by repeated interrogation of respondents on their expectations and
understandings of a particular topic. A summary of results
from an initial interview is fed back to respondents who may
confirm or revise their previous opinions. In some cases,
justification is sought for deviant opinions, and these are
also fed back to the respondents as stimuli for re-examining
their original judgments. Eventually, individual views tend
to converge and group consensus is achieved. This method of
repeated questioning with controlled feedback has been shown
to yield a more accurate consensus of opinion than do the responses obtained from a single survey.

Subjects

Round 1. The sample used in the first round of the present
study consisted of 250 medical practitioners randomly selected
from the various professional registers. The sample included
general practitioners, obstetricians, gynecologists, nurse-
midwives, pharmacists, and traditional medicine men and midwives. The actual numbers selected from each group were:

-- Medical doctors (general practitioners,
   obstetricians, and gynecologists)   100

-- Paramedical personnel (nurse-midwives,
   pharmacists)   100

-- Traditional medicine men and midwives   50

                                            Total   250

        To ensure geographical representativeness, the medical
and paramedical personnel were selected from three areas:
West, East, and Northern Nigeria (Ibadan, Enugu, and Kaduna).
The 50 native doctors were selected from the Ibadan area, making a grand total of 250 subjects.

Round 2. Subjects for round 2 of the survey were 30 medical
practitioners selected from the Ibadan and Lagos areas. This
second stage of the study was confined to these areas mainly
because the initial analysis of the round 1 questionnaire
showed the responses of the medical practitioners from the
three areas of the country to be extremely similar. Nothing
new was therefore to be gained by covering the entire country
again. Moreover, because mailed questionnaires are practically
a waste of time and money in Nigeria, especially with busy
professionals, the respondents had to be individually interviewed. Hence it was found more expedient in terms of logis-
tics and in terms of the time and funds available to confine
round 2 to these 30 medical practitioners who are recognized
to be specially knowledgeable about the abortion issue.

                        Interview Schedules

        The round 1 interview schedules were adaptations of
questionnaires originally developed for the Jamaican study
conducted jointly by the University of the West Indies and
the Transnational Family Research Institute (see chapter 11).
The schedules contained questions on various aspects of the
abortion issue, such as the incidence of abortion as compared

with that of some other common ailments, the types of persons
performing abortion, the characteristics of women seeking it,
the methods used, the common complications that could occur,
the fees charged, and the attendant problems from the woman's
and from the doctor's viewpoint. The schedules also included
major questions on the legalization of abortion, the restrictions that should be imposed in the event of its legalization,
the acceptability of new fertility-regulating methods, and the
overall effect of eventual legalization on the country's family planning program. Respondents were not asked directly
about their own practice but about their view of the general
situation.

The round 2 questionnaire was prepared following a
preliminary analysis of round 1 data. It supplied feedback to
respondents in the form of frequency distributions of answers
to selected questions. Respondents then had the opportunity
to reconsider their initial opinions in the light of the
views of their anonymous colleagues. The round 2 questionnaire also provided the opportunity for clarifying ambiguous
responses and for following up intriguing leads produced by
the first round.

Procedures

Both rounds 1 and 2 questionnaires were individually
administered to the respondents in face-to-face interviews.
A few questionnaires were left with respondents to be completed
in their own spare time. The interviewers then returned to obtain the completed questionnaires.

Whenever a respondent selected into the sample was not
available, another one was selected randomly from the register
as replacement. In all, completed questionnaires were obtained from 100 doctors, 48 nurse-midwives, and 49 pharmacists
in the country-wide survey.

In analyzing the results, frequency counts were made
of the responses to the various questions and a content analysis was made of the responses to the open-ended questions.

RESULTS

Incidence of Illegal Abortion

One of the major objectives of the present study was
to obtain the perceptions of medical and paramedical personnel
on the incidence of illegal abortion in Nigeria relative to

other common diseases. As has been mentioned, induced abortion is illegal in the country, and thus it is practically impossible to obtain actual figures of its incidence either from
those who perform it or from the women who have experienced it,
One of the conventional ways to get around this problem is to
elicit judgments from medical and paramedical personnel concerning the comparative frequency of illegal abortion and
other common ailments. Such judgments are known to be closer
to clinical experiences and therefore more reliable than actual quantitative guesses of incidence.

In round 1 of the survey respondents were provided
with a list of 18 diseases and medical conditions common in
Nigeria. They were then asked to judge whether the occurrence
of illegal abortion was mcre or less common than the diagnosis
and treatment of each of the diseases on the list. In round
2 of the survey, the list was confined only to diseases on
which there were no clear-cut agreements or for which further
confirmation of the estimated incidence was thought necessary.

In analyzing the results, a 50 percent cut point was
adopted and the only diseases recorded for further discussion
were those that 50 percent or more of the respondents thought
occurred more or less frequently than abortion. Table 12-1
shows the diseases that at least 50 percent of the respondents
believe to occur less frequently than abortion. Table 12-2
shows those thought to occur more frequently than abortion.
Of course, Table 12-1 is more important for estimating the seriousness of illegal abortion as a public health hazard. It
shows that there is agreement among at least two of the three
groups (physicians, midwives, and pharmacists) that abortion
is more frequent than toxemia of pregnancy, miscarriage, and
vaginal infections. It also shows that doctors (who perhaps
are in the best position to know) also feel that abortion is
more frequent than placenta previa and joint diseases.

Results from round 2 of the survey indicate that there
is substantial agreement that abortion is more frequent than
toxemia of pregnancy, ectopic pregnancy, and joint diseases.
It is as frequent as miscarriage and less frequent than worm
infestation.

It is, of course, clear that in order to obtain a more
accurate picture of the magnitude of illegal abortion as a
public health problem, it would be necessary to have actual
figures for the incidence of at least those diseases that are
the same or are less in frequency than illegal abortion itself.
However, such exact figures are not available for these diseases, and therefore a quantitative estimate of the incidence
of illegal abortion cannot be made. Still, it is possible to

Table 12-1

Relative Incidence of Abortion: Diseases Thought
to Be Less Frequent than Abortion

Diseases	Respondents (raw frequencies in parentheses)		
	Doctors (N=100)	Midwives (N=48)	Pharmacists (N=49)
Toxemia of pregnancy	59% (59)	52.08% (25)	
Miscarriage	59% (59)	77.08% (37)	58.33%
Placenta previa	60% (60)		
Joint diseases	51% (51)		
Urinary tract infection		52.08% (25)	
Ectopic pregnancy		60.41% (29)	
Vaginal infection		52.08% (25)	58.33%
Venereal disease		50.00% (24)	
Anemia		50.00% (24)	
Coronary Thrombosis			50.00%

reach the qualitative conclusion that since illegal abortion
is more frequent than diseases that are themselves known to
be public health problems, illegal abortion in Nigeria is perceived by these medical and paramedical personnel as a relatively common phenomenon and a definite public health problem.

The Abortion Phenomenon

Another major objective of the present study was to
obtain from medical and paramedical personnel in Nigeria their
own perceptions of various aspects of the abortion phenomenon.
Besides providing data that are hard to get in any other way,
such perceptions also provide an additional indication of the
magnitude of illegal abortion as a public health hazard. This
is because, to a large extent, the perceived magnitude of illegal abortion as a public health problem is influenced by
such factors as the category of personnel thought to perform
it, the methods used, and the common complications that arise.

Table 12-2

Relative Incidence of Abortion: Diseases Thought
To Be More Frequent than Abortion

	Respondents (raw frequencies in parentheses)		
	Doctors (N=100)	Midwives (N=48)	Pharmacists (N=49)
Respiratory infection	69% (69)		55.10% (27)
Urinary tract infection	73% (73)		
Hypertension	64% (64)	58.3% (28)	
Fungal skin infection	71% (71)	58.3% (28)	
Vaginal infection	61% (61)		
Venereal disease	54% (54)		
Anemia	54% (54)		
Eye infection	56% (56)		55.10% (27)
Ear infection	52% (52)	47.9% (23)	61.22% (30)
Appendicitis	56% (56)		
Common childhood disease	60% (60)	66.6% (32)	
Malaria	66% (66)	56.25% (27)	48.97% (26)
Sickle cell anemia	50% (50	52.08% (25)	
Coronary thrombosis		54.16% (26)	
Diabetes mellitus		68.71% (33)	
Placenta previa		54.16% (26)	
Joint diseases		58.3% (28)	
Worm infestation		79.16% (38)	

Persons Performing Abortion. Three groups of respondents--
doctors, pharmacists, and native healers--agree that medical
practitioners top the list of those who perform abortion;
midwives, in complete disagreement with these other groups,
feel that druggists top the list. Of particular importance,

however, is the fact that all respondents believe that people
of little or no medical training (druggists, native healers,
nurses) feature largely among those who perform abortion, The
fact that the overwhelming percentage of abortion seekers go
to these people (because of their larger number, greater accessibility, and lower fees) indicates the great danger to
which abortion seekers are exposed in Nigeria,

Methods Used in Procuring Abortion, Tables 12-3 and 12-4 show
the common methods used in procuring abortion at different periods of the pregnancy cycle, Doctors, midwives, and pharmacists attest to the predominant use of dilatation and curettage
during the first three months of pregnancy and to the slight
decrease in the importance of this method after the first three
months of pregnancy. Especially noteworthy is the collection
of rather strange methods used by native healers, shown in
Table 12-4. A glance at this table shows that the ingestion
of many of the materials indicated (e.g., potash, rough limestone, indigo blue) constitute a great threat to human life.

Common Complications of Illegal Abortion. The common complications of abortion when performed at different periods of the
pregnancy cycle are shown in Tables 12-5 and 12-6. Perforation
of the uterus during the first three months of pregnancy and
hemorrhage after the first three months are the complications
most frequently mentioned by doctors, midwives, and pharmacists
alike. The rather weird list of complications (e.g., death,
insanity, and swollen chest) mentioned by native healers and
the very fact that death looms large in this collection are
hardly surprising judging by the methods used by this group to
induce abortion,

It is also noteworthy that most respondents agreed
that the risk of complications increases with the lack of medical expertise of the person performing the abortion, For instance, the majority of respondents felt that the risk of complications is less than 1 in 4 cases when the abortion is
performed by a physician, about 1 in 4 if performed by a midwife, about 3 in 4 when performed by a pharmacist, and more
than 3 in 4 when performed by a native healer, They also
agreed that the risk of complications increases with the delay
in seeking and obtaining an abortion, The respondents' perceptions of why women delay having an abortion included: (a) lack
of awareness about the risks of abortion late in pregnancy;
(b) difficulty of dinding someone or a method to use; (c) fear
of legal consequences; and (d) use of ineffective methods before finding one that worked,

Since it appears that most women in Nigeria seek illegal abortions from those with little or no medical training,

Table 12-3

Methods Used in Procuring Abortion:
First and Second Trimesters

Method	Doctors[a] (N=100)	Midwives[a] (N=48)	Pharmacists[a] (N=49)
First Trimester			
Dilatation and curettage	93% (93)	91.7% (44)	87.76% (43)
Saline in uterus	4% (4)	-	-
Prostaglandins	1% (1)	12.5% (6)	4.08% (2)
Vacuum aspiration	-	-	6.12% (3)
Second Trimester			
Dilatation and curettage	30% (30)	52.08% (25)	57.14% (28)
Vacuum aspiration	13% (13)	2.08% (1)	6.12% (3)
Prostaglandins	10% (10)	20.08% (10)	28.56% (14)
Saline in uterus	5% (5)	6.25% (3)	4.08% (2)
Operative procedure other than D&C	4% (4)	2.08% (1)	4.08% (2)
Others	5% (5)	6.25% (3)	-

Note. [a]Raw frequencies in parentheses

including native healers who use dubious and unsafe methods, they risk serious physical harm from the procedure. That many delay having the abortion only adds to the dimensions of what is evidently a grave public health problem.

Problems of Illegal Abortion from the Woman's and the
Doctor's Viewpoint and Suggested Solutions

The present survey also sought the opinions of re-spondents on the problems associated with illegal abortion from the standpoint of the woman who is seeking the abortion and from the standpoint of the doctor who is called upon to provide the service. This approach provides a fresh perspec-tive on the problem because it highlights--from the woman's side--the personal-emotional cost of seeking an illegal abor-tion. Table 12-7 shows respondents' perceptions of the rela-tive importance of the problems associated with illegal abor-tion from the woman's standpoint. Round 2 survey results

Table 12-4

Methods Used by Native Healers in Performing Abortions

Method	Respondents (raw frequencies in parentheses)
First 3 Months	
Native medical power	40% (20)
Bark of tree	32% (16)
Vegetable concoction	12% (6)
Native medicinal soap	12% (6)
Rocksalt	10% (5)
Indigo blue	8% (4)
Rough limestone	6% (3)
Herbs	6% (3)
Illicit gin	4% (2)
After 3 Months	
Native medical powder	28% (14)
Cooked bark of tree	22% (11)
Native medicinal soap	12% (6)
Vegetable concoction	10% (5)
Insertion of foreign object into vagina	6% (3)
Potash	4% (2)
Incarnated water	2% (1)
After 6 Months	
Medicinal loin belt	6% (3)
Native medicinal soap	4% (2)
Vegetable concoction	4% (2)
Native medical powder	4% (2)
Tobacco leaves	4% (2)
Bark of tree	4% (2)

confirm that doctors perceived that "finding someone to do it" and the "embarrassment" are the two most serious problems associated with abortion from the woman's standpoint. Doctors also perceive that the problems associated with abortion from their own standpoint are "infection," "problem of quacks," "hemorrhage," and "high mortality," in that order of importance.

Table 12-5

Common Complications of Abortion: First Trimester
and After First Trimester

Complications	Doctors[a] (N=100)	Midwives[a] (N=48)	Pharmacists[a] (N=49)
First Trimester			
Perforation of uterus	59% (59)	72.91% (35)	32.65% (16)
Infection: local and systemic	53% (53)	28.1% (13)	4.29% (7)
Hemorrhage, shock, and anemia	52% (52)	58.33% (28)	51.02% (25)
Septicemia	41% (41)	25.00% (12)	34.07% (17)
Retention of placental tissues	31% (31)	39.58% (19)	28.57% (14)
Laceration	-	10.42% (5)	-
Salphingitis	-	6.25% (3)	-
Urinary tract infection	-	-	18.37% (9)
After First Trimester			
Hemorrhage	73% (73)	20.83% (10)	22.45% (11)
Hemorrhage, shock, and anemia	30% (30)	50.00% (24)	-
Retention of placental tissues	54% (54)	12.5% (6)	12.24% (6)
Septicemia	43% (43)	22.91% (11)	30.61% (15)
Perforation of uterus	45% (45)	22.91% (11)	34.7% (17)
Urinary tract infection	15% (15)	-	8.7% (4)
Bowel obstruction	-	14.58% (7)	-
Salphingitis	-	8.33% (4)	-

Note. [a]Raw frequencies in parentheses

In regard to the line of action respondents would support to combat these problems, round 2 survey results show that 96.42 percent of respondents would insist that abortion be performed by medical personnel only; 84.62 percent would support the legalization of abortion. Only 53.84 percent would support the establishment of authorized panels for legal abortion, perhaps because such panels might limit availability of services and slow the decision-making process.

Table 12-6

Complications of Abortion when Performed by Native Healers
at Different Periods of Pregnancy

	Respondents (raw frequencies in parentheses)
Between 1st and 3rd Month	
Excessive loss of blood	44% (22)
Death	18% (9)
Swollen abdomen	8% (4)
Dizziness	8% (4)
Insanity	2% (1)
Irregular menses	2% (1)
Venereal disease	2% (1)
Weakness	2% (1)
Persistent emaciation	2% (1)
Swollen chest	2% (1)
Between 4th and 5th Month	
Death	22% (11)
Swollen stomach	16% (8)
Loss of blood	14% (7)
Dizziness	10% (5)
Infertility	8% (4)
Madness	4% (2)
Reduced energy	4% (2)
Between 7th and 9th Month	
Death	38% (19)
Retained placenta	18% (9)
Bleeding	10% (5)
Swollen stomach	10% (5)
Infertility	6% (3)
Ill health for about 3 months	6% (3)
High fever	4% (2)

On the whole, the findings in this section bring into
focus the personal-emotional costs to the woman seeking an
abortion. This factor, when considered along with the relative incidence of illegal abortion and its attendant complications discussed earlier, further highlights the seriousness
of the abortion phenomenon as a public health hazard. The
subsequent section of this report focuses more exhaustively

Table 12-7

Problems of Procuring an Abortion, from the Woman's
Standpoint (Respondents' Ranking)

Problem	Doctors	Midwives	Pharmacists
Finding someone to do the abortion	1	2	2
The embarrassment	2	1	3
The pain	3	3	4
The expense	4	4	1
Unwillingness	5	6	5
Ambivalence	-	5	6
Outcome of the operation	6	-	-

on the opinions of all groups of respondents on some of the
measures cursorily suggested above for combating this problem,
i.e., legalization of abortion, restrictions to be imposed in
the event of legalization, and the perceived impact of legalization on the existing health delivery systems.

Legalization of Abortion, Suggested Restrictions
and Impact on Existing Health Delivery Systems

One other major objective of the present study was to
ascertain if Nigerian medical and paramedical personnel would
favor a liberalization of the existing abortion law in the
country. Table 12-8 shows that the majority of doctors (83
percent) and pharmacists (69 percent) are in support of liberalizing the existing laws, although quite a number of the
latter group abstained from giving any opinion. The doctors'
position on this issue was also confirmed by the results of
round 2 of the survey, where 76 percent of the doctors expressed support for the move. Midwives (58 percent) and native healers (52 percent) appear to be more lukewarm in their
support for liberalization. Perhaps one of the major reasons
for the response of the midwives is that this group, composed
mostly of women, believes in the sanctity of the unborn child.
The majority of the native healers, on the other hand, appear
to feel that abortion is against traditional customs and beliefs

Table 12-8

Respondents' Attitude toward Legalization of Abortion

	Doctors (N=100)	Midwives (N=48)	Pharmacists (N=49)	Native Healers (N=50)
Yes	83%	58,33%	69.38%	52%
No	17%	41.66%	18.37%	48%

      When respondents were asked to give reasons for their positions, those who supported legalization noted that if abortion were performed under hygienic conditions by competent, medically trained personnel, complications and mortality would be greatly reduced, They also observed that there is great demand for abortion in the country--whether legal or not, abortions will be provided. One respondent puts this succinctly: "We should accept the inevitable. If it has to be done, it might as well be done properly." Legalization will also enable more control to be exercised on the conditions under which it is performed; it will "save women from quacks." Supporters of legalization also mentioned that abortion will constitute a veritable method of keeping the country's population under control. Those who oppose legalization say, for example, that abortion is tantamount to genocide and promiscuity. They also say that it will overstretch the very limited and meager resources of medical personnel now available and will distort the health delivery system because the majority of doctors will tend to concentrate on performing abortions.

Who Should Perform Abortions If Legalized? In answer to this question, 97 percent of the doctors, 73 percent of the midwives, and 77 percent of the pharmacists contend that only doctors should be allowed to perform legal abortions. Curiously enough, 10 percent of the pharmacists say that midwives should also be allowed to perform abortions.

Where Should Abortions Be Performed? Doctors, midwives, and pharmacists are all agreed that the hospital, the doctor's office, and special abortion clinics will be the most suitable places for performing abortions, in that order of preference.

Should Abortions Be Provided Free? Respondents were also asked whether, if abortion is legalized, it should be provided

free to those who cannot afford to pay. This is a very important question in the Nigerian context, Because the greater
majority of the people still have a very low per capita income, they cannot afford very high prices--even for medical
treatment, Therefore, even if abortion is legalized, the desired effect of saving women from the quacks may not be
achieved. People will tend to go where the prices are cheap-
est, and most of the quacks charge very low prices. Native
healers, in fact, very often charge fees only in food items--
chickens, yams, and palm oil--so they have a continuous stream
of clients. Within the context of such reasoning, the answer
to the question of whether abortion should be free assumes
very great importance. Results of round 1 show that only 57
percent of the doctors, 43 percent of the pharmacists, and 35
percent of the midwives endorse free abortion. More midwives
(48 percent) said no than said yes. However, the sizable proportion of respondents (7 percent of doctors, 17 percent of
midwives, and 24 percent of pharmacists) who expressed no
opinion may indicate a rather undecided attitude regarding the
issue. Round 2 of the survey, directed only to doctors, provided a slightly more definitive response. Only 38 percent of
the doctors now say that abortion should be provided free; 62
percent say it should not. It appears, therefore, that the
major trend of opinion among respondents is that abortion
should not be provided free to those who cannot afford to pay
for it. Reasons given for this negative response center
around the greater likelihood of abusing the privilege, taking
freedom for license, and paying no regard to the use of contraceptives (and the consequent increase of repeated abortions)
that will be caused by offering abortion free of charge. Whatever the reasons respondents might have for their reluctance
to advocate free abortion, the effect of that position can be
disastrous. Women who cannot afford to pay high fees for procuring safe, medical abortions will gravitate towards unqualified abortionists.

Restrictions that Should Be Placed on
Abortion if Legalized

Respondents were also asked about the restrictions
that should be placed on abortion if it is legalized. Table
12-9 shows the restrictions suggested. There is general
agreement among respondents that abortion should be insisted
upon where the child is very likely to be deformed. Other
restrictions advocated include limiting the number of abortions a woman can have, forbidding abortion after 12 weeks of
pregnancy, and providing legal protection for physicians performing abortions on minors. Doctors and pharmacists advocated abortion in cases of contraceptive failure; doctors
were alone in advocating the approval of at least two physicians before an abortion is done. The midwives were unique

Table 12-9

Conditions Suggested for Legalized Abortion

Suggestions	Respondents		
	Doctors (N=100)	Midwives (N=48)	Pharmacists (N=49)
Insist on abortion when there is high probability that the child will be deformed	49%	87.50%	73.50%
Discourage repeated requests by limiting the number of abortions a woman can have	44%	75.00%	68.90%
Provide legal protection for physicians performing abortion on minors	45%	68.75%	51.00%
Forbid abortion after 12 weeks of pregnancy	41%	64.60%	57.14%
Provide abortion in cases of contraceptive failure	44%	-	42.90%
Require the approval of at least two physicians for an abortion	34%	-	-
Discourage repeated requests by requiring sterilization after several abortions	-	64.60%	-
Do not change the law; concentrate on improving Family Planning Programs	-	50.00%	-
Leave abortion decision solely to the woman and her doctors	-	-	46.90%

in advocating sterilization after several abortions in order
to discourage repeated request for abortions; 50 percent of
them also advocated concentrating on improving family planning
programs rather than changing the abortion law. Such suggestions indicate the midwives' essential opposition to liberalization of the existing abortion law. It is important to
note that the type of restrictions suggested in this section
will be very useful to policy makers when a liberalization of
the existing abortion law in Nigeria is contemplated.

Circumstances Under Which Doctors Will
Perform an Abortion

          Even if abortion were legalized, the personal attitude
and convictions of the individual doctor will still be one of
the important factors determining whether or not an abortion
will be performed. Such personal attitudes and convictions
will therefore be among the factors moderating the availability of services to abortion seekers. To identify such attitudes, respondents were asked under what circumstances they
would perform an abortion if the decision were left to the
woman and her doctor. Table 12-10 shows the situations in
which respondents would perform an abortion. All respondents
would agree to perform an abortion in situations where having
the child would endanger the mother's life, where the child
might be deformed or mentally retarded, and where the woman is
mentally ill or retarded. It is noteworthy that doctors and,
to a limited extent, midwives would agree to perform abortions
in cases of contraceptive failure. Other situations in which
much smaller proportions of the respondents would perform an
abortion are also shown in Table 12-10.

Perceived Impact of Legalization

          As shown in Table 12-11, doctors and pharmacists ex-
pect the impact of legalization to be advantageous because,
rather than discourage the use of contraceptives, the opportunity to choose between contraception and abortion would
stimulate interest and increase awareness of all birth control
methods. Nurses, however, are not as optimistic. They believe that the impact of legalization would be adverse because
women now using contraceptives would become careless in their
use. Round 2 found 54 percent of the doctors firm in their
expectation of the advantageous effects of legalization.

          If the opportunity to choose between contraception and
abortion is expected to stimulate public interest and increase
awareness, it is important to learn whether respondents see a
place for abortion in the National Family Planning Program.
Table 12-12 shows the opinions of respondents on this issue.

Table 12-10

Circumstances under which Respondents Will Perform
an Abortion

Circumstances	Respondents			
	Doctors (N=100)	Midwives (N=48)	Pharma-cists (N=49)	Native Healers (N=50)
When having the child would endanger the woman's life	88%	92%	82%	50%
When there is a reasonable likelihood that the child will be deformed or mentally handicapped	82%	69%	59%	50%
When the mother is mentally ill or retarded	77%	75%	51%	50%
When the pregnancy was due to rape or incest	72%	NA[a]	NA	50%
When the woman does not have the physical or emotional health to adequately care for the child	62%	64%	NA	46%
When the woman has been using a contraceptive but got pregnant anyway	62%	37%	NA	NA
When having another child would result in serious economic hardship for the family	NA	NA	35%	NA
When the woman has already had all the children she wants	NA	NA	29%	NA
When having a child would interfere with job or education	NA	NA	NA	46%

Note. [a]Data not available

Table 12-11

Perceived Impact of Legalization

Type of Impact	Respondents		
	Doctors (N=100)	Midwives (N=48)	Pharmacists (N=49)
Advantageous, because the opportunity to choose between contraception and abortion may stimulate interest, increase awareness of all birth control methods	44%	41.3%	46.9%
Adverse, because women now using contraceptives may become careless or irregular in their use	26%	45.8%	32.7%
No effect, because there would be no increase in the number of abortions performed	24%	14.0%	32.7%
Adverse, because women not using contraceptives now may accept abortion as a method of birth prevention	14%	31.5%	24.5%

Apparently only the doctors and the pharmacists see abortion as part of the National Family Planning Program. Nurses, consistent with their lukewarm attitude towards legalization of abortion and related issues, do not feel that abortion services should be provided within the family planning context. However, the large number of respondents in the "Don't Know" and "No Response" categories show that the final word is yet to be said on this issue.

Attitudes of the Medical Profession
Toward New Abortion Procedures

It is legitimate to expect that following the legalization of abortion there will be an upward surge in the number of abortions performed within the medical system. It seems

Table 12-12

Respondents' Opinion on the Place of Abortion in the
National Family Planning Program

Is there a place for abortion in the National Family Planning Program?	Respondents		
	Doctors (N=100)	Midwives (N=48)	Pharmacists (N=49)
Yes	66%	12.50%	42.85%
No	23%	37.50%	22.45%
Don't Know	7%	29.16%	26.54%
No Response	4%	20.83%	8.16%

clear, therefore, that the health services would have to
undergo some change or reorganization in order to accommodate
the increased demand. One particular aspect of the health
care delivery system that would need to change is the method
of performing abortions. A quicker, more efficient, and safer
method of performing abortion would mean that more clients
could be accommodated. A simpler method would mean that paramedical personnel could be employed to provide abortion services. Respondents in the present survey were therefore questioned about their attitudes to two specific innovations in
the abortion service: the use of menstrual regulation for
early abortion and the wider employment of paramedical personnel in providing this service.

After providing respondents with a brief description
of menstrual regulation, they were asked if they had heard of
the technique prior to the interview. It was found that 60
percent of the doctors, 83 percent of the midwives, and 86
percent of the pharmacists had not. Over 80 percent of all
respondents did not know if the method was being used anywhere
in Nigeria at the time. Since one important determinant of
the future widespread use of the technique in Nigeria would be
whether nurses and other paramedics could use it, respondents
were asked under what conditions they would favor a nurse or
other paramedic performing menstrual regulation. The majority
of respondents (54 percent of doctors, 65 percent of midwives,
50 percent of pharmacists) would favor paramedics performing
menstrual regulation only under a doctor's supervision,

Typical of their traditional conservatism, 41 percent of the
doctors would not favor paramedics performing it under any
condition. Such conservatism might be due to respondents'
limited familiarity with the technique; whatever the reason
might be, it must be overcome if the method is to be widely
used in the country.

On the basis of the brief description of menstrual
regulation provided to respondents, they were also asked what
they thought were the main advantages and disadvantages of the
technique. All categories of respondents felt that the reduced risk of complications and the early relief of the woman's
anxiety about delayed menses were the main advantages of the
technique. For doctors, the two most frequently mentioned
disadvantages of the technique were the possible complications
or injury that could arise from repeated use, and the fact
that women might come to rely heavily on menstrual regulation
at the expense of contraception. Midwives most frequently
specified the possible complications resulting from repeated
use and the guilt feelings the woman might have when she considered the process to be an abortion. Pharmacists, on the
other hand, most frequently mentioned the guilt feelings and
the heavy reliance on the technique at the expense of contraception as the major disadvantages.

Because the successful use of menstrual regulation
depends largely on the woman's early recognition of a missed
period, respondents were also asked about the ability of their
clients to realize when their periods are overdue. Over 70
percent of all respondents believed that most of their clients
(i.e., over 50 percent) know when their periods are delayed
by about seven-to-ten days--well within the recommended time
limit for the safe application of menstrual regulation.

Finally, respondents were asked about their overall
favorability to the use of menstrual regulation in Nigeria.
Although 34 percent of the doctors, 12 percent of the midwives,
and 41 percent of the pharmacists were favorably disposed towards the method, 16 percent of the doctors and 15 percent of
the midwives were clearly against it. (In round 2 of the survey, the doctors' position was confirmed. Thirty-five percent
of the doctors were favorable, 42 percent were neutral, and
23 percent were unfavorably disposed.) The large number of
respondents who were neutral or who volunteered no opinion at
all appears to reflect a general lack of familiarity with the
technique and a reluctance to pass judgment on a process about
which respondents know very little. Thus, as could be easily
predicted, when respondents were asked if menstrual regulation
should be subject to the same legal restrictions as abortion,
56 percent of the doctors, 48 percent of the midwives, and

70 percent of the pharmacists said it should. This, again, could be said to be due to a "fear of the unknown," and indicates the need for some sort of intervention to make menstrual regulation better known to medical and paramedical personnel in Nigeria.

DISCUSSION AND CONCLUSIONS

The findings of the present survey have shown that abortion is more common or is at least as common as some other diseases whose incidence or seriousness is of great concern to medical people in Nigeria. Beyond the high incidence, the categories of people who perform abortion and the methods used constitute a cause for alarm. Although medical doctors are believed to top the list of those who perform illegal abortions, pharmacists, nurses, people with little or no medical training, and native healers also are featured largely among those who provide abortion services. The methods used range from the conventional dilatation and curettage, vacuum aspiration, and prostaglandins, to native healers' rather dubious prescriptions for the ingestion of such things as potash, rough limestone, and indigo blue. Consequently, the complications have been shown to vary from perforation of the uterus, local and systemic infection and hemorrhage, to swollen chest, insanity, and death.

The toll taken by illegal abortion is not confined to physical complications alone. It also entails some high personal-emotional costs. The doctors, for instance, constantly worry about the complications, the high mortality, and the problem of quacks. The women seeking abortion suffer from embarrassment and ambivalence about the pregnancy. Finding someone to do the abortion and the expenses related to the operation are major worries.

On the whole, therefore, the present study has clearly shown that illegal abortion in Nigeria constitutes a public health problem in more senses than one. In such a situation, the medical profession on the one hand and the Nigerian Government on the other have a joint responsibility to safeguard the people's health. That the medical profession has been living up to its responsibility in this regard is demonstrated by the fact that a number of Nigerian doctors (e.g., Akingba, 1971) have called for positive action on the abortion issue. The Nigerian Association of Obstetricians and Gynecologists has also called for the liberalization of the existing abortion law. The same action was endorsed at the 1975 Annual Conference of the Nigerian Medical Association in which the findings of the present survey were first presented. An announcement by the Nigerian Government (Nigerian Daily Times, October 25,

1975) that it planned to promulgate a decree to legalize abortion was designed, in part, to test public reaction, Strong opposition could be reliably predicted from religious bodies, parent associations, and even from a few dissenting members of the medical profession,

In the face of such opposition, the findings of the present survey--that illegal abortion already exists on a large scale and that it constitutes a serious health problem that largely could be solved by legalization--definitely will reinforce the Nigerian Government in its proposed action, Additional reinforcement will also come from the findings showing that the majority of medical and paramedical personnel supports the legalization of abortion, At the very least, the present findings can be expected to close the ranks of the medical profession itself behind legalization, Dissenting voices now become aware of the consensus of opinion among colleagues. Individual doctors who support legalization but who have been inactive because they did not perceive the relatively high support among their colleagues now can be expected actively to support legalization,

If abortion becomes legalized, it is reasonable to expect that the government will not give a blank check to abortion practitioners to proceed as they like, Rather it can be expected that certain conditions will be tied to the legalization, In that case, the conditions and restrictions suggested by medical and paramedical personnel in the present survey will provide policy makers with a useful starting point from which to devise the official conditions for legal abortions, For instance, there is consensus among respondents in the present survey that, when legalized, abortion should be performed only by medical doctors--preferably in hospitals, but also in the doctor's office or in special abortion clinics (in that order of preference). The wisdom of setting up special abortion clinics is, however, rather questionable because they could easily acquire a stigma that would further embarrass the abortion seekers, This eventually could lead to nonuse of the clinics.

One important question to which both the Nigerian Government and the medical profession must perforce address themselves sooner or later is whether abortion should be provided free to those who cannot afford to pay for it. Respondents in the present survey have come out categorically against free abortion. To hold rigidly to this opinion might well defeat the whole purpose of legalizing abortion, for those who are too poor to pay the medical fees (and these lie in the majority) will seek the cheaper services of quacks and native healers. The result might well be that, despite legalization, the physical and emotional toll of illegal abortion would continue unabated. A workable compromise must therefore be found on the issue of providing free abortion services to those who cannot afford to pay.

Other restrictions that should be placed on abortion in the event of legalization, as suggested by medical and paramedical respondents in this survey, could be very useful. Among these are: (a) limiting the number of abortions a woman can have; (b) forbidding abortion after 12 weeks of pregnancy; and (c) seeking the approval of at least two physicians before an abortion is done, However, the midwives' advocacy of sterilization after several abortions in order to discourage repeated demands should be subject to further discussion.

Finally, the findings of the present study indicate that doctors and pharmacists expect the overall impact of legalization to be advantageous, The midwives, however, had consistently shown a rather lukewarm acceptance of legalization and related issues, The present findings concerning the favorable attitudes of doctors and pharmacists should help close the ranks of midwives behind legalization. There will be need, however, to spread information on the new technique of menstrual regulation, which will be very useful in coping with the increased demand for abortion that legalization is expected to engender. As of 1977, medical and paramedical personnel in Nigeria are not fully aware of the immense possibilities of the technique and are therefore still tentative in its acceptance.

REFERENCES

Akingba, J. B, The problem of unwanted pregnancies in Nigeria today. Lagos, Nigeria: University of Lagos Press, 1971,

Akinla, O., & Adadevoh, B. K. Abortion--a medico-social problem. Journal of the Nigerian Medical Association, 1969, 6(3), 16-22.

Dada, B. A. L.I.M.H. Statistical Report for 1974. Unpublished manuscript, University of Lagos, 1974.

Johnson, R, L,, Friedman, H. L., McCormick, E. P., & David, H. P. Gatekeeper studies: Information for management forecasting and planning of fertility-regulating services. A prospectus for research. Washington: Transnational Family Research Institute, 1973.

Onifade, A. Attitude towards abortion in Nigeria. Nigerian Medical Journal, forthcoming,

13

Contraception and Abortion Services at Barros Luco Hospital, Santiago, Chile*

Anibal Faundes and Ellen Hardy

Editors' Note: As Latin American policy makers
begin to give increasing recognition to the
consequences of inadequate fertility regulation,
it seems appropriate to recall the pioneering
contraception and abortion services developed
at the Barros Luco Hospital in Santiago between
the 1940s and early 1970s. Faundes and Hardy
offer a vivid description of the attitudes of
a unique group of medical and paramedical personnel whose efforts instilled a more humane
view of abortion among other staff and the
general public. The public health importance
of the epidemiology of abortion and fertility-
regulating practices in Latin America was recently recognized when the Pan American Health
Organization published its first monograph on
the topic (PAHO, 1975).

INTRODUCTION

The development of family planning programs over the
last two decades at Barros Luco Hospital in Santiago, Chile,
constitutes a unique case study of the dynamics of the social
change process. It is the purpose of this chapter to record
a slice of history in which we participated as observers and
occasional actors. The focus is on attitude changes and on
changes in family planning practice in the Department of Obstetrics and Gynecology of the Barros Luco Hospital (which in
1965 was administratively merged with the Trudeau Hospital
and is now officially known as the Barros Luco-Trudeau
Hospital).

CONTRACEPTION

The Department of Obstetrics and Gynecology of the Barros Luco Hospital was already known at the beginning of the 1950s for the freedom with which surgical sterilizations were performed. Located in an area of rapid population growth, the hospital serves a population of low socioeconomic status and high fertility. About 35 percent of the maternity patients were grand-multiparae (having given birth to five or more babies before their present delivery). A high proportion were over 35 and even over 40 years of age. These factors, plus nutritional problems, high abortion incidence, and others, led to a great frequency of pregnancy and delivery complications. For these reasons there was a tendency to be more liberal in accepting requests for surgical sterilization than was usual in other hospitals in Santiago or elsewhere in Chile. At that time--mid-1950s--there were no modern contraceptives for effective family planning so there was no alternative but to agree to requests for terminating fertility when a couple already had more children than desired.

The most important aspect of Barros Luco procedures was its considerable sensitivity towards the requests made by the women, plus understanding the idea of preventing new pregnancies when they had great probability of ending in pathology. This was to become a tradition in the maternity department and would have a decisive influence on the evolution that occurred during the following years. Dr. Hernan Sanhueza Donoso, chief of maternity, and Dr. Manuel Moreno (one of the most experienced gyneco-obstetricians of the department during those years) are the persons responsible for impelling this line of action.

With the prospective increase of abortions observed during that decade (Armijo & Monreal, 1964), probably noted to a greater degree by the Barros Luco Hospital than by other hospitals, it became more and more evident to many physicians of the maternity department that women who were having induced abortions must be given some possibility of contraception. However, only a small number of physicians took the initiative and offered a few patients diaphragms or spermicides.

This situation continued until the end of 1959. At that time an article published in the American Journal of Obstetrics and Gynecology caught the attention of Dr. Jaime Zipper, who conducted clinical activities in the maternity department and taught and did research in the Institute of Physiology of the University of Chile. The article was Oppenheimer's first publication describing his experience with

metal intrauterine rings used as contraceptives. Based on
this description, Dr. Zipper designed a ring made of nylon
thread, wound several times around two fingers, in which one
of the ends was used as a tail. The latter was an original
innovation designed to overcome the difficulty, previously encountered with tailless IUDs, of removing the device or check-
ing if it was in situ.

The availability of a method comparatively easy for
the patients to use brought a fundamental change. Through
Dr. Zipper's initiative, a free public contraceptive service
was started in the Prenatal Clinic of Barros Luco Hospital.
Dr. Hernan Sanhueza was responsible for the opening of the
first contraceptive clinic in which IUDs were inserted. It
is necessary to call attention to this decision, as the responsibility assumed was considerable. At the end of 1959
there was no other clinic of this kind in the region and the
insertion of an intrauterine device was as much if not more
criticized by the Chilean medical and gyneco-obstetrical establishment as was "therapeutic abortion" 13 or 14 years later.

During these years, the International Planned Parenthood Federation Western Hemisphere Region was mostly an idea,
with few activities. Development assistance programs of the
United States did not include support for fertility regulation
and, with very few exceptions, no private or governmental institution nor United Nations organization had any funds for
family planning. In this sense, the Barros Luco Hospital has
always been proud of the fact that its activities in contraception anticipated international trends and so could not have
been the result of external pressures or of financial incentives from some foreign institution. Activities resulted from
the demand of the patients served in the maternity department
and from the concept of preventing pregnancies that constituted a risk for the woman.

From the start, the Barros Luco/Contraceptive Clinic
functioned with midwives more than with physicians. This, we
think, was the most important factor in giving it the contin-
uity, large number of patients, and the national as well as
international importance it achieved.

When the first Comite Chileno de Proteccion de la
Familia was founded in 1962, the Barros Luco Maternity Department was amply represented. Since this organization developed into the Asociacion Chilena de Proteccion de la Familia,
the maternity department has had several permanent represen-
tatives on the board of directors.

As demand for service grew and the acceptance of IUDs
by physicians increased, the small clinic became insufficient.

During 1963-1964, it moved to larger premises in the maternity department basement. During this same period, contraceptive clinics were established in the maternal and child health centers of the health area associated with the hospital.

The growth of the clinic's activities was not confined to an increase in the number of patients. Although unplanned, Barros Luco, almost from the beginning, became a training center for physicians, midwives, and other health workers. At the same time, in part because of the immediate attacks from many sides, it became indispensable to do a very careful clinical evaluation of the first patients. This led to the development of one of the most important centers for clinical evaluation of contraceptives in Latin America, not so much because of the number of patients but because of the quality and reliability of the results.

RESEARCH AND TRAINING

At first, research and training activities were limited to contraception. After a few years of activities specifically designed to reduce abortions, it was observed that abortions continued to increase. It was then necessary to add socio-demographic research to verify the hypothesis that induced abortion could be reduced by family planning.

The informal training that had been given to anyone who asked for it, focusing almost exclusively on the practice of IUD insertions, was formalized in a Family Planning Training Program. The program was financed through the Association Chilena de Proteccion de la Familia and sponsored by the Graduate School of the Faculty of Medicine, University of Chile.

The first courses for Latin American physicians (other than Chileans) were held during 1965. The program included demography, public health, and biology of reproduction, besides theory and practice of contraception. CELADE (Latin American Center for Demography), the School of Public Health of the University of Chile, and the J. J. Aguirre Hospital Obstetrics Clinic collaborated with these courses. In 1967, paramedical personnel were trained; later on, Chilean health professionals were also accepted. When the government officially incorporated family planning in the maternal and child health programs (Valdivieso, 1967), these courses were used to train National Health Service physicians, midwives, social workers, and public health educators from all over the country. This training program, which continued until the early 1970s, had an influence in Chile and in all of Latin America. It can safely be said that the great majority of physicians and paramedical workers who started their own programs in different centers in Chile and Latin America were trained in Barros Luco and in its Family Planning Clinic.

From the point of view of the development of family planning in Chile, perhaps more important than these post-graduate courses and theoretical teaching was the participation in the training of medical students who lived the experience of contraception as part of the routine work of the maternity department during the practice period. When these students graduated and moved to another city or town to work, they felt the need of preventing a new pregnancy after delivery of a chronically hypertensive woman or of a grand multipara with postpartum hemorrhage, or after an induced abortion. They felt this need the same way they felt the need for measles vaccination or for essential medicines. As a result, they themselves looked for a way to provide contraceptive services where they did not exist, in contrast to the weak and not always effective motivation of the physician who was not trained in this way of perceiving the problem.

During all those years, .the clinic was a center of research for new contraceptives. The biological basis was developed by Dr. Zipper in his laboratory at the Physiology Institute, such as the inclusion of metal ions in the IUDs and tubal occlusion by transcervical citotoxic injection.

Dr. Horacio Croxatto made his first experiments in recovering eggs and sperms from the uterine cavity and the Fallopian tubes in this clinic and in the Department of Obstetrics and Gynecology. His experiences would mean a great advance in the knowledge on the transport of gametes in the female genital tract.

Barros Luco also was the base of studies that demonstrated the possibility of greatly reducing induced abortion through education and by providing easy access to effective contraceptive methods for women at high risk of pregnancy.

The available literature demonstrates that these studies had, and continue to have, an importance that transcends the borders of the country and, in some cases, of Latin America.

To the list of pioneers at Barros Luco must be added the name of Mrs. Laura Partene, a midwife who participated in the creation of the first clinic and the making of the first nylon rings and who was also a victim of the hard initial criticism. Involved in every aspect of service, training, and research, she had been in charge, officially or unofficially, of the Contraceptive Clinic since its creation. Her name is linked with that of Dr. Zipper and others in the research and in the innumerable pre- or postgraduate, national or international, family planning courses conducted there.

ABORTION

Although abortion was the irritating thorn that justified the family planning program, the problem was approached at Barros Luco with greater interest and sympathy than in many other hospitals in the country. In 1965, educational programs on the risks of abortion and the possibilities for prevention offered by contraception were started in the maternity and abortion wards of the Department of Obstetrics and Gynecology. Initiated with only a single social worker, the program was subsequently strengthened through the efficient cooperation of a group of women volunteers.

This educational program plus the contraceptive services provided by the network of clinics already existing in the area did not reduce abortions in the quantity expected. To improve the efficiency of the program, insertion of post-abortion IUDs was started in 1967.

In July 1970, a more extensive program was initiated. A new group of family planning volunteers presented a daily lecture to the group of post-abortion patients and interviewed each one to clarify doubts, reinforce motivation to use a contraceptive, and inculcate the serious health hazards of having an induced abortion. Each patient was offered a contraceptive on discharge and was asked to come to the hospital's family planning clinic a week later. At the clinic, those using contraceptives were checked; those not using anything were offered a method. Those with infertility problems or who had suffered spontaneous abortion (and wanted a child) were also assisted. This visit also served as a post-abortion check. At the same time, the clinic's medical personnel was increased to make certain that every post-abortion patient was seen the same day she came. The same volunteers, supervised by the program's paid staff, made sure that all patients came for this first check. If they did not arrive, one or more letters were sent to the available addresses and, in exceptional cases, patients were summoned through public notices in the press or were visited at home.

As the program was evaluated at the same time, some mistakes that influenced patients not to come to the clinic were corrected. The lecture was modified to exclude mention of legal sanctions against those who had an induced abortion. Such sanctions were never enforced but instilled fear about

returning to the hospital. A social worker made arrangements
so that patients who had no social security and were too poor
could legally leave without paying. Previously, many women
unable to pay left the hospital unchecked and did not dare to
return to the clinic. Finally, after the beginning of 1971,
contraceptive pills given to patients at the time of discharge
from the abortion ward were added to the service.

What justified all these efforts to reduce abortion?
The number of abortions admitted to the Barros Luco had been
reduced from over 5,000 a year during the mid-1960s to a little
over 3,200 in 1972. Nevertheless, it was impossible to feel
satisfied for various reasons: (1) during 1972, 15 patients
died from septic post-abortion complications, some after having undergone a treatment long and painful for the patient
and costly for the hospital--this meant that the mortality
rate of 1 per 200-250 abortion patients continued unchanged;
(2) even in those cases in which the patient did not die, secondary abortion complications forced mutilations that left
young childless women sterile; and (3) multiple cases of repeated abortions continued to be identified, in spite of educational efforts to motivate the women to use contraception.

One fact related to the organization of the department
needs to be mentioned. During this period, in order to stress
the relationship between abortion prevention and contraception,
it was decided that the Contraceptive Clinic would form part
of the Abortion Section (one of the three functional units
that constituted the maternity department). This meant that
the doctors of the Abortion Section and of the Contraceptive
Clinic were completely integrated and rotated their functions
weekly.

The reorganization strengthened the abortion prevention
program and also reinforced the medical staff's motivation, because the total program could now be better perceived.

There was one other unplanned result from this situation. At this point, the public was better informed about
abortion and its social meaning was changing. Mass media, especially the press, started to call attention to this situation.
Paula, a modern woman's magazine directed and written almost
exclusively by women, had a particularly humanitarian and sensitive approach to abortion. In several issues, the magazine
referred to abortion as a problem that was affecting Chilean
women. One long article, published in 1971, stands out, describing how upper- and middle-class women experienced induced
abortions. What most readers over age 30 knew and what younger
women guessed was described openly and in detail. During 1972,
another article decidedly in favor of liberalizing abortion

laws was published. It was well received by the readers and evoked little negative reaction.

At the same time, the government had pointed out that the fighters against induced abortion had to consider an "eventual legalization of abortion. . .,and more immediately. , , an extension of the indications for therapeutic abortion, as in the cases of contraceptive failure for example. . .(Allende, 1971).

This overall situation of public attitude change toward abortion and the incidence of unwanted pregnancies due to contraceptive failures led a group of physicians to decide in 1971 to start performing free therapeutic abortions for needy patients referred by contraceptive clinics from the hospital's health area, whose pregnancies were the result of contraceptive failure. At first they were done only by one of the maternity department emergency teams. There was no effort to conceal what was being done. That the pregnancy was unwanted and had occurred during use of a contraceptive was stated on the patient's record, together with the note that the abortion was "inevitable," in the sense that the patient would inevitably have an induced abortion and that it was better to have it in the clean and safe conditions of the hospital than in the dirty and dangerous conditions of an unskilled abortionist's "office."

All those who knowingly participated in these first trials to liberalize abortion were willing to jointly assume their legal responsibilities and even go to prison if necessary, in the hope that the resulting scandal would move public opinion toward abortion laws that came closer to reflecting the reality of Chilean society.

In spite of the large number of people with different philosophical and religious ideals who knew what was going on (nurses aides, nurses, physicians, medical and obstetrical students, etc.), nobody attempted any legal or administrative denunciation. Soon, abortions were performed during the mornings as a normal part of the ward's work. At this point, the chief of the department had to admit officially that he was aware of what was going on. A series of private and public meetings were held in the department and a committee consisting of the head of the whole department and the chiefs of both the obstetrical and gynecological sections was designated. This committee was to accept or reject each application for therapeutic interruption of pregnancy. In this way the conditions of the Chilean law that allow therapeutic abortion when the pregnancy seriously imperils the patient's health or life were fulfilled, in that the abortions were documented with the

signature of at least two physicians (Isaacs & Sanhueza, 1975).
That a pregnancy ended by illegal abortion, done by an amateur
abortionist, imperils the health and lives of the women in the
socioeconomic group coming to Barros Luco is well documented
in Chilean experience.

Prof. Onofre Avendano, head of the department, communicated with the National Health Service authorities regarding
this decision through regular channels. He included considerations such as the ones presented in this chapter and proposed
a pilot plan. The authorities, who knew what was happening,
did not reply. Even though they agreed, they feared that such
a measure would demand that many resources be diverted from
other priority programs.

The situation continued thus for a few months but, as
the committee became excessively strict, a series of dramatic
cases that moved all the maternity's personnel occurred: a
young woman committed suicide after her application was rejected and left a letter claiming injustice had been done; a
nurses aide from the hospital was admitted with serious post-
abortion sepsis after her application was rejected. Other similar though less dramatic cases produced a reaction from the
supporting staff of the abortion ward. They called for a
meeting of all the personnel, including physicians. (As a result of the "democratization of the National Health Service,"
supporting personnel had acquired the right to give their
opinion regarding problems that directly affected their work.)

This meeting occurred in March 1973 and was attended
by the Chief of the Obstetric Section and all the physicians
from the abortion ward. The following agreements were reached:
(1) the decision to accept or reject an application to interrupt a pregnancy would depend on the Abortion Section; (2) all
those cases in which the woman could not be dissuaded from her
decision to interrupt the pregnancy would be accepted; and
(3) the only conditions set were that gestation could not be
over 12 weeks, that the women could prove they lived in the
hospital's health area, and that they would accept the use of
an effective contraceptive (pills, IUDs, or subdermal implants)
or surgical sterilization after the abortion, if not contra-
indicated.

All the people who participated in making this decision were completely aware of two fundamental facts: (1) the
legal and social significance of the step they were taking,
the possible direct or indirect criticism, official administrative sanctions or attacks that each of them could receive,
and (2) the much larger amount of work that this decision
would mean for each of them.

The great pressure exerted by the patients, facilitated by the good rapport existing between them and the maternity department personnel, added to the traditional sensitivity toward the needs of the community, was stronger than the well-founded fears. Those who were also moved by public health principles and who for many years had believed that family planning on its own was the solution to the abortion problem realized that, although contraceptives represent the first ideal level of prevention in avoiding pregnancies with a high risk of ending in induced abortion, they are not the entire solution. At the present stage of development, it is impossible to succeed in eliminating the abortion problem through family planning. So long as perfect methods are not available there will be pregnancies due to contraceptive failure; so long as education programs do not reach every place, there will be couples who do not practice contraception because of ignorance; so long as service and distribution are not made sufficiently accessible, there will be people who will not be able to use contraceptives even if they have the knowledge and wish to do so; so long as appropriate sexual education is not started early, there will be young girls pregnant before quite realizing what happened. And even if all these ideal conditions are fulfilled, there always remains the woman who wanted a child, got pregnant, and because of subsequent circumstances, such as abandonment, no longer wants the child and must have an abortion. If we accept the irrefutable reality that abortion does exist in our society, then the only way to prevent serious health consequences and death is by improving the conditions in which it is performed. Faced with an unwanted pregnancy that will inevitably end in abortion, we must resort to this second level of prevention--abortion under good conditions.

Meanwhile, the press continued reflecting the changes that were occurring in Chilean society. In March 1973, Paula published a series of interviews with about 20 women from different social levels, from lawyers to workers, who were not afraid to state publicly (with their picture, name, profession, etc.) why they were in favor of legalizing abortion. Following this example, Paula published another article in September 1973, in which five physicians, four of whom were university professors, expressed opinions openly favorable to the legalization or liberalization of abortion.

By this time, two of the most widely circulated newspapers of Santiago, La Tercera de la Hora and La Segunda, had already published outstanding page-long articles objectively reporting that pregnancies were being interrupted in a hospital in Santiago for women who fulfilled certain prerequisites, so as to prevent them from resorting to illegal abortion and all its consequences.

Finally, in an October 1973 edition of Paula, there appeared a six-page report titled: "In the Barros Luco Hospital they are doing 500 therapeutic abortions per month." The problem was clearly described, the names of the doctors who declared themselves responsible for what was being done were given, an explanation was presented of how they reached their decision, and some positive results were mentioned. In general, a 100 percent favorable and approving opinion was given to this form of action. When we consulted the journalists of La Segunda and Paula (both females) who wrote these articles, they agreed that there had been an incredible lack of public reaction, considering that until a short time ago the interruption of pregnancy in any condition was categorically rejected by the vast majority of opinions expressed publicly.

Nevertheless, there was an official reaction to the article published by La Segunda. Two members of Parliament asked for an investigation of the practice of "therapeutic abortions" in Barros Luco and a petition of inquiry was sent to the Ministry of Health so that it would inform the Parliament. This petition followed the usual procedure and arrived at the maternity department, where it was answered. The answer never reached Parliament, which was dissolved shortly afterwards.

What happened in Barros Luco during the first eight months of 1973? During January, 89 abortion-related operations were performed, including curettages after spontaneous and induced abortions and "therapeutic interruptions of pregnancy." In July, the number of these operations rose to nearly 500 and the demand was so great that even though all the personnel multiplied their efforts many women were obliged to wait up to one week for their turn to have a "therapeutic abortion." How is this demand explained? It was evident that in a short time the usual clientele had expanded in two directions. On the one hand, women who really lived in the geographic area corresponding to the hospital, but who had never used its services because of their higher economic level, now came to ask for pregnancy interruption. They waited for a long time along with many other women, often in little comfort, wearing cheap and sometimes torn nightgowns in the typical conditions of collective care, in preference to individual attention by a physician or midwife acting as a professional abortionist in a private clinic. The economic factor is one that could explain this preference, but many patients (university students or professionals) said that, in spite of the disadvantages described, they preferred the honesty, positive psychological atmosphere, and technical quality of the hospital. There they felt the psychological support of the group that shared the same problem and the understanding of the personnel who acted with the same naturalness as if providing any other medical treatment. These conditions were more favorable than the clandestine hiding and the feeling of commercial exploitation of their problem in the hands of an abortionist whose primary orientation was financial and who many times was not technically competent.

On the other hand, women came not only from all over Santiago but from all over the country. All attempts to verify their addresses were continuously foiled. It was not difficult to obtain a certificate that "proved" the patient lived at a given address. The police gave a certificate after visiting the address and asking if Mrs. X lived there. It was only necessary to have a friend in the neighborhood and ask her to tell the police that she did live there. This way our clientele grew both in terms of social level and geographic area.

Naturally, this increase in the number of operations meant a great increase in the work to be done in the sector. But it would be a mistake to believe that work increased in the same proportion as the number of abortions, because it is very different to do a semi-ambulatory curettage by aspiration, with paracervical anesthesia, than to take care of a patient with septic shock or a post-abortion peritonitis. Although the first group increased five or six times, the latter were reduced to almost none (the one exception came from outside our area). There were then no problems regarding medical hours, though one of the reasons for the lack of problems was the willingness of everyone to do any kind of task in the sector with great dedication. This dedication originated in the fact that all understood that they were leading the way, fulfilling a mission that went further than the usual work. If physicians did not have much extra work, midwives and nurses aides did. It is impossible to overemphasize the devotion to work and the human solidarity toward that group of women with problems shown by the nurses aides whose work easily tripled. Their only complaint was that Barros Luco was doing the job of other hospitals and that each one should face up to its own responsibilities.

This possibility was brought to the attention of the head of the National Health Service's Technical Department. He recommended that in those areas where all stages of abortion prevention through family planning had been exhausted, therapeutic abortions could be prescribed for cases of contraceptive failure. This recommendation probably never left the Technical Department before the change of government.

From January through August 1973, there was only one maternal death due to post-induced abortion complications in

the Barros Luco maternity department. This patient had had
an induced abortion in another area and was transferred from
another hospital. During the same period in 1972, nine women
had died because of abortion complications. During the preceding years the intensive care ward was continuously occupied
by infected women and many times patients who required more
care had to be discharged to make room for others in more
critical condition. From April 1973 on, the intensive care
ward was almost exclusively occupied by a few patients with
post-Cesarean section or post-vaginal delivery infections. Not
one of all the personnel who worked in the section had the
slightest doubt that they were doing a most fair and honest
job, and they unanimously felt the satisfaction of saving lives
and preventing suffering. There were a few negative reactions
from physicians belonging to other sections. Some were very
direct and sincere and were considered with respect. Those
objecting strongly to therapeutic abortion did not dare to at-
tack the principles on which it is based, but tried to bring
the physicians working in the section into disrepute. They
accused them of being paid with funds coming from international
or private institutions and from the United Nations. The false-
ness of these accusations could be demonstrated easily, but
they were never made openly or directly but always in a concealed way through a third person.

CONCLUDING COMMENT

The experience at Barros Luco shows that abortion is
no longer rejected by Chilean society and that it is not absolutely necessary to modify the actual legislation. What was
being done in Barros Luco was known by the Supreme Court, the
Parliament, the Executive Branch, the University, the Catholic
Church, and the national press. All the different political
and philosophical ideas were represented in these institutions
and they had the power to stop it or to start a campaign
against it. The fact that nothing was done demonstrates that
the existence of abortion as a social phenomenon can no longer
be denied and that nothing justifies keeping it sordid, criminal, clandestine, and at such a high cost for Chilean women.

REFERENCES

Allende, S. Primer mensaje del Presidente de Chile al pais en
    la inauguracion del periodo ordinario de Sesiones del
    Congreso Nacional. Santiago: Government of Chile, 1971.

Armijo, R., & Monreal, T. Epidemiologia del aborto provocado
    en Santiago de Chile. Revista Medica de Chile, 1964, 92,
    548.

Isaacs, S. L., & Sanhueza, H. Induced abortion in Latin
America: Legal perspective. In Pan American Health Organization, Epidemiology of abortion and practices of
fertility regulation in Latin America: Selected reports.
Washington: PAHO, 1975.

Pan American Health Organization. Epidemiology of abortion
and practices of fertility regulation in Latin America:
Selected reports. Scientific Publication No. 706.
Washington: Author, 1975.

Valdivieso, R. Discurso de apertura. In H. Romero (Ed.),
Proceedings, VIIIth Conference, International Planned
Parenthood Federation. Santiago: IPPF, 1967.

PART SIX

COMMENTARIES

14

Methodological Issues
in Psychosocial Abortion Research*

Herbert L. Friedman and Raymond L. Johnson

*Editors' Note: The final section of the mono-
graph begins with comments on methodological
issues and recommendations that emerged from
the experience of cooperative studies described in previous chapters. The perspective common to all these efforts is the
recognition of the importance of identifying
critical points in the sequence of events
over time, and the study of human interaction
using those nodal points as a behavioral
focus.*

INTRODUCTION

A number of the studies reported in this volume (e.g.,
Czechoslovakia, Dominican Republic, Hungary, Israel, Jamaica,
Nigeria, Switzerland, and Yugoslavia) formed part of the Cooperative Transnational Research Program in Fertility Behavior,
one of the tasks of which was the evaluation of a conceptual
framework. Over a period of five years, several workshops and
seminars (cited in chapter 1) were held, which focused on this
objective and the methodological approaches it spawned. The
purpose of this commentary is to summarize key features with
special reference to abortion.

To understand, predict, and modify psychosocial factors surrounding induced abortion, it is best to consider
abortion not in isolation but as one event in a sequence of
events having important and describable antecedents, occurring

---

*A portion of this material is reprinted with permis-
sion from Family Planning Perspectives, 1974, 6, 184-186.
Segments also appeared in reports of workshops coordinated by
the Transnational Family Research Institute.

in a situation of human interaction, and having consequences
dependent on certain characteristics of preceding events. A
sound conceptual framework facilitates the cumulation of findings, the testing of hypotheses, and the attraction to the
field of capable researchers. With these objectives in mind,
a psychosocial model of fertility choice behavior was developed
with Jean Kellerhals of the University of Geneva (Friedman,
1972; Friedman, Johnson, & David, 1976). In interaction with
the evolving research program, this model led to the development of general guidelines for fertility research design and
specific designs for specific studies, some of which are cited
in this volume (e.g., chapters 4, 6, 11, and 12).

RESEARCH GUIDELINES

The research guidelines distilled from the project activities in the evolved conceptual framework (Friedman, 1974)
may be summarized as follows:

1. The focal point of fertility behavior is the couple. Where possible each partner should be separately studied,
providing data for a four-way comparison of the validity of
responses, the accuracy of mutual perception, and the degree
of congruence. If that is impracticable, then at least data
about the partner's views as seen by the respondent should be
solicited.

2. It is important to know not only what fertility-
regulation methods and services are available, but what is believed to be available.

3. It is important to identify each respondent's view
of alternative courses of action, the psychosocial costs attached to each alternative, the outcomes expected, and how
the outcomes are valued (Janis & Mann, 1977).

4. Fertility choice behavior is dynamic. Each outcome leads to a new situation and each situation or choice
point may be identified in advance and utilized for research
purposes. The timing of research in relation to the individual's choice situation may critically affect the generaliza-
bility of the findings to other situations.

5. Choice points lie in a branching chain, and a key
feature of successful fertility-regulation behavior (in the
eyes of the couple) may well lie in the degree to which the
individual recognizes likely outcomes, plans for them, and
has contingency plans available for what to do in the event
of failure.

6. The position of the couple in their overall fertility career is of great importance in the selection of populations for study, and their sampling. If couples are selected without regard to this dimension, opposing factors may be mixed and confound the interpretation of the findings. Major positions in the long-term fertility career, from which sampling can be considered, include individuals who are at menarche, single, engaged, newly married, married and childless wanting no children, married and childless wanting children, married with children wanting more, married with children wanting no more, divorced or widowed, approaching menopause. Selecting samples along this psychosocial fertility continuum rather than by purely sociodemographic characteristics is recommended.

7. If the selection of the population for study is derived from the method or service they are using, the sampling procedure should attempt to reach individuals as close as possible to the decision-making process. Thus, a woman with a positive pregnancy test and an unwanted pregnancy is a better source of information about abortion-seeking dynamics than a nonpregnant woman drawn from the general population at risk.

8. Research designed to evaluate services should gather data from both users and providers of the service, with special attention to the psychosocial costs and benefits to the client as each perceives them, along with objective data about the same phenomena. These data are important for modifying services, for examining the discontinuity of use, and for determining the extent to which others will choose the service.

9. In the study of couple choice behavior, hypotheses ought to be confirmed or disproven insofar as possible on the basis of behavioral events. Prospective studies permitting the prediction of subsequent identifiable events such as pregnancy, request for abortion, abortion, childbirth, or the choice of a new contraceptive are recommended for this purpose.

10. There are circumstances in which a service is available but illegal, or when consideration is being given by policy makers to introducing or legalizing a service. This is often true of induced abortion. Research is required to determine the manner in which such services are being utilized where illegal, and to provide information about the likely demand for the service if it were introduced or legalized. Valuable data may be drawn from the "gatekeepers" of such services--the medical or paramedical personnel who are or would be involved, the service administrators, and the policy makers. A design for such studies is outlined in chapter 11.

11. Although most studies will focus on the findings of the majority within the sample, it is sometimes of great value to examine the "deviant" behavior of the minority in the sample. What makes the minority differ from the majority, when environmental factors are held constant, may be an important clue to mutable characteristics of the population, and an advance indication of future trends.

12. The urgency of the population problem, and the limitations on environmental manipulation from an experimental point of view, makes especially valuable the use of "natural" experimental situations utilizing culturally different conditions. Successful studies can be developed with careful consideration of the selection of different cultures--cultures comparable to one another on the self-selected psychosocial dimension of their position in the long-term fertility career stage or in the short-term procreational phase. These studies can measure the impact of cultural factors, which exert different kinds of pressures upon couples' fertility choice behavior. In any setting, the individuals primarily responsible for the research should be a part of the society being studied. At the same time, however, the quality of the research will be enhanced by its prior exposure to design, theory, and experience drawn from a cross-cultural and integrated approach.

Although not unique, the approach described in these guidelines is reinforced by the cooperative experience reported in the monograph. For example, the Swiss study focuses on an early choice point by selecting a sample of women who have requested an abortion but have not yet made a decision. The Yugoslav studies begin with the woman at the time of a clinic visit for an abortion or contraceptive service, and follow with couple interviews. The Dominican study is concerned with the immediate after-effects of an illegal and incomplete abortion. The Czech study considers the long-term consequences of denied abortion requests. The Jamaican and Nigerian studies report the views of service providers, both actual and potential, in countries where there is some discussion of liberalizing abortion legislation. The Israeli studies utilize couple-oriented techniques and information obtained from multiple sources, including policy makers, service providers, and service users.

CONCLUSION

The focus of this brief commentary has been on design and sampling in abortion research rather than on measurement instruments. Standardized designs and sampling procedures based on psychosocial dimensions can be developed in transnational research; but within those constraints, measuring instruments must be sensitive to sociocultural settings, with great care devoted to standardization. Thus, psychosocial costs may fall into the same categories, cross-nationally, but may have unique manifestations in diverse settings; an abortion index which reflects the rate of abortion over time of exposure can provide standardized information on comparable bases if used judiciously.

If a single common perspective may be said to exist in the methodology that has evolved to study psychosocial aspects of abortion in diverse circumstances, it is perhaps that of the identification of critical points in sequence of events over time, and the study of human interaction using those nodal points as a behavioral focus.

REFERENCES

Friedman, H. L. An approach to psychosocial research in fertility behavior. Unpublished paper, 1972.

Friedman, H. L. Fertility choice behavior: Some recommendations for research design. Family Planning Perspectives, 1974, 6, 184-185.

Friedman, H. L., Johnson, R. L., & David, H. P. Dynamics of fertility choice behavior: A pattern for research. In S. H. Newman & V. D. Thompson (Eds.), Population psychology research and educational issues. Bethesda, Md.: Center for Population Research (NICHD), 1976.

Janis, I. L., & Mann, L. Decision making: A psychological analysis of conflict, choice, and commitment. New York: The Free Press, 1977.

15

Issues in Service Implementation*

Malcolm Potts

Editors' Note: The evidence is persuasive
that the demand for family planning services
outruns supply in most countries. Resources
currently invested in family planning, if
reallocated, might be sufficient to meet
latent demand at the world level. Achieving such a goal would require political will,
technical insights, and elimination of re-
dundant activities. Within such a context,
the contributions of research and educational
programs will be valued only to the extent
that findings can be utilized for the improvement of service programs.

INTRODUCTION

Genitally and cerebrally we are more sexually active
than most other animals. But sexual activity rarely involves
more than two individuals at any one time. For this, or some
other reason, we seem to find the division of labor necessary
for birth control more difficult than for death control, and
the community as a whole rarely recognizes and assists the individual to achieve his or her fertility goals in the most
rational way possible.

Biologically, man has to exert effort to turn off reproduction rather than to choose to conceive a child. Unfortunately, law and social custom usually reinforce this tire-
some fact. For example, all too often society forces a couple
to have a number of unplanned pregnancies as a token of the
fact they really want to be sterilized.

---

*Adapted with permission from the Proceedings of the
Royal Society (London), 1976, 195, 213-224.

The political will to alter the status quo is weak.
Although the need to bring birth rates into step with death
rates is self-evident to biologists and apparent to most parents, it is an issue easily lost in political decision making--
where a week is said to be a long time.

Clearly, family planning is one aspect of, and necessarily related to, other facts of socioeconomic development.
But although fertility declines are linked to economic development, trends can nevertheless be accelerated.

CURRENT SITUATION

The majority of the developing world's population (75
percent, or over 2000 million people) now live in countries
with governmental family planning policies, most of which also
have explicit demographic goals (Nortman & Hofstatter, 1975).
Another 15 percent of the third world lives in countries which
endorse family planning, although they will fight shy of stating specific demographic targets. Yet for most of the people
covered by these programs, access to modern contraceptives is
as remote as the possibility of going to university and the
option of the surgical means of fertility control as unlikely
as owning a car.

Only one in six population programs is more than 10
years old. But the logic of population change is that any
communal response is better made early than late. Therefore,
the judgment of history on the past 10 years of family planning is likely to be exacting and the obligation to learn from
successes and mistakes imperative.

In the decade 1966-1975 much was claimed for family
planning, but too little attempted. In country after country,
dire results were predicted if population growth was not
curbed: western governments began to donate money, beginning
with Sweden, followed by American funding. The World Health
Organization, after a lamentable delay, managed to develop a
partial philosophy justifying family planning activities. International Planned Parenthood Federation (IPPF) budgets ex-
ploded. The United Nations Fund for Population Activities was
created as a special source of money in an area where rapid
action was perceived to be necessary.

But a world that looked for action was largely given
conferences, study tours, inappropriate training programs, and
a general dissipation of effort; services frequently came second to administration, education, research, and buildings. An
exception has been the aggressive program of contraceptive

purchases by the United States Agency for International Development (USAID), averaging about 100 million cycles of pills annually since 1973 (US Agency for International Development, 1974).

In the past decade, the birthrate has fallen in most developing and nearly all developed countries (Ravenholt & Chao, 1974). The challenge is to quicken this fall by the wise management of the resources the world is willing to allot to this one topic, foreseeing perhaps some increase in total budgets, but without assuming an order of magnitude leap in available money (Rosenfield, 1974; Potts, 1974).

We must recognize that the declines in birthrate that have taken place are not necessarily due to structured family planning programs. In the 1960s in countries like Korea (Hong & Watson, 1972), Tunisia (Vallin, 1971), and India, illegal abortionists have often provided a service as numerically significant as, or more significant than, the overt national family planning program. Even today breastfeeding averts more births than all the structured family planning programs put together (Rosa, 1976).

One country, the largest in the world, is an outstanding exception. The Chinese birthrate was estimated as 26 per 1,000, to give a natural increase of 1.6 percent. Lower claims have been made. Probably even the Chinese themselves do not know accurately. But one thing is agreed: namely, public programs have been more successful in China than in any other developing nation (Potts, 1972).

PUBLIC ACCEPTABILITY VERSUS PRIVATE USEFULNESS

The gap between need and achievement, particularly in western society, is best explained as part of the painful process of social evolution in which the privileged have tried to extend help to vulnerable groups in society. In the conflict between individual need and what society finds itself able to permit at any particular time, both family planning methods and programs fall into a clear hierarchy of acceptability. Thus pills and IUDs surface in the ocean of public approval before condoms, sterilization remains submerged longer, and abortion is the iceberg that breaks surface last. Similar contraceptives supplied by physicians (especially if from a tiled clinic with a euphemistic sign outside) always prove socially acceptable sooner than an over-the-counter sale of the same commodity; health "justifications" for family planning become substantiated earlier than social reasons; sterilization for a medical "indication" receives public approbation

before the same operation is made available "electively"
(heart disease always receives greater public sympathy than
poverty).

The key to understanding the implementation of family
planning programs is to appreciate that the order in which
services and techniques surface is not related to their usefulness, either to the individual or to the program adminis-
trator. Indeed, social elites instinctively permit the least
effective methods and programs first. Therefore the problem
facing those in family planning is twofold: to push methods
and services to the level of public approval as soon as possible; to prevent programs crystallizing at an incomplete
stage.

It is dangerously easy for a program devised to promote that combination of actions that proved possible at a
particular instant of history to itself become a barrier to
the addition of other necessary components. In many developing countries, for example the Philippines, Kenya, and India,
no new family planning activity can be funded by an external
agency without the approval of a centralized family planning
board. Thus, the declaration of a national population policy
can inhibit innovation in services and the administratively
reasonable concern for liaison and integration leads to
rigidity when it is least needed.

METHODS AND PROGRAMS

The final shape family planning programs will take can
be seen with clarity and certainty. In a developed country
they will look something like the USA, where access to reversible methods of contraception is backed up by elective sterilization and abortion, and services to the poor are often free
or subsidized. In developing countries they will look something like that in the People's Republic of China: access to
all methods including abortion, each through logistically appropriate channels and combined with social policies to promote the status of women in a traditional society, such as
raising the age of marriage.

Methods

Traditionally, methods have been reviewed in terms of
effectiveness and continuation rate. It is also useful to
list them in terms of political acceptability and administrative appropriateness, considering the latter in relation to
poor countries like Thailand or Ghana and very poor countries
like Bangladesh or Ethiopia.

1. The diaphragm was useful in the western world when services had to be based in clinics and before IUDs or pills were invented. It is a Model-T Ford, still running in a few places, but insignificant at a world level.

2. The IUD has been acceptable to doctors and decision-makers--a nice sterile piece of plastic not obviously related to coitus--but it has proved disappointing to women. It requires a trained person to insert it and to provide after-care. Therefore it is difficult to administer in poor countries and impossible to make work in very poor ones. The history of its use did not recognize this fact.

3. Condoms remain underutilized. It took a hundred years to realize they could add to, instead of detract from, the fun of sex. USAID purchases rose from a few tens of millions in 1968 to 500 million in 1974-1975. The experience of Population Services International demonstrates that social marketing is possible in any developing country, has been successful where tried, and is exceptionally easy to administer.

4. Systemic contraceptives have a worse public image than their side effects justify. They are the only method with the potential of controlling the biological hazards of infertility (e.g., postponing the first pregnancy raises the risk of breast cancer). When prescribed by physicians they are expensive to administer and therefore of limited value in poor countries and practically none in very poor ones. In programs of community-based distribution, pills are easy to administer, costs are acceptable, and they go well in both poor and very poor countries (Bailey & Correa, 1975). Again, in Bangladesh, PSI sold 105,000 cycles of pills in two-and-a-half months.

5. Vaccination against pregnancy would be simple to administer and likely to be acceptable in many cultures. It could be the basis of an urgently needed leap forward in methods.

Programs

Just as family planning methods have passed the gate of social approval in a particular order, so programs have been developed to meet something of the same political needs. And again, the order of program evolution does not reflect those things which are administratively most useful or rational. The earliest example of this trend was found in the ritual of family planning clinics.

Clinics were a necessary response to the problems of providing fertility care between the two World Wars in Europe and North America. For Marie Stopes and other British pioneers, they represented an island of sane care in a sea of hostile and sometimes hysterical communal antagonism. For Margaret Sanger in the US, they were a way to pour the balm of medical respectability on the religious and political wounds she had opened. After the war they retained a modest relevance for Britain and the US, but offered little for the developing world (MacCorquodale, 1977). Yet family planning clinics from Rio de Janeiro to Kuala Lumpur are depressingly similar to those in Los Angeles or Leamington Spa. Family planning clinics (1) have resulted in too much physician involvement in the reversible methods of contraception; (2) have often concentrated on a single method—even where the so-called "cafeteria" approach has emerged, it still assumes you must go to the restaurant to choose the menu, yet most family planning, like most cooking, is done at home; (3) nearly always assume family planning is a task for women, not men; (4) use personnel inefficiently; and (5) soak up heavy capital investment, but have an outreach limited to a few kilometers radius.

In summary, clinics are expensive and culturally inappropriate. They are also demonstrably unnecessary. The Philippines has over 1700 clinics, Sri Lanka 504, but in Taiwan there is not a single specialist family planning clinic in the whole country. Yet in Taiwan 14.3 percent of women (15-49) receive contraceptives through program sources, while in the Philippines it is only 8.3 percent (Nortman & Hofstatter, 1975). In Taiwan all the work was achieved by the practical expedient of recruiting nearly 900 private practitioners on an item of service basis, to insert IUDs in their own surgeries—a device the British Government has recently discovered. Paradoxically, the Philippines is poorer than Taiwan and therefore, ex hypothesis, should be less able to afford sophisticated clinics.

The next most politically acceptable program is that relating family planning to maternal and child health (Taylor & Berelson, 1971). Such programs tend to be pursued in those countries (such as African or Latin American nations on the threshold of accepting family planning) and by agencies (such as the World Health Organization) whose policies are most diluted by political pressures.

No one denies it is responsible, reasonable, and necessary for maternal and child health services to offer postpartum and post-abortion contraceptive advice. Often the option of sterilization is particularly valuable. But such an

outlet can only be a minor part of any program. Unhappily,
maternal and child health/family planning services all too
readily become a sentimental byway, diverting attention from
the routine but central task of distributing contraceptives
and providing cost-effective surgical fertility-regulation
services. In Kenya, a $36 million four-year program has been
launched, largely using World Bank and other donor money. The
target is to recruit 640,000 new acceptors and avert 150,000
births. There are 298 clinics in the country. In 1974 they
inserted an average of one IUD per week and began one new pill
user every 3 days. In the new plan it will cost $240 to avert
a birth and the final effect will be to reduce the population
growth rate by only 0.25 percent by 1978 (Nortman & Hofstatter,
1975). Yet women who have had criminal abortion in Nairobi
lie two in a bed. The over-the-counter sale of condoms already
serves approximately one-quarter of the national program achievement. (The total subsidy received by the public sector activity
is only $6,000 a year from Population Services International.)

Maternal and child health services are rarely cost-
effective because: (1) they cannot help in the necessary task
of raising the age of maternity from the teens to twenties;
(2) they are inappropriate in assisting in the major problem
of controlling fertility in the long interval after the last
wanted child; (3) the majority of the world's deliveries are
unattended by any trained person and therefore outside maternal
and child health care; (4) they are exclusively female oriented;
and (5) administrators and practitioners put the immediate demands on curative medicine before the long-term advantages of
family planning.

The political compromise produced by the Bucharest conference with its emphasis on "integrated development" is the
most recent diversion of funds from the obvious. It is a
jargon, which in organizational terms is as relevant as attempting to assemble motor cars on a railway station because
both happen to be means of transport.

In the search to make programs respectable certain
generic activities are more acceptable than others. Sometimes
the term research covers a valid activity, sometimes it is a
welcome camouflage for an action program, but too often it
is--to use a piece of American slang-- a "cop out." Intellec-
tually, the fascination of human fertility control is that it
involves a wide range of variables and brings together so
many disciplines, from anatomy to sociology and anthropology
to statistics. Unhappily, much research is a narrow, monoto-
nous series of studies on a limited range of methods or turgid
demographic analysis that establishes the need for action yet
again, but contributes little to the decision making that must
precede any solution.

That complex of program activities called "I&E"--
information and education--is all too often another "cop out"
area. A calendar, or a poster about "small families being
happy families" is always easier to put around than a condom,
although a condom is demonstrably a better advertisement, as
well as being a useful contraceptive. Armies of young university graduates now work in national and international agencies,
doing work which is often of no proven use and, even if it is
necessary, would be better and more cheaply subcontracted to
experienced advertising agencies.

CHOICES IN POLICY

There are two schools of practice in family planning.
The first has been termed that of the demandologists. It
claims that in all countries there is a large unmet market for
family planning goods and services and that if underutilization
exists it is because of some defect in the services themselves,
which perhaps is more easily visible to the consumer than the
provider.

To the demandologists the essential step in implemen-
tating a family planning program is to ensure an adequate supply of pills and condoms in every village and easy access to
abortion and sterilization.

The second school may be called culturologists. While
demandologists claim that the same basic rules for good family
planning apply to nearly all societies, culturologists emphasize the differences between societies, often advising a
relatively slow, cautious approach; they are afraid of the
dangers of a backlash if programs develop too rapidly. In
contrast, the demandologists are impatient to move. Culturologists emphasize education and information programs. They often build up large numbers of field workers (but usually do
not give them contraceptives to distribute). The demandologists use many more community resources, building on existing
skills and the commonsense good will of a villager who will
set aside a little time each week to help his friends and
neighbors and distribute contraceptives.

The demandologists' case has rarely been proved wrong
and there are some dramatic instances where the hypothesis has
proved correct. In 1968, the Humanity Association of Howrah
began an oral contraceptive distribution project. Howrah is
a cancer of poverty and despair that has metastasized across
the Hoogly River from Calcutta. Half a million people live
there with only two metalled roads (neither wider than a man's
arm span) and without a sewer between them. Over 4 years,
in a sample population of 30,000 persons, 2,552 women enrolled;

4 out of 10 of all fertile women, or 67.7 percent of all women
menstruating regularly accepted the pill. Seventeen hundred
were still using the method when the project was discontinued
in 1972 (Majumdar et al., 1972). (It proved impossible to get
large organizations to support the project even though over
$100 million was spent on family planning in India that year.)

One-quarter of the pill users had two children and the
remainder were equally divided between those with three-to-
four and those with five or more. These remarkable results
are contrary to every stereotype of the illiterate poor of the
third world recklessly reproducing, often, according to the
experts, because they fear their children will die before
reaching maturity. Indeed, one wants to question everything,
including the accuracy of the data. It is interesting that
a follow-up survey was carried out in 1973 and 1,529 of the
former users traced. Two-thirds of the women still did their
best to go on using some form of contraception. For those not
using anything the reason was almost exclusively "nonavail-
ability." Close to 95 percent said they would use oral contraceptives if still available. Six hundred women went on to
purchase pills over the counter. In western terms, they were
spending 10 percent or more of their disposable income on
family planning (Mullick et al., 1976).

On the whole, individual couples make rational choices
concerning achieved family size. They perceive the likelihood
of child survival and their own economic capacity to support
their families with reasonable accuracy. But at present, in
nearly all countries, achieved family size exceeds desired
family size (Lapham & Maudlin, 1972).

It is important not to misinterpret the demandologists'
case. It is not that everyone in the developing world wants
to control fertility. It is that more people want to have the
services. It is that the resources available for family planning are limited. It is that those resources should be used
to fill unmet needs. In a sentence, it would be possible to
put all the available resources into services and still not
fill all the needs of the market.

Clearly, culturologists concede there must be some supplies for a successful program and the demandologists do not
deny the usefulness of broad educational campaigns or the
value of making the reversible methods of contraception available in hospital and clinic settings. However, the duality in
implementation of family planning programs must be brought out.
There are real conflicts that have to be resolved. Most of the
money used and the majority of the professional personnel currently involved in family planning belong to, or were brought
up in, the culturologist tradition.

To the demandologist one of the problems facing family planning programs in the mid-1970s is overpopulation--there are too many family planning specialists, nationally and internationally. The largest slice of nearly all budgets goes to professional personnel, their travel and support. If overmanning exists then it is wasting resources that could provide more goods and services at the consumer level.

Overmanning has a number of consequences: it diverts potential resources from the individual man or woman for whom they are intended. It undermines morale in service organizations, because most people are aware when they are not working to capacity. Those with least insight begin to complicate simple tasks and those with more insight become frustrated.

Perhaps donor agencies would do better to strengthen the university base for research and the provision of consultant skills. In turn, action organizations should trim their staff numbers. In this way teams of people could be assembled rapidly and more cheaply than at present, and the dead restraint of desire for promotion, or fear of loss of tenure of office, would be eased a little.

Time is running out. It may be that the day of compromise is also passing. Some compromises are self-defeating. The illusion of action, which does not carry assistance to the socially and economically desperate, or promise demographic change, is dangerous. Unhappily, several of the biggest international organizations working in family planning have well-developed conjuring skills when it comes to portraying weak or effective programs as if they were of value.

SURGICAL ASPECTS OF FERTILITY CONTROL

The most straightforward indicator of realism in family planning programs today is the willingness to make sterilization and abortion services available.

At a world level voluntary sterilization may already prevent more births than any other single method. Eighty million sterilizing operations may be needed globally in the next 10 years to catch up on a backlog of neglect and to maintain the level of prevalence society seems willing to choose (Ravenholt, 1976). Fortunately, recent developments in female sterilization (mini-laparotomy) now make this operation, if not as simple as vasectomy, at least of a comparable nature (International Fertility Research Program, 1976).

The technique and the program that is last to emerge is that of elective early abortion. Communist China, capitalist

America, Moslem Tunisia, and Catholic Austria have it to varying degrees, but much of the world still does not. In a rational program, abortion would be the first component to be
introduced: (1) as a hindsight method immediately understood
and almost universally acceptable--it requires no high promotional investment; (2) with simple contraceptives it provides
the combination of reversible methods presenting less risk to
the life of the user (Tietze, 1969); (3) without access to
abortion a program of reversible contraception is rapidly dis-
credited by the failures that inevitably occur (Potter, 1971);
(4) conversely, access to abortion is an effective way of recruiting people into the use of reversible methods; (5) women
will travel considerable distances to get abortions; (6) even
people of limited income will pay toward the cost; and (7) aux-
iliary workers can be taught early abortion.

        In short, early abortion is safe, effective, cheap,
and potentially the easiest method to administer. To call it
"a second best" or "a back-up method," as is so often done, is
to believe a mythology made up for political reasons, which
runs directly counter to the needs of women, the welfare of
existing children, and the future prosperity--or maybe
survival--of mankind.

                        CURRENT CONFUSION

                        National Problems

        Briefly, communities rarely get the family planning
programs they need or deserve. Instead, as a result of selective pressures applied by social elites, doctors, politicians,
legislators, and churchmen, they get an arbitrary and commonly
unworkable selection of techniques and program designs.

        In 1974, in Peninsular Malaysia, 87 percent of family
planning program users took oral contraceptives and abortion
was illegal. In India, 0.3 percent of users took pills but
abortion was legal. At one time British women flew to Stockholm for their abortions; more recently, Swedish men have been
flying to London for their vasectomies. In Eire it is illegal
to sell a condom but no one remembered to pass a law forbidding
sterilization, so at least vasectomy (because it can be performed outside hospital) is available. In Japan the condom
is the most used method, abortion is cheap and safe, but
sterilization is uncommon and the pill illegal.

        This procession of paradoxes does not represent any-
thing profound about the cultural acceptance of different methods as much as the arbitrary attitudes of the medical profession and administrators and historical accidents of law.

Ironically, the groups who create these bottlenecks
themselves have ready access to the abortions and sterilizations they deny others. Neither do they use the clinics or
the maternal and child health/family planning services they
impose on others. They are not disadvantaged by having the
pill on prescription. To complete the injustice, they alone
can afford to live with the mistakes in fertility planning
they themselves make. Although the record of Christendom is
particularly bad, even the People's Republic of China coyly
refuses to preach to the rest of the world what it practises
at home.

The task of meeting unmet needs in family planning,
which would have been difficult if begun in the 1950s-1960s,
now borders on the impossible in the 1970s-1980s. For some
parts of the world the demographic momentum that has built up
in the past decade is such that increasingly radical solutions
become necessary the longer the latent period before action.

International Aid

Currently, rich countries transfer about $500 million
annually to poor countries for family planning programs. The
total money spent globally on fertility control has been estimated to be perhaps $4000 million--much of which flows in
private sector activity or is spent, as in Latin America, by
governments on cleaning up the appalling consequences of illegal abortion: the individual and the state both pay to get
a dangerous, painful, wasteful service (Robbins, 1974).

These moneys are not comparable with such important
human endeavors as taking one-hundred-odd passengers to
Bahrain at twice the speed of sound, but it is money that
could and should be made to go further. The money required
for important changes in direction is not large. Only approximately $100 million spent over five years would be needed to
set up the services necessary to do that proportion of 80
million sterilization operations that will require subsidized
facilities. Or, to take an hypothetical but useful example:
every day there are 220,000 excess births over deaths. With
a moderate use of contraceptives it takes approximately 1.5
abortions to avert one birth. In one day one operator (or
sequence of part-time operators) can do about 25 early abortions. On average such a person might cost $3,000 a year and
would require equipment worth a few hundred dollars. Therefore staff costs for a hypothetical world abortion service to
achieve global zero population growth would be $26,400,000,
less than the total budget of one organization such as the
International Planned Parenthood Federation.

Organizational Needs

In order to implement family planning service programs, the world needs action organizations prepared to harness the resources of the community to meet the needs of the individual, especially the most underprivileged. This means making goods and services available across social classes and between rich and poor countries. Action programs can be successful only if they are consumer orientated. Voluntary organizations have a record of being more sensitive to consumer needs, and have an essential role to play in all countries. In developed societies a voluntary association needs to criticize services constructively and to be an advocate for the consumers. In developing countries this consumer advocacy role is usually one step removed from those most in need of services, but it is probably equally important.

To be successful family planning agencies should have:

1. Tight-knit, efficient, and flexible administration.

2. The ability to develop resources and then divide them equitably; there is always a danger problem to be looked at according to frontiers rather than population distribution. Botswana easily gets more per capita than Bangladesh.

3. The machinery to expand successful programs.

4. The ability to measure success by hard criteria of cost-effectiveness.

5. The machinery to cut back on unsuccessful programs-- a more difficult but just as necessary task. Family planners on the whole are "nice people," they suffer from a surplus of good will, but in the end any lack of business-like efficiency hurts the unseen but very real poor of the developing world, whose welfare is more important than any interruption in the career of a civil servant.

6. Develop the capacity to innovate. The only factor uniting "experts" in the field of family planning is that each one has a different solution. Therefore every program is no more than a test-tube experiment, and the unlikely combination may turn out more significant than the predictable.

Calls for greater professionalization and administrative sophistication in programing are currently being made (Korten, 1975). They are not always what is wanted: unlike building a railway or improving agriculture, family planning is rarely doing what is wanted or is logistically possible. Too much programing sophistication runs the risk of fixing the picture before all the elements have been added.

Politics is the art of the possible and must control the implementation of family planning programs, just as it does of other affairs. It is not possible to set up a world abortion service today. But to play the political game well one must be clear about the rational optimum; then it can be "packaged" as economically as possible. The problem in family planning is that too many people have come to believe their own invented mythologies.

REFERENCES

Bailey, J., & Correa, J. Evaluation of the profamilia rural family planning program. Studies in Family Planning, 1975, 6, 148-155.

Hong, S. B., & Watson, W. B. The role of induced abortion in fertility control in Korea. Clinical proceedings of IPPF/ SEAOR medical and scientific congress. Sydney: Australian and New Zealand Journal of Obstetrics and Gynaecology, 1972.

International Fertility Research Program. Female sterilization: Current trends and techniques. Chapel Hill, N.C.: Author, 1976.

Korten, D. C. Population programs 1985: A growing management challenge. Studies in Family Planning, 1975, 6, 178-187.

Lapham, R. J., & Maudlin, W. P. National family planning programs: Review and evaluation. Studies in Family Planning, 1972, 3, 29-52.

MacCorquodale, D. A study of family planning clinic effectiveness in the Philippines. Proceedings of the International Population Conference, 1976. Washington: World Population Society, 1977.

Majumdar, M., Mullick, B. C., Montra, A., & Mosley, K. T, Use of oral contraceptives in urban, rural, and slum areas. Studies in Family Planning, 1972, 3, 227-232

Mullick, B. C., Cheng, C. I., Pachauri, S., & Kessel, E, Follow-up study of oral contraceptive acceptors in Howrah District, India. Author, 1976.

Nortman, D., & Hofstatter, E. Population and family planning programs. Reports on Population/Family Planning, 1975, 2, 1-86,

Potter, R. G. Inadequacy of one-method family planning programs. Studies in Family Planning, 1971, 2, 1-6,

Potts, M, Family planning in the People's Republic of China. Report on first official IPPF visit. IPPF Medical Bulletin, 1972, 6, 1-3.

Potts, M. The implementation of family planning programmes. Journal of Reproduction and Fertility, 1974, 37, 475-485.

Ravenholt, R. T. World epidemiology and potential fertility impact on voluntary sterilization services, Third International Conference on Voluntary Sterilization, Tunis, 1976. In M. E. Schima & I, Lubell (Eds.), New advances in sterilization. New York: Association for Voluntary Sterilization, 1976.

Ravenholt, R. T., & Chao, J. World Fertility trends, Population Report, 1974, Series J, 21-40,

Robbins, J. Estimated total cost of fertility control: Survey of world needs in family planning. London: IPPF, 1974,

Rosa, F. Breast feeding: A motive for family planning, People, 1976, 3, 10-13.

Rosenfield, A. Family planning programs: Can no more be done? Studies in Family Planning, 1974, 5, 115-122,

Taylor, H. C., & Berelson, B, Comprehensive family planning based on maternal/child health services: A feasibility study for a world program. Studies in Family Planning, 1971, 2, 22-54.

Tietze, C. Mortality with contraception and induced abortion, Studies in Family Planning, 1969, 1, 6-8,

US Agency for International Development, Office of Population, Family planning service statistics: Annual report. Washington: Author, 1974.

Vallin, J. Limitation des naissances en Tunisie. Population, 1971, 26, 181-204.

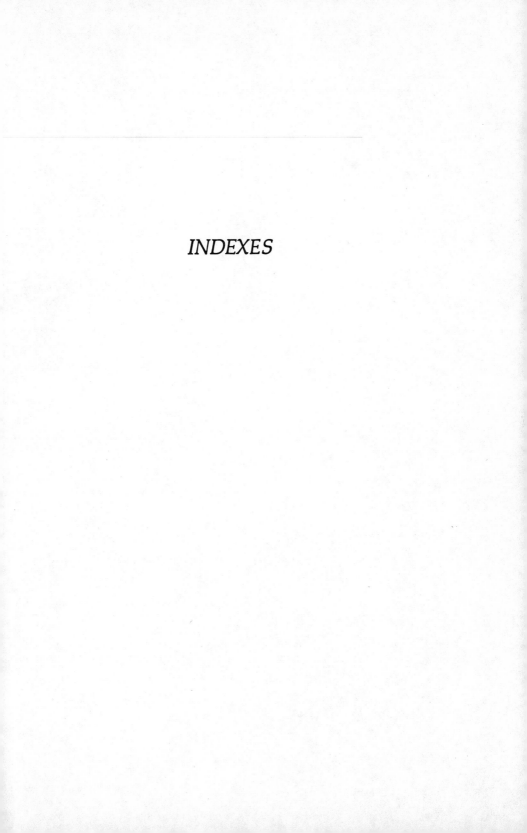

INDEXES

NAME INDEX

SUBJECT INDEX

United States Agency for International Development, 308, 310, 320
User-System Interaction Design, 66

Vaccination against pregnancy, 310
Vasectomy, 59, 163, 316

Virginia, 78

Washington State, 78
Women, status of, as factor in abortion decision, 16
World Health Organization, 11, 307, 311

Yugoslavia, 3, 4, 5, 6, 7, 8, 119-144, 304